ON THE FRONTIER

ON THE FRONTIER

Letters from the Canadian West in the 1880s

William Wallace

edited by KEN S. COATES
and BILL MORRISON

Printed and bound in Canada at Marquis.
COVER AND TEXT DESIGN: Duncan Campbell, University of Regina Press
COPY EDIT: Anne James
INDEX: Patricia Furdek
COVER PHOTO: "Old lock on an old grey weathered barn door" by Valerie Hunter.

Library and Archives Canada Cataloguing in Publication
–Wallace, William, active 1881-1886
["My dear Maggie—"]
  On the frontier : letters from the Canadian West in the 1880s / William Wallace ; edited by Ken S. Coates and Bill Morrison.
A republication of "My dear Maggie—" published in Regina by Canadian Plains Research Center, University of Regina, 1991. With new cover, layout, introduction and front matter.

Includes bibliographical references and index.
Issued in print and electronic formats.
ISBN 978-0-88977-408-7 (paperback).—ISBN 978-0-88977-410-0 (html).
—ISBN 978-0-88977-409-4 (pdf)

 1. Wallace, William, active 1881-1886—Correspondence. 2. Pioneers—Manitoba—Correspondence. 3. Immigrants—Manitoba—Correspondence. 4. Frontier and pioneer life—Manitoba. 5. Manitoba—Social life and customs. I. Coates, Kenneth, 1956-, editor II. Morrison, William R. (William Robert), 1942-, editor III. Title. IV. Title: ["My dear Maggie— ".

FC3367.2.W34 2015 971.27'3 C2015-904221-6 C2015-904222-4

10 9 8 7 6 5 4 3 2 1

University of Regina Press, University of Regina
Regina, Saskatchewan, Canada, S4S 0A2
tel: (306) 585-4758 fax: (306) 585-4699
web: www.uofrpress.ca

We acknowledge the financial support of the Government of Canada. / Nous reconnaissons l'appui financier du gouvernement du Canada. We acknowledge the support of the Canada Council for the Arts for our publishing program. This publication was made possible through Creative Saskatchewan's Creative Industries Production Grant Program.

CONTENTS

PREFACE..*vii*

INTRODUCTION...*ix*

1881..*I*

1882...*63*

1883...*137*

1884...*191*

1885..*247*

EPILOGUE..*297*

INDEX..*305*

PREFACE

We first heard of the Wallace papers in 1985 when we were teaching history together at Brandon University. At that time, Tom Mitchell, a friend and colleague (later archivist) at Brandon University, brought them to our attention. They had been in the university archives since 1941, but apparently had been largely unexamined. A glance at them, however, was enough to convince us of their historical value, and after some false starts, we were lucky to be able to convince the Canadian Plains Research Center to publish them.

We were also fortunate in our research assistants: Roberta Kempthorne, who did most of the research on which the maps are based, as well as collecting much local information, and Bruce Stadfeld, who transcribed many of the letters into readable copy in the summer of 1986. Glenn Iceton provided research support for the new introduction to the letters. Brandon University and the University of Victoria provided logistical support for the preparation of the original volume. Tom Mitchell kindly scanned the original maps and photos for the second edition. Monica Ball of the Manitoba Legislative Library provided the population statistics for Shellmouth.

Another source of good fortune was the fact that when we started working on the papers in 1986 there were still members of the Shellmouth community who remembered the Wallace family. Isabel Joy, then in her nineties, had known William Wallace for decades, and had acted with him in amateur theatricals during World War I. She appears with him in the 1914 picture of the Shellmouth Amateur Dramatic Society contained in this book, and she was able to give us personal reminiscences of him. Another long-time resident of the community was Sarah Wileman, the daughter of a man who had worked for Wallace later in his life, and who had lived in the house with him for some years as a young girl. Local residents Earl Morrison (no relation) and Emile Busch gave us photographs of the Wallaces that they had saved. This was also a stroke of luck, because none of the Wallaces had children, and since William died in 1943, we could easily have been without images of any of them. Now, in 2015, these personal connections have vanished, and there must be few if any people in the district with direct memories of the Wallace family.

These papers are a treasure, possibly a unique Canadian collection. They consist of twenty years of long descriptive letters, not like a diary, but more like a series of articles written for distribution or publication. Reading them is akin to reading a realistic novel about early prairie settlement, albeit one totally lacking a love story.

On the Frontier: Letters from the Canadian West in the 1880s was published in 1991 by Canadian Plains Research Center, in a small edition under the title *My Dear Maggie: Letters from a Western Manitoba Pioneer*, and soon went out of print. We are delighted that the University of Regina Press has agreed to republish this fascinating collection of letters.

INTRODUCTION

By 1880, the Dominion of Canada, formed in 1867, had grown from a confederation of four provinces into an ambitious transcontinental nation that stretched from Nova Scotia to the west-coast province of British Columbia. In between lay a vast stretch of territory, home to First Nations and Metis people, massive herds of bison, and millions of acres of grasslands. The vast prairie lands of Western Canada held the key to a grand national dream of the country's future. Canadian nation builders, particularly in Ontario, saw in the western lands the promise of endless opportunity and the greatest of all dreams, the chance to build a country stretching from sea to sea, enriched by the millions of farmers who would populate the prairie expanse.

This was no original plan, no made-in-Canada strategy for national greatness, for a template existed south of the border. The United States of America, once locked into a North-South set of coastal states that stretched from Maine to Florida, had unleashed its commercial and entrepreneurial potential when it started to expand westward after the Civil War to the central plains. Through the later decades of the nineteenth century, America built a network of railways that reached, like an eager hand, into the western interior. The new infrastructure, coupled with the promise of free or cheap land to those who ventured into the region to establish farms, captured the imagination of Europe and attracted millions of immigrants. In short order, America's population and economic output grew dramatically.

And now it was Canada's turn. The acquisition of Rupert's Land in 1870 led to the creation of the postage-stamp-sized province of Manitoba and the nationally controlled Northwest Territories. The other pieces quickly fell into place. The Dominion Lands Act of 1872 dangled the prospect of free land in front of prospective settlers. A series of treaties with First Nations—Treaty One in 1870 to Treaty Seven in 1877—removed the original peoples as a threat to would-be settlers, a promise enhanced with the creation of the North-West Mounted Police in 1873. The promise to British Columbia that a railway would be built as a link with eastern Canada promised western settlers access to markets and supplies. Canada had copied the American example, with the notable exception of using treaties rather than the army to deal with Aboriginal occupation of their traditional territories. Where the westward expansion of the United States was marked by long and bitter Indian wars, Canada's was destined to be dominated by treaties, reserve lands, and Indian agents.

But the flood of settlers did not come as early as planned. The American west still had land available, with better railway networks and a warmer climate. Not until the 1890s, with the closing of the American frontier, would the promise of western expansion south of the 49th parallel start to fade. Canada expected and planned for millions of immigrants and settlers. They came at first only in the thousands, well below the grandiose vision of a western landscape transformed from prairie grasslands to prosperous farms. Canada's day in the prairie sun came later, following the danger of the 1885 Rebellion on the plains and after the election of Wilfrid Laurier and the Liberals in 1896 and the development of an aggressive immigrant promotion campaign targeted at Eastern Europe. The period in between, from 1870 to 1896, was one of national stagnation, marked by the Pacific Scandal over railway contracts that toppled the Conservative government of John A. Macdonald, low rates of settlement, weak economic returns from prairie agriculture, wild speculation in railway construction, and tensions with Metis and First Nations that culminated in an aggressive and nasty campaign against the First Nations and the 1885 Metis uprising led by Louis Riel.

This period, between the excitement of creating a transcontinental nation and the promise of the late-nineteenth-century settlement boom, is somewhat of a blind spot in the understanding of Canada's past. The challenges and responses of the First Nations and Metis have attracted a great deal of attention. James Daschuk's 2013 work, *Clearing the Plains: Disease, Politics of Starvation, and the Loss of Aboriginal Life*, is but the latest in an impressive list of books describing government perfidy, Indigenous determination, and conflict over the west's future. But there was settlement during this period, especially in western Manitoba. Starting before 1870, and particularly after 1880, newcomers came west, seeking land and opportunity in the British-Canadian territories north of the American republic. Soon the settlers outnumbered the Indigenous peoples.

To settle in the West in the 1870s and 1880s, particularly if it meant venturing west of the relative security of the Red River valley and the growing city of Winnipeg, was a risky gamble. Disappointing it may have been for the country as a whole, but this was also one of the most fascinating and challenging—and little known—episodes in Canadian history. Getting inside the life histories of these early settlers, understanding the risks and survival strategies of the first Europeans trying to create lives for themselves on the western plains, has been difficult. A window into them was opened, however, when William and Andrew Wallace, two brothers from England, arrived in western Manitoba with their father, Peter. Immediately they started writing regular letters to their sister, Maggie. In the process, they produced one of the classic testimonials about the early history of Canada. *On the Frontier* tells, in their words, the remarkable, harrowing, funny, and sometimes daunting experiences of the early western settlers.

The Wallaces were among the first settlers to western Manitoba and what is now eastern Saskatchewan, part of the "Manitoba land boom" of the early 1880s. When they moved from their first homestead near Brandon to the Shellmouth district, they were one of the first farm families in the district. They were the pioneers, the heroes, the builders, and the land they came to was, to their minds, "empty." They stayed throughout the boom, the early years, and long after, the last of them living until 1948. Their own history mirrors that of settlement in that part of the prairies, and this alone makes these letters a valuable historical source. As well, they are just fun to read. They are long, descriptive, informal, humorous, and very personal, like extended diary entries, but meant to be read and passed around rather than kept secret.

Since these letters were first published as *My Dear Maggie*, research on prairie history and settlement has turned away from people like the Wallaces. Instead, much of the new scholarship deals with prairie settlers who were very much unlike the Wallaces and their neighbours: women,[1] Mennonites,[2] Ukrainians,[3] Metis and First Nations,[4] other

---

1   Anne C. Gagnon, "En Terre Promise: The Lives of Franco-Albertan Women, 1890–1940" (PhD dissertation, University of Ottawa, 1998); Nanci L. Langford, "First Generation and Lasting Impressions: The Gendered Identities of Prairie Homestead Women" (PhD dissertation, University of Alberta, 1994); Sandra Rollings-Magnusson, "Hitched to the Plow: The Place of Western Pioneer Women in Innisian Staple Theory" (master's thesis, University of Regina, 1997); Sandra Rollings-Magnusson, "Canada's Most Wanted: Pioneer Women on the Western Prairies," *Canadian Review of Sociology and Anthropology* 37, no. 2 (May 2000): 223–238; S. Leigh Matthews, "Bound to Improve: Canadian Women's Prairie Memoirs and Intersections of Culture, History, and Identity" (PhD dissertation, University of Calgary, 2002); Lesley Erickson, "The Unsettling West: Gender, Crime, and Culture in the Canadian Prairies, 1886–1940" (PhD dissertation, University of Calgary, 2003); Catherine A. Cavanaugh, "'No Place for a Woman': Engendering Western Canadian Settlement," in *Women and Gender in the American West*, eds. Mary Ann Irwin and James F. Brooks (Albuquerque: University of New Mexico Press, 2004), 183–209; Sarah Carter, *Capturing Women: The Manipulation of Cultural Imagery in Canada's Prairie West* (Montreal & Kingston: McGill-Queen's University Press, 1997); Sarah Carter, "Categories and Terrains of Exclusion: Constructing the 'Indian Woman' in the Early Settlement Era in Western Canada," in *In the Days of Our Grandmothers: A Reader in Aboriginal Women's History in Canada*, eds. Mary-Ellen Kelm and Lorna Townsend (Toronto: University of Toronto Press, 2006), 146–169.
2   Roland Meyer Sawatzky, "The Control of Social Space in Mennonite Housebarns in Manitoba, 1874–1940," (PhD dissertation, Simon Fraser University, 2004).
3   Roman Paul Fodchuk, *Zhorna: Material Culture of the Ukrainian Pioneers* (Calgary: University of Calgary Press, 2006); John C. Lehr, "Governmental Coercion in the Settlement of Ukranian Immigrants in Western Canada," in *Immigration and Settlement, 1870–1939*, ed. Gregory P. Marchildon (Regina: University of Regina and Canadian Plains Research Center, 2009), 267–284.
4   Gerhard J. Ens, *Homeland to Hinterland: The Changing Worlds of the Red River Metis in the Nineteenth Century* (Toronto: University of Toronto Press, 1996); Sarah Carter, *Lost Harvests: Prairie Indian Reserve Farmers and Government Policy* (Montreal: McGill-Queen's University Press, 1990); Stephen George Sliwa, "Standing the Test of Time: A History of the Beardy's/Okemasis Reserve, 1876–1951" (master's thesis, Trent University, 1993); Sarah Carter, *Aboriginal People and Colonizers of Western Canada to 1900* (Toronto: University of Toronto Press, 1999); Maureen K. Lux, *Medicine that Walks: Disease, Medicine, and the Canadian Plains Native People, 1880–1940* (Toronto: University of Toronto Press, 2001).

non-British immigrants,[5] and ranchers[6] among them. We could add to this list a substantial number of publications on law enforcement and other topics.

But little or none of this applies to the Wallaces. The elder Wallace was a widower, and his sons were lifelong bachelors, neither of whom seems to have had any personal relations with women at all, though the letters are full of coy references to matrimony. Nor were they involved with non-Anglo settlers, for as the table below shows, their neighbours were almost all white, British, and Protestant. They had almost no contact with First Nations, except to observe some of them nervously and unsympathetically during the 1885 Rebellion. To place the Wallaces in historical context, one needs to look at research dealing with prairie settlers who were like them, came at the same time, and had much the same experiences. Lyle

5   Jason F. Kovacs, "Con Artist or Noble Immigration Agent?: Count Esterhazy's Hungarian Colonization Effort, 1885–1902," in *Immigration and Settlement, 1870–1939*, ed. Gregory P. Marchildon (Regina: University of Regina and Canadian Plains Research Center, 2009), 285–313; Fred Stambrook and Stella Hryniuk, "Who Were They Really? Reflections on East European Immigrants to Manitoba before 1914," in *Immigration and Settlement, 1870-1939*, ed. Gregory P. Marchildon (Regina: University of Regina and Canadian Plains Research Center, 2009), 457–482; John M. Cobb, "German Lutherans in the Prairie Provinces Before the First World War: Their Church Background, Emigration and New Beginnings in Canada" (PhD dissertation, University of Manitoba, 1991); Wendy Lee Karhoffer, "Visions of a New Land: Government Recruitment of Norwegian Immigrants to Alberta, 1870–1930" (master's thesis, University of Calgary, 1991). Stella M. Hryniuk and Neil G. McDonald, "The Schooling Experience of Ukrainians in Manitoba, 1896-1916," in *The Prairie West: Historical Readings*, 2nd edition, eds. R. Douglas Francis and Howard Palmer (Edmonton: The University of Alberta Press, 1992), 289–307; Maureen A. Pedersen, "Wherever Two or Three are Gathered: A Study of the Finnish Settlement at New Finland, Saskatchewan, 1888–1945" (master's thesis, University of Regina, 2004). Allan Rowe, "Prairie Shamrock: Irish Settlement and Identity in Western Canada, 1870s–1930s" (PhD dissertation, University of Alberta, 2009).

6   David H. Breen, *The Canadian Prairie West and the Ranching Frontier, 1874–1924* (Toronto: University of Toronto Press, 1983); W. M. Elofson, "Not Just a Cowboy: The Practice of Ranching in Southern Alberta, 1881–1914," *Canadian Papers in Rural History* 10 (1996): 205–216; A. B. McCullough, "Eastern Capital, Government Purchase and the Development of Canadian Ranching," *Prairie Forum* 22, no. 2 (Fall 1997): 213–235; Warren M. Elofson, *Frontier Cattle Ranching in the Land and Times of Charlie Russell* (Montreal & Kingston: McGill-Queen's University Press, 2004).

Dick's study of early settlement around Abernethy, Saskatchewan,[7] is one of the best examples of such work.

Readers familiar with the literature mentioned above will find the Wallace letters to be a perfect example of the world view that is now called the "settler mentality." The phrase is often used pejoratively these days, but it was of course the way that the Wallaces and all their neighbours viewed their world. The prairies were a *tabula rasa* to them, a blank slate on which to write their futures. It never would have occurred to them that First Nations had any rights to the land, or that that land had any history before their arrival.

An important thing to note about the Wallaces, who arrived in Manitoba in the spring of 1881, is that they were not "men in sheepskin coats," to quote Clifford Sifton's famous description of the ideal prairie settler. When the three Scotsmen,[8] Peter Wallace, aged fifty-nine, and his sons William, twenty-two, and Andrew, fifteen, came to Manitoba intending to establish a farm on the frontier, the more famous period of settlement was fifteen years in the future. They did not arrive in the west during the great wave of European migration that occurred between 1895 and 1914, but two decades earlier, during the Manitoba land boom of 1880–1881.

This period of migration was of vital importance to the prairies, and especially to the new province of Manitoba, for it was during these years that much of the region's basic social pattern was set. Yet it is much less well known than the later one, and has been ignored in a general assumption that the important immigration occurred at the time when Wilfrid Laurier declared that the twentieth century would belong to Canada. In 1883 there were actually 133,000 immigrants to Canada, a good percentage of whom came to the prairies. In 1890 the figure had declined to 75,000, and in 1896 to

7   Lyle Dick, *Farmers "Making Good": The Development of Abernethy District, Saskatchewan, 1880–1920* (Ottawa: National Historic Parks Sites, Canadian Parks Service, Environment Canada, 1989).

8   On Scottish settlement in the prairie provinces, see Alan R. Turner, "Scottish Settlement of the West," in *The Scottish Tradition in Canada*, ed. W. S. Reid (Toronto: McClelland and Stewart, 1976). For a popular account of prairie settlement, see Barry Broadfoot, *The Pioneer Years 1895–1914: Memories of Settlers Who Opened the West* (Toronto: Doubleday Canada, 1976); Pierre Berton, *The Promised Land: Settling the West 1896–1914* (Toronto: McClelland and Stewart, 1984).

just under 17,000, after which time the "sheepskin coats" period began, with the number rising to over 400,000 in 1913.[9] It is often thought that the important migration to Canada began in 1890, but the previous decade was of greater significance: over 849,615 came to Canada in the period 1880–89, and only 372,474 in the period 1890–99.[10] The roots of the Manitoba farm economy in particular go back into the late 1870s and early 1880s, and the Wallaces were in on the ground floor of it.

The period of prairie history that saw the arrival of the Wallaces can be seen as a transition between the earliest days of European settlement—the largely unregulated era when the farm population clustered around the Red River colony—and the later boom period that began in the late 1890s. When Manitoba joined Confederation in 1870, the Metis made up the majority of its settled population. By 1880 the Metis were a minority in their own land, swamped by an influx of settlers from eastern Canada, most of them English-speaking Protestants from Ontario and the Maritimes, and by increasing migration from Great Britain. The aggressive white Anglo-Saxon population had little place for the Metis, who were, with government complicity, deprived of lands promised to them under the Manitoba Act.[11] By 1885–1886, at the point where this collection of letters ends, the population of Manitoba was overwhelmingly of British ethnic origin. In the Elton district near Brandon, where the Wallaces first took up land, the proportion of British settlers was almost 95%, and in Russell and Shell River districts, where the Wallaces eventually settled, the proportion approached 100%.[12] It was during this period

---

9   R. D. Francis et al., *Destinies: Canadian History Since Confederation* (Toronto: Holt Rinehart and Winston, 1988), 112; "Room to Spare," an article by David J. Hall in *Horizon Canada*, 7, no. 76, uses the same table.

10   The figures, taken from *Historical Statistics of Canada*, eds. M. C. Urquhart and K. A. H. Buckley (Toronto: Macmillan, 1965) are 1881—47,991; 1882—112,458; 1883—133,624; 1884—103,824; 1885—79,169.

11   D. N. Sprague, *Canada and the Métis, 1869–1888* (Waterloo: Wilfrid Laurier University Press, 1988).

12   The Wallace farm was on the border of the two districts. These tables were prepared by Bruce Stadfeld at Brandon University from Canadian census data. The "Irish" were mostly Irish Protestants. The First Nations population is not included.

that the first great increase in the province's population took place—
from 12,000 in 1870[13] to 66,000 in 1881 to 109,000 in 1886.[14]

ETHNIC ORIGINS OF THE POPULATION, 1885–1886, PERCENTAGES

	MANITOBA	ELTON	RUSSELL	SHELL RIVER
English	27.3	28.3	32.2	35.8
Scottish	27.0	32.0	41.1	28.2
Irish	22.3	34.6	24.9	34.9
Total of 3	76.6	94.9	98.2	98.9
French	7.0	0.0	0.0	0.0
German	11.7	0.0	0.0	0.0
Icelanders	2.6	0.0	0.0	0.0
Other	2.0	3.0	1.8	1.1

Other statistics show the almost totally Anglo-Protestant nature
of the Shell River district during the period the Wallace family
was pioneering there, even compared to the rest of Manitoba. For
instance, in 1885 the four largest religious denominations in the
province were Presbyterian (26.1%), Anglican (21.4%), Methodist
(17%), and Roman Catholic (13.5%). Roman Catholics made up
only 0.7% of the population of the Shell River district, and the
Presbyterians (47.8%), Anglicans (36%), and Methodists (9.8%)—
93.6% in total.

Thus the region of the prairies to which the Wallaces came in 1882
was not a welter of different races and languages—the traditional image
of the west during the settlement era; on the contrary, it was almost
totally homogeneous in ethnicity and language, and was to remain so
throughout this early period—it was some years before William Wallace
noted the arrival of the first Ukrainian settler. It was not that all the

---

13 Or 19,000, taking the same area in 1870 as in 1881 and 1886.

14 The figures, which include the English- and French-speaking Metis population,
are from Gerald Friesen, *The Canadian Prairies: A History* (Toronto: University of
Toronto Press, 1984), 202. By 1886, 20,000 people, nearly 20% of the population,
lived in Winnipeg.

settlers in the district were overseas immigrants, for the majority of them had been born in Canada: two-thirds came from other provinces and almost all the rest from the British Isles—the figures for 1885–1886 are Canada (62.2%), England (14.4%), Ireland (10.5%), Scotland (10%), other (2.8%). But they all spoke the same language, had the same racial and cultural background, and went to the same three churches. Their economic position also fell within a fairly narrow range; some had hardly any money at all, and had a very difficult time establishing themselves, and there was the occasional magnate—Col. Boulton[15] was the local example, though he was deeply in debt most of the time. But most of the settlers seem to have been in the same situation as the Wallaces— enough money to make a success of things, provided they applied a good deal of hard work and had a reasonable amount of luck.

One thing that was not homogeneous in the Shell River district was the gender balance. Though the population of Manitoba in 1885–1886 was 55% male and 45% female, the figures for Shell River were 62% and 38%, and most of the females were either married or children. There were very few women of marriageable age in the district, and William Wallace expressed keen interest every time a new one arrived. But since neither he nor his brother, Andrew, seem to have been particularly enterprising in this respect, they ended their days as did many other pioneers—as old bachelors living with a housekeeper—in this case Maggie, their widowed sister.

The pioneering careers of the Wallaces and the hundreds of thousands of other immigrants who came to the prairies in those years were governed by the Dominion Lands Policy, based on the public land system of the United States, and first enunciated in the Dominion Lands Act of 1872.[16]

---

15 D'Arcy Boulton was born in 1841 in Cobourg, Ontario and served in the Royal Canadian Regiment from 1857 to 1867. After participating in the Red River Resistance he settled in western Manitoba, and was one of the first residents of Russell and Shellmouth. During the 1885 rebellion he raised "Boulton's Scouts," a force of mounted irregulars, from the Russell district. He was appointed to the Senate in 1889, but never received the government plums he felt he deserved, nor was he very successful in business. He died in Shellmouth in 1899.

16 Statutes of Canada, 35 Vic., c.23. There are many descriptions of the Dominion Lands Policy; this material is based on John L. Tyman, "Patterns of Western Land Settlement," *Historical and Scientific Society of Manitoba Transactions*, Series III, no. 28 (1971–72), and James. M Richtik, "The Policy Framework for Settling the Canadian West, 1870-1880," *Agricultural History*, no. 4 (October 1975).

LEFT TO RIGHT: William Wallace, c. 1930; Andrew Wallace, c. 1905; Peter Wallace, c. 1905. Photo of William courtesy of Emilie Busch and Brandon University. Photos of Andrew and Peter courtesy of Earl Morrison and Brandon University.

Under this act, any head of family, or a single man twenty-one years of age, could claim a quarter section (160 acres) of public land. The settler would gain title to the land "upon proof, to the satisfaction of the Land Officer that he ... resided upon or cultivated the land for the three years next after the filing of the affidavit for entry." This meant that the homesteaders could not speculate on their land; they had to live on their land and work it, then satisfy a government official that they had fulfilled the conditions of the law before they could gain title to it. These regulations were changed from time to time. In 1874 the age limit was lowered to eighteen; Andrew Wallace was quick to claim a quarter section as soon as he reached that age, and the regulations requiring residence on the land were relaxed somewhat in 1884. Another feature of the land policy was the pre-emption, which enabled a person who entered for a quarter section to obtain an interim entry for an adjoining unclaimed quarter section, with the right of purchasing it when he got his farm established; the Wallaces took advantage of this provision as well.

Why the Wallaces left Scotland is not known, since William Wallace was very much a man who looked to the future rather than the past, and his letters say almost nothing about his life in the old country; in fact, we know very little about their lives before the family came to Canada. Very likely, however, the reason was like that of the hundreds of thousands of other Britons of their class who emigrated to the colonies in that period—it was simply to improve their fortunes; a parallel case is that of Turner Bone, a civil engineer from Glasgow who came to Canada in 1882, a year after the Wallaces, and found work with the C.P.R. His choice seemed fairly straightforward:

> As my apprenticeship was nearing an end, I was giving serious thought to the question of my future. Finally, I made up my mind to try my fortune in Canada. One of the other apprentices in the office ... who had already finished his apprenticeship, was of the same mind; so we agreed to go together to Canada, and made our preparations accordingly.[17]

Why the Wallaces chose Canada over the United States, where so many immigrants were flooding in the 1880s, is clear enough—they were proud Britons who had little use for the United States and Yankee ways, a disdain which a short stay in New England on their way west did little to reverse.

The Wallaces came to Manitoba in a period when many in Canada hoped that it and the rest of the prairies might become the "Britain of the West."[18] Canadian expansionists of the 1870s and 1880s, men such as George Grant, Presbyterian clergyman and ardent patriot, felt that mere growth in Western Canada was not enough. Canada should be more than just a huge country, a North American version of Russia; Canada's western empire needed a strong moral as well as a physical foundation. "A country is great," wrote Grant, "not from the number but the quality of its people."[19] Canada was developing the west to "build up a nation on the British plan"[20]:

---

17 P. Turner Bone, *When The Steel Went Through: Reminiscences of a Railroad Pioneer* (Toronto: Macmillan, 1947), 14.

18 The phrase is from Doug Owram, *Promise of Eden: The Canadian Expansionist Movement and the Idea of the West, 1856–1900* (Toronto: University of Toronto Press, 1980). See especially chapter 6, "The Character of Empire: The Britain of the West."

19 National Archives of Canada, Grant Papers, vol. 24, "Thanksgiving and Retrospect," 227, quoted in Owram, 125.

20 Thomas Cross, "Canada and the Empire," *Rose-Belford's Canadian Monthly*, VII (Sept. 1881), quoted in Owram, 126.

The British Empire was thought to represent man's highest achievement in the development of governmental and social institutions. The North West, promising great economic wealth, seemed to give Canada a unique opportunity to implant firmly these noble institutions in a rising world power. ... The vast territory of the West offered a canvas large enough to be appropriate for the moral grandeur of British institutions.[21]

Eventually Canada would not only become a partner of the mother country, but might someday replace it as the carrier of civilization's torch. For this to happen it was essential that the prairies, where Canada's future lay, be made as British as possible. To that end, British immigration should be encouraged, and the Britons who settled there should also be encouraged to preserve a close connection with their former homes:

> Canadians also felt that British institutions were the most reliable in terms of both social welfare and social stability ... The stability of Canada and thus its ability to inherit the mantle of Great Britain depended to a large extent on its ability to develop and maintain a social fabric as strong as that of the mother country ... If Canada was to achieve its destiny within the Empire it would have to seize the opportunity offered by the North West in such a way as to ensure that its benefits lasted beyond the frontier period. The very success of Canada's historical mission depended on it developing a society of sufficient strength and stability to survive the transition of the North West from frontier to mature community.[22]

This historical mission would not be based on urban centres like Winnipeg, but on the economic and social strengths of the individual farmers. The ideal people for such a mission were the British, particularly British tenant farmers and farm labourers. Such men,

---

21 Owram, *Promise of Eden*, 126.
22 Owram, *Promise of Eden*, 129.

with their wives and children, would cement the strength of British institutions on the prairies, would avoid the lawlessness and disorder which seemed always to be a feature of the American frontier.

People like the Wallaces were exactly what was wanted—ambitious and energetic people with a background in agriculture. They had the "right stuff" for the 1880s—hard workers with a thoroughly British outlook and a disdain for American ways.

The corollary of strengthening British institutions in the west was weakening non-British ones, a policy first applied to the Metis and then to others, particularly during the suppression of Roman Catholic schools in Manitoba after 1890. The British tone of William Wallace's letters, and his impatience with things that were not British, is a clear precursor of the notorious Manitoba Schools Question that so bedevilled national unity in the 1890s.

The exact route taken by the Wallaces from the eastern seaboard to Manitoba is not known, since a crucial letter from Winnipeg is missing from the collection. Since they landed at Halifax and then travelled to Boston it is likely that they followed the route of the majority of travellers in that period—by train from the east through Chicago, Minneapolis, and down the Red River valley to Winnipeg, then west over the new C.P.R. or, in their case, since snow had blocked the trains, on foot to the Brandon district.[23] Their homestead, part of section 19, township 11, range 19, was railway land, purchased from the C.P.R.

The Wallaces arrived at the beginning of the western Manitoba land boom of 1881, which coincided with the beginning of the serious push to build the railway through to the west coast.[24] A land office was opened in Brandon that year, and when it was realized that the railway was about to arrive there was a wave of land speculation, particularly in town building lots:

Nearly everyone had speculative dealings in land—hotel-keepers, shopmen, clerks, even the barber—and wished

---

23 The city of Brandon was born when the C.P.R. arrived on the west bank of the Assiniboine in 1881. The Wallaces got to the district shortly before the railway did.

24 A detailed history of settlement in this period is John L. Tyman, *By Section Township and Range: Studies in Prairie Settlement* (Brandon: Assiniboine Historical Society, 1972).

either to buy or sell. Some worked their farms by hired labour ... Every hotel-bar was placarded with advertisements and crowded with people crazy to sell town-lots. It mattered nothing to these people if these lots were at the bottom of the Assiniboine, or in the middle of a pond, or even if they had no existence at all; so long as they were eagerly bought by persons willing to give enormous prices for the prospect—usually a good one—of selling them again at a handsome profit. Inspecting them was an altogether superfluous accompaniment either of sale or purchase.[25]

On March 21, 1881, a few weeks before the Wallaces arrived in Brandon, the boundaries of the province were extended to include western Manitoba, and in that year and the next, settlers began to arrive in the province in substantial numbers—over 44,000 in 1882 alone. Despite the end of the boom that year, settlers continued to come to the province, so that by 1891 its population, including Indigenous people, had passed 150,000.

Although the Wallaces shunned speculative ventures, they did take a considerable chance when in 1882 they sold their land near Brandon and set out to the northwest, heading for the Qu'Appelle district. Assuming that the railway would follow to their new home (local boosters assured them that it would) was a real gamble. Because it was extremely difficult to reach anything more than a purely local market without ready access to a railroad, it was vital to be within reasonable hauling distance of one. Here the Wallaces lost their gamble; in 1882 they settled six miles southeast of Shellmouth expecting a railway to go through that town within a year. But fulfillment of this hope was to be long delayed. At the beginning of their life near Shellmouth they had to go to Moosomin for rail service, a distance of over seventy miles. In 1886 the railway reached Birtle, forty miles to the southeast, and a year or so later a line was built from Binscarth to Russell, twelve miles southeast of the Wallaces' farm. But the railway did not reach Shellmouth until 1909, 27 years after the family settled in the district. Despite the fact that

---

25 Robert M. Christy, *Manitoba Described* (London: Wyman, 1885), quoted in Tyman, 42.

they farmed for five years (1882–87) with a railroad no closer than forty miles, they did manage to sell most of what they produced, much of it locally, though at discouragingly low prices—but it was not until the railroad came to Russell that they saw a degree of prosperity.

The Wallaces, arriving in the Shell River district in 1882, were one of the first pioneer families in the part of the province to the north and west of Brandon, an area that included Neepawa, Minnedosa, Birtle, and Russell. Since the most important period in the taking up of Manitoba lands was 1881–1882, the years in which the Canadian Pacific Railway crossed the province, the Wallace papers are an invaluable record of that crucial era in the province's history.

This, then, is the record of a vital period in the history of Manitoba—an era of growth in which, as Gerald Friesen points out, a new provincial and regional consciousness was taking shape:

> … it resulted in the establishment of a stable community and reasonable prosperity. This was a grain-growing province, but its farmers had sufficient animals and gardens to sustain their families in difficult times … 'The greatness of the break made by the newcomers had created a strong sense of identity … and the strange new land became familiar quickly because of its distance from the old homes. … With a speed which was often amusing the new settler of yesterday became the Manitoban of the morrow. But under these more brilliant stars and amid these wider horizons the farmsteads continued the rural life of Ontario to which the British settlers were assimilated.'[26]

What distinguished this family from the thousands of others that came to Canada in this era was that the elder son, William Wallace, was an unusually assiduous writer of letters, with a fine eye for descriptive detail. The men had left a sister, Maggie, back in Scotland, and every three or four weeks Willie Wallace wrote her a letter describing his life in Manitoba. These letters began in March 1881 aboard the ship taking the Wallaces to Canada, and ended

---

26 Friesen, *The Canadian Prairies*, 218–219.

early in 1904, when Maggie and her husband left Britain to join the family in Canada. Maggie carefully saved the letters, bringing them to Canada with her. William Wallace, like many other pioneers, had what Heather Robertson calls an "intuitive historical sense."[27] He knew instinctively that he was engaged not just in making a living, but in something of lasting importance—an extraordinary human event that would one day be important to later generations—and he preserved his letters, giving them to a university shortly before his death.

Neither William, nor Andrew, nor Maggie Wallace had children, and there are no other relatives in Canada, so it has proved impossible to obtain information on the family's history in Scotland other than what is alluded to in the letters. Nothing is known, for instance, of Mrs. Wallace, except that her last name was Stevenson, her people were farmers, and there was an uncle, Hugh Stevenson, presumably her brother, who was a prominent Presbyterian clergyman. For some reason William does not once mention her in all his letters, but judging from reminiscences of people who knew the family in Canada it seems likely that she had died a few years before they emigrated. On his application for a homestead patent, Peter Wallace stated that he had been "farming since boyhood."[28] At the time the family emigrated, William was a clerk, Andrew was in or just out of school, and Maggie was training to be a teacher.

The history of the Wallace family shows many of the themes that ran through the experiences of thousands of other pioneers. One was the element of sheer chance that determined much of their lives. Though recent studies have shown that in many instances the choice of location depended on contact with people already in the region,[29] this does not seem to have been true of the Wallace family. They came to the Brandon district in the spring of 1881 for reasons which the letters do not make clear, perhaps because it was on the edge of settlement and they had heard or read that good

---

27 Heather Robertson, *Salt of the Earth: The Story of the Homesteaders in Western Canada* (Toronto: Lorimer, 1974), 7.
28 A copy of the application, dated 25 April 1886, is in the Wallace Papers in the Brandon University Archives.
29 D. M. Loveridge, "The Settlement of the Rural Municipality of Sifton 1881–1920" (master's thesis, University of Manitoba, 1977), 190–205.

LEFT TO RIGHT: John and Maggie (Wallace) Bond, Andrew Wallace, c. 1905.
Photo courtesy of Brandon University.

land was to be had there. But for some reason, possibly the quality
of their land, they found it not to their liking. So in the next year,
1882, they struck northwest for the Qu'Appelle district. Reaching
the Assiniboine north of present day Russell, they found the river in
flood. Rather than wait weeks for the water level to fall, they explored
their surroundings, and decided that the country in the Shellmouth
district suited them. There William Wallace stayed for the next sixty-
one years. Such considerations swayed many decisions in that era.

Another theme was the alternation between optimism and
despair that runs through the letters. William Wallace was by nature
an optimist, and when things were going well, he bubbled with
enthusiasm about the future of the country. But then came drought,
or low prices, or blizzards, and he was plunged into gloom. A soft
spring day, a well-timed shower, or a glorious sunset, and he was
again ebullient about his prospects.

A third theme is that of physical effort. The Wallaces worked
hard at farming, and made few serious mistakes—the worst one was
building a new house in a location where they had not tried to dig a
well. When the house was built and water not forthcoming, they had
to dismantle the house and move it. They ploughed, sowed, reaped,

cut logs for their house, built the house, burnt lime for plaster, cut trees for fence posts, milked cows, made butter, baked, cooked, repaired their clothes. Besides this William Wallace had time for civic duties, music, theatricals, and lengthy letter-writing.

William Wallace's letters demonstrate that it was easier to be a pioneer if one had some money and settled on good land. In his studies of pioneering in the Abernethy district of Saskatchewan, which began about the same time as at Shellmouth, Lyle Dick effectively disproved the old myth that the major factor in success as a homesteader was perseverance.[30] More important factors were the quality of the land, general economic conditions, and previous experience in farming (98% of the British nationals and 96% of the non-British nationals reporting their previous vocations on the homestead application forms in the region Dick studied said they had been farmers).[31] Those who came first were also able to profit tremendously by a rise in the price of land: acquiring their lands virtually for free, they saw the value of a quarter section rise to several thousand dollars in twenty years or so, a capital gain that could be used for expansion or farm improvements, or, as in the Wallaces' case, for a comfortable retirement. The most important factor, though, was accessibility to a railroad. In three adjacent townships studied by Dick, the cancellation rate of homestead entries was 51% for the one closest to the railroad, 57% for the one next farther away, and 75% for the farthest one. It is clear that "the risks of homestead failure increased with distance from the railway, particularly beyond twenty to twenty-two miles."[32] The Wallaces were probably lucky that the railway arrived in Russell when it did. They felt that the railroads were extortionists, but at the same time they were anxious to have a

---

30 Lyle Dick, "Factors Affecting Prairie Settlement: A Case Study of Abernethy, Saskatchewan in the 1880s," Canadian Historical Association, *Historical Papers* (1985). The greatest number of homestead entries in the Abernethy district occurred in 1882. No comparable study has been made of the Shell River district. See also his "Estimates of Farm-Making Costs in Saskatchewan, 1882–1914," *Prairie Forum* 6, no.2 (1981), and Lewis H. Thomas, "A History of Agriculture on the Prairies to 1914," *Prairie Forum* 1, no. 1 (1976).

31 In the three townships in the Abernethy district studied by Dick, 59% of all homestead entries were not "proved up."

32 Dick, "Factors Affecting Prairie Settlement," 20.

Shellmouth Amateur Dramatic Society, 1914. William Wallace is seated to the right of the bearded man with the cane. Photo courtesy of Isabel Joy and Brandon University.

railroad nearby. Next to William's desire for his sister Maggie to join him, longing for a railroad is the most prevalent theme in the letters.

Dick's work establishes "a statistical relationship between early arrival, acquisition of good, cheap, accessible land and long term success." Nonetheless, there was also something to be said for hard work. The Wallaces had a neighbour or two of the remittance man sort, and they did not last long.[33]

Though it is not known how much money they brought with them to Canada, the Wallace family was able to make an initial purchase of land near Brandon, and then to sell that land and use the proceeds to help get them started near Shellmouth. They were also able to buy oxen, horses, a wagon, a binder, and some comforts. Though they were perennially short of money—one of the main themes of the letters—and had to be helped by periodic small loans from Maggie, they were never really poor, and they were able to weather the difficulties of the early years of settlement.

33 The remittance man is described in Patrick Dunae, *Gentlemen Immigrants: From the British Public School to the Canadian Frontier* (Vancouver: Douglas and McIntyre, 1981).

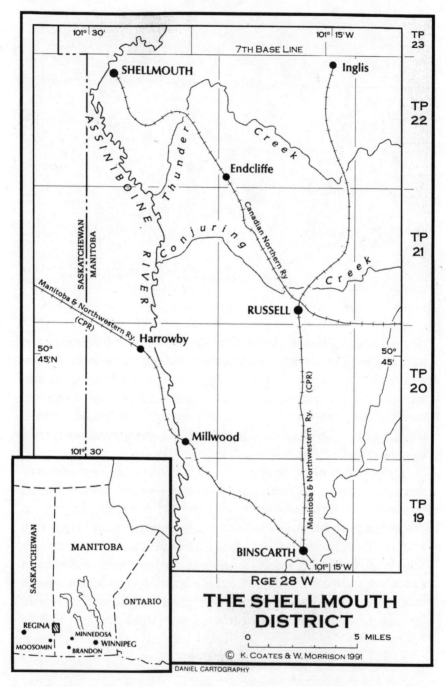

The Shellmouth District. Map by Daniel Cartography, courtesy of Brandon University.

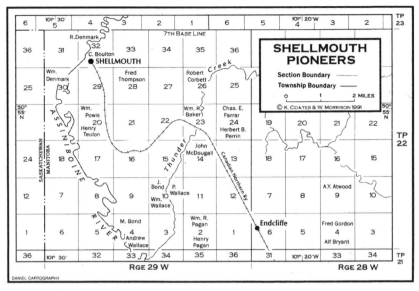

Shellmouth Pioneers. Map by Daniel Cartography, courtesy of Brandon University.

It did not take long for immigrants to Manitoba to discover the painful inequities of the Canadian economic and political system, particularly as they learned how the national protective tariff and transportation systems worked from the producers' end. Their protests, which started over railways and tariffs, led settlers south of Brandon to form a Farmers' Protective Union in 1883. The gathering farm anger, which focused on the Canadian Pacific Railway's monopoly, the need for provincial control over land and resources, and the elimination of the hated tariff, among other issues, was slowed by the introduction of partisan politics, particularly the attempt by western Liberals to co-opt the movement. The Wallaces, like so many of their neighbours, were highly critical of the government. They resented being taxed for the maintenance of officials in Ottawa, they complained of the lack of a post office, but most of all they had the typical love-hate relationship with the railroad. Like many Manitobans, William Wallace was so infuriated by the Macdonald government in the early 1880s that he talked openly of secession of the west and the formation of a new country. Though this came to nothing—an upsurge of patriotism during the 1885 Rebellion dampened it—such outbursts show that "western alienation" has a long history, beginning as soon as the west was settled. W. L. Morton, in fact, claimed that the rise of the Farmers'

Protective Union was Manitoba's counterpart to the 1885 rising of First Nations and the Metis.[34]

The letters of William Wallace are thus not only a fascinating social document, but a valuable record of the formation of a regional consciousness and identity in rural Manitoba, a consciousness that owes much to hostility to the federal government and to the difficulties of the early 1880s. This identity did not of course remain static—its exclusively British nature began to change as early as the 1890s with the arrival of Ukrainian and other European migrants and the departure of the less successful pioneers—but it remained distinctively regional, particularly in its suspicion of government and its ambivalent attitude towards railroads.

William Wallace was a steady man who shunned the crazes of his day. He witnessed the real estate boom of 1881, but correctly predicted that many who participated in it would regret doing so. When traces of gold were discovered in the Shellmouth district he declined to become a prospector. His philosophy was one of hard work and slow but steady progress towards prosperity—he thus was scornful of neighbours who spent what he considered to be excessive time in sports and games.

But he was also a man who enjoyed life. Despite the long hours of labour, there was also much recreation in the early years in western Manitoba. Going to town for the mail and supplies was a holiday, and the letters give evidence of the tremendous amount of visiting between neighbours that went on in the early days.

Shellmouth, just at the beginning of settlement when the Wallaces arrived in the spring of 1882, was, though newborn, by no means without cultural amenities. Because many of the earliest pioneers had, like the Wallaces, been well educated in Britain, there were from the beginning concerts, plays, and other performances, in which William took a large part. These served not only to alleviate hardship and loneliness, but also to emphasize that a British country was being founded on the prairies—an evening of recitations and Gilbert and Sullivan songs in Shellmouth had symbolic as well as entertainment value. William Wallace was a great reader, with a hunger for news of

34 See K. S. Coates, "Western Manitoba and the 1885 Rebellion," *Manitoba History*, 19 (Autumn 1990), 32–41.

the world, and thus appeals for books, newspapers, and magazines occur in many of his letters. His love of music was particularly strong, and one of his earliest purchases in Shellmouth—and the only extravagance of these early years—was a parlour organ, for which he paid the large sum of fourteen pounds sterling.

Residents of Shellmouth still alive in the late 1980s who remembered William Wallace only as a middle-aged and old man expressed surprise that in his youth he was a hard-working farmer, for his manner after he retired from farming at the age of fifty suggested a man of urban rather than rural origins. But as a young man he and his brother worked as hard as any pioneer. Not all of the Wallaces' neighbours were successful. Many failed through ineptitude, inexperience, or bad luck, and there was a sizeable turnover of population in the early years. But many others, including the Wallaces, succeeded and established themselves as prosperous citizens of the new land.

Because an edition of the complete letters would have necessitated a volume four times the length of this one, it was decided to publish only those written in the first five years of the Wallaces' life in Canada. These give a picture of the earliest, and in many ways the most interesting, years of pioneering in the Brandon and Shellmouth regions. The letters in this volume begin with the transatlantic voyage in 1881, and end early in 1886 with the aftermath of the Riel Rebellion. Nothing that pertains to Canada has been omitted from the text; the material that has been left out, indicated by ellipses, comprises in almost every case answers to Maggie's letters about relatives or events in the homeland, which have no relevance to Canada or Manitoba, and which would only burden the text with repetitious family details.

Because William Wallace was a good speller and a competent writer, virtually no changes have been made in the text of his letters. The only exception is that the originals of the letters are lacking in punctuation. Even periods are missing in many cases, and the letters flow in a stream of consciousness that makes them difficult to read. Virtually all the punctuation has been added by the editors, who have tried to use it as sparingly as possible. In the cases where words are illegible, the editors have either guessed at the meaning or left them out—in either case the guesses and omissions have been indicated by the use of square brackets. Other than this, nothing has been added; all the words, with the exception of a few postscripts from Andrew, are those of William Wallace.

Ken S. Coates, Johnson-Shoyama Graduate School of Public Policy, University of Saskatchewan

Bill Morrison, Emeritus Professor of History, University of Northern British Columbia

1881

S.S. Prussia[n]
22 March 1881

My Dear Maggie,

I was very sorry that I did not get meeting you as I proposed from Milngavie. Since leaving Glasgow we have had a very pleasant time of it, although the voyage has been what sailors style a rather rough one, quite worthy of the time of year it was undertaken. I could not think of keeping a journal but will just now write what I recollect.

After we had a last look for sometime at you and the other friends, we proceeded down the river very pleasantly although slowly ... We came to anchor at Greenock and waited there till about 4 o'clock on the purser with the ship's papers. On his coming aboard we sailed down the Firth of Clyde, the sea as smooth as glass. One saw the coast very indistinctly owing to a foggy haze. We did not see Arran, although we saw Holy Isle quite distinctly. When dusk came Pladd's light beamed forth brilliantly and it was kept [to the] right until it dropped down in the horizon. Then we picked up the Campbelltown light and shortly afterwards the Mull of Kintyre. By this time it was getting cold and we determined to go to bed. So taking a last look at Scotland in the form of the red light of Kintyre and the indistinct outline of Ailsa Craig we went below. You saw our berths; Papa took the single one near the window, Andrew the low one opposite, and I the top one for my own. My mind was puffed up with nautical valour, but alas, we got into our bunks after a great deal of merriment, considering the peculiarity of our surroundings.

We were just getting on with our first snooze when a rap comes to the cabin door and the pale, brown-whiskered visage of the Second Steward was inserted. "Are you feeling yourself comfortable?" he said. "Yes," the others said. I ventured out a very "where is a vomiter?" With that he exposed to view a large mongrelled looking specimen

I

of a spittoon with [?] attached. I ventured to ask him if it would be required. He said we would know that best ourselves, the steamer would likely be pitching a little in the morning, and [he] put in a quiet smile when Papa remarked that he felt it a little already. However, gentle sleep fixed our thoughts and eyelids.

When the awakening came, alas, I don't know how long I had been feeling uncomfortable, but I at last realized that a queer feeling was about my forehead and a queerer one about my grist mill. . . . The boat was swinging in a desperate manner—everything betokened a great storm. Up I determined to get, so getting one foot on to the basin stand I, after difficulty getting the notion of what I styled these confounded ticky bed clothes, got on to the cabin floor. And if I did not make the place lively for a bit, no one ever did—I was like a cat on a hot plate. Of course the others, though they were sick as I was, had to show their courage by pestering me with any number of ridiculous questions. But I at last silenced them and myself with that same vomiter, and after that, with some degree of comfort, proceeded to thoroughly complete my toilet. And when I got to the open air I felt all right. The others rose after me, and, notwithstanding their sickly attempts to laugh at me, were as bad if not worse than I was.

When I got on deck the scene was very grand—big peaking white crested waves all round as far as the eye could see and no land in sight, the steamer rolling about among them like a "tee totum."[1]But the 3rd mate assured us this was nothing, it was quite tolerable, and I have since learned to believe him.

Since writing the above when crossing the banks of Newfoundland we have called at Halifax. I trust you will be enabled to read it. The steamer was pitching a good deal and the saloon table was shaking very much with the working of the engine. Just now the sea is quieter and I am writing on top of the bunk bedclothes so [as] to legibly resume the story.

We had passed Tory Island on Sunday morning about four o'clock; we had not therefore the pleasure of seeing Ireland. The sea gradually became more stormy all day, and we just had to sit and hang on. My only difficulty was going below for meals, but this was

---

1   A teetotum is a child's four-sided top, or any top spun with the fingers.

all managed to do regularly. My breakfast was the only one I gave to the fishes and it did not trouble me in the slightest degree. I got two or three bad tumbles; one of them I did seawards and had my legs through the rail. I slightly skinned my shins and learnt to more desperately hang on the ropes they had run all along the decks to grasp by.

Next day the sun was shining very brightly and it dried up the decks and made it more pleasant. Our only employment was sitting away astern and watching the steamer's nose slapping at the waves deluging her front with great quantities of water and raising volumes of spray. The only vessel we saw on the voyage to Halifax passed. It was generally supposed to be the "Waldensian," but she could not be made out. On Tuesday, Wednesday and Thursday we very seldom got on deck it was so wet and stormy, the two latter days especially. She rolled and pitched about at an awful rate, shipping great quantities of water. When at tea on Thursday, the sea came in and deluged everything, bringing the meal to an abrupt conclusion. It had not been so very stormy in the morning when we arose, so we ventured to our breakfast by way of the deck. We had not far proceeded when a huge wave took a thundering slap at her. Papa was first and I last on the lee side of the engine room. Andrew, being about the centre, escaped with a soaked cap and collar, but Papa and I, being each nearer the ends, caught it. I was thoroughly soaked, every bit of me, to the skin. My only consolation was that it being salt water would soon dry out and would not give me the cold. So I took my breakfast as comforted as I could.

Soon after dinner, when the process of drying was nearly completed, something tempted me to go up on deck again. I crept along the safe and dry side of the funnel to what I considered a safe standing point. I had not been many minutes there when again the thundering noise was heard. I saw the whole cloud of water coming over the bow but did not move, as I expected the roll would throw it off, but it didn't. Along it came at what must have [been] a depth of three feet of water, lifting me quite off my feet. Had I not had a good catch of rope I should most assuredly have been swept overboard. If I was wet before, I was drowned now. I went below sad in mind and soaked in body. A talkative Yankee standing in the companion way told me to "say nothin' but come in and wipe your nose."

3

On Monday the gale was exchanged for a thick Newfoundland fog that delayed us very much and kept the steam whistle constantly a-booing. Tuesday was very much clearer, and everything was got ready for steaming into Halifax at nightfall, but down came the fog again and brought the steamer to a dead stand. I remained out of bed until about 10 o'clock to get my first view of the New World, but then had to turn in disappointed, as the fog showed no signs of lifting during the night. I understand they fired two guns or small cannons but none of us heard them, so you may judge how we slept.

Early in the morning, about two o'clock, I gradually awakened to the fact that the engines were again going, and the port light was again letting in a bright light. I got up quickly, and the first bit of America I saw was a queer lantern-looking lighthouse; but it was too cold and early to rise, so I got back to my old quarters and for two hours listened to the interesting work of porting a steamer.

I got up about 6 o'clock and had a pleasantly surprised look at Halifax. Learnt Russia was at her old tricks, shivered a bit and then determined on a walk before breakfast round the town. It was an exceedingly bright frosty morning and everything was gilded with a bright sun that would have made our place look pretty. The houses are principally built of wood with shingle fronts and slates, that is, thin square bits of hard wood all painted white or cream colour. Some of them are very nice and tasteful. On the opposite side of the bay is a town called Dartmouth, and its white-painted, straggled-looking houses with the green waters of the bay in the foreground and dark, pine-covered hill in the background made a particularly fine appearance. The bay narrows away to a point almost and then again opens into what is called the New Bedford Basin, capable of holding all the vessels of the British navy; but I will stop the description as I am not doing it justice. I will continue the story when I am more comfortable than sitting on my knees.

We expect to be at Boston tonight (Thursday) and will land tomorrow forenoon. We are all in splendid health and capital spirits. I did not write from Halifax as the Boston post is quite as early. I do not expect to be able to write you again until we get to Winnipeg. Do not criticise this letter too much; glean the sense and be thankful. Andrew will write a post script. We will call for your eagerly longed-for letter at Winnipeg post office. We all trust you are being reconciled to our absence. Every now and then I have a look at our watches and consider what Maggie will be doing this morning. When sitting on the deck cold and hungry for breakfast we came to the conclusion that you would be [?] your midday apology. I was exceedingly sorry that I did not again get writing Uncle Hugh. You might do so at a leisure time. Enclose the photographs—tell him I got the Bible and one of the books. The other I could not get but expect to be more fortunate at Boston, and let him know what you learn from this letter. By the bye, Papa wishes you to call at Higgins the Jeweller, pay him [?] and in return get a pin he intended for Andrew—bring it with you when you come.

We are now opposite the Bay of Fundy and expect to be anchored near Boston about 8 o'clock tonight. . . .

Your most affectionate brother
Willie

[postscript from Andrew]

I suppose by the time this reaches you, you will be getting very anxious to know how we liked our journey. As Willie has written nearly all the details I will make this a very short letter. After having taken our last look at you and the rest, we proceeded very slowly down to Greenoch, where we had to lie about four hours waiting for the Purser. After he came aboard we steamed down the Firth and at about 9 o'clock we made up our minds to go to bed. Shortly after we had turned in, the second steward came and stuck a vomiter on the side of my bed right at my nose, the same as if I was the only one that was going to be sick. In the morning when I awoke and felt awfully uncomfortable, and when Willie commenced to vomit I had to follow his good example. After that I felt quite well and was troubled no more with sickness.

For the first two or three days I enjoyed myself nicely, but then novelty of the thing wore away, and time hung very heavily on my hands. Learning that there was a small library aboard I was not long in making use of it. Yesterday morning we arrived at Halifax and I had a walk through the town. The roads were in a frightful condition and I did not think very much of the town at all. Shortly after two o'clock we sailed for Boston. The policemen at Halifax were the funniest looking objects you ever saw and I would not be the least frightened of them. After we left Halifax it was reported that there was a large number of whales about, although I did not see any. As this is all I have got to say at present I will close with love from all.

I am

Your most affectionate brother,

Andrew

P.S. I neglected to describe the policemen. They were awfully white-faced, wore full cheesecutters, white fronts, tailed coats and waddled about with small batons in their hands.

[post card to Maggie]

Minnedosa, NWT

29 April 1881

Today bought Railway Land Section 19, Township 11, Range 17. Address letters to Post Office Grand Valley, North West Terr. Write all news. Will move to land and begin before end of week. Land is 36 miles from here, eight from Grand Valley City, and 4 to 6 from Railway to be running this year. Will write fully when settled next week. All well and happy. Will receive your first letter in less than fortnight.

WSW

Springcreek Farm

Grand Valley

3 May 1881

Dear Maggie,

You must excuse the long time that has elapsed since I wrote you last. We have been so very busy getting the farm made comfortable that it is only now I have the opportunity of breaking the silence. I presume you have now received my post card and know that we have got fixed.

Since writing you at Winnipeg[2] we have seen and experienced a great many interesting things that would, I am sure, interest you very much. I do not know whether in the short time at my disposal I would do them justice, but I will try.

Until the morning we started west we were not sure if we would team all the way from Winnipeg, but owing to the rail track having been snowed up for some time and the consequent scarcity of cars we determined to hitch up and start. You would have laughed had you seen Andrew and I each with our yoke of oxen stepping it over the streets of Winnipeg with the waggon. We did not very well understand the cattle, and certainly they showed that we to them were incomprehensible. I was bad at leading them but very much worse at driving, keeping them on the straight. They went tolerably, but turning corners was the beginning of the fun. When near the loading point I have an uncomfortable recollection of being jammed hard in between the brutes and the corner of a stable and seeing Andrew and his yoke turning a corner with a rapidity that would have done any Epsom course credit. But we did at last get ready for starting.

Bryant[3] with his waggon took the lead after a bit. He had his four oxen attached and was accompanied by a hired man we called [?]. Our waggon followed and behind it was our cow commonly called "Maggie." Immediately behind was a waggon belonging to two young seamen who accompanied us on the steamer from Glasgow. Such is a description of the train—now for its experience.

Snow was over and around all things, except here and there patches on the trail, and, where snow was wanting, mud—dirty, soft, sticky mud that defies a brush was in abundance. We got over the first nine miles well enough but after that we had hard work. The snow was very deep sometimes, in fact almost all the remaining distance I was wading along side the oxen almost up to the knees. Before the remaining six miles were over I was ready to drop down with fatigue. I never welcomed anything so much as the sight of our sleeping place for the night. I was actually asleep twice when

---

2   This letter is not among the Wallace papers.

3   The Bryant family came over on the same ship, and later settled in the Shellmouth district near the Wallaces.

unyoking. Never before had I such a relish for my supper or enjoyed the night's rest, and since that time I have never had [the same] satisfaction of either food or bed.

The deep snow broke up the continuity of the train. Bryant arrived a short time before us, and Shaw and Walker did not turn up till late in the evening without their waggon, which they had been forced to leave five miles back. Both of them had their feet badly frozen. They were not able to go any farther, and Shaw will not likely be able to work for a year.

Next morning we started from Headingly and got along very pleasantly all day, arriving in the evening at Houses.[4] We passed on the way a stopping place called Jerusalem owned by the only Jew in the country. We met him in the evening; a comical genius he was with his "tousands and tousands" and unceasing praise of "Lundeen" as being the place to make money.

Our next stage was Poplar Point. We again had hard driving getting there. The snow was very deep and the waggon was often off the trail right away into the snow up to the axles. The sun was shining very powerfully; the effects of it are still to be seen on Andrew. He got a terrible burning; his face was swollen beyond recognition up till a week ago. Now he is more like what he was, but still the lower part is speckled with hard scabs. The skin has twice completely come off my own, and for a time it was very sore.

This stopping place was a miserable hole, everything dirt and pork grease, but it is all over now. I think anybody who experiences some of the western sloppery with pleasure would enjoy a horsetail in their soup. Next day we arrived at Portage la Prairie, having accomplished the distance of 60 miles in 3 and a half days. Very good time considering the state of the roads. But time will not permit of my further continuing the story.

I will just shortly tell you how we are now situated. We have bought a quarter section, 160 acres of Railway land that we mean to make our centre, our home. It is splendid land with every advantage. A creek or stream of splendid water runs on one side. On the banks of it is a spring of water that is said never to freeze. We are sure to have a railway station within four miles. Grand Valley (Florence

---

4   That is, stopping houses.

City I understand is soon to be its name) is sure to be one of the great western cities and is about seven miles from here. We will have the advantage of church services there and possibly nearer during the summer. We already have got up a nice proud house of one apartment. It will be thoroughly finished in a day or two.

Our animals are getting along very well. The cow will be calving in a day or so and then we shall have abundance of milk. The beast is a regular petted nuisance—her nose must be into everything. I expect that any amount of thrashing will not keep her outside the premises when she is loose at the grass. We have also got a nice dog called Jess, about three months old. She is shy like a ducking spaniel. We already have abundance of friendly neighbours.

After we have done with the spring work I may possibly go farther west and take up homestead and pre-emption rights for Papa and myself; so with 500 acres we should do very well for time. Tomorrow I purpose going to the Valley for paper to cover the inside of our house and will at the same time post you this letter, and next day we will likely begin to the ploughing. Now you must excuse my stopping this letter. It is getting late and things are not just yet comfortably fixed up, but soon you will get a more complete epistle. I really wish to hear from you. I suppose you will have quite a budget of surprising news, particularly about Uncle Hugh. I trust—we all trust—that all the friends are well and prospering. We all unite in sending our kindest love to Cousins Henry, Agnes, and yourself.

Your most affectionate brother
Willie.

P.S. Do not address letters to Spring Creek Farm. The people about here do not understand that kind of nonsense. Just address to Post Office, Grand Valley, NWT. We will likely have a post office within a mile of us in a day or two. I may receive your first letter tomorrow.

Grand Valley
19 May 1881

My Dear Maggie,

I with the others have just finished my evening repast and I daresay you would just between ourselves like to know something about it. Try and picture to yourself a rolling prairie and at a particular position of it, a stream or creek of running water . . . with here and there deep ponds of water. Not far from these imagine a house, size 12 ft. by 12 ft., built of wood and rather comfortable-looking. Outside of it, numerous farming implements, and not far off, cattle grazing and two oxen ploughing. Along with them, two young men often times sadly troubled and perplexed with their work and mosquitoes, and very much relieved when their work is over. Quickly they unyoke, hobble the oxen, trot down to the creek, wash their hands, and return to the aforementioned house where you may, if you can in your imagination, follow them.

A large-looking stove in the centre of the floor is the first thing to catch the attention. On the right hand a long high table occupies nearly the whole length of the interior. Underneath, three chests are ensconced, bearing the marks of a long journey; above, two shelves covered with numerous useful articles. On the left hand side are barrels built over with some bags, and right in front are three beds, two pretty high up and one underneath. The division is marked by two boards on which soon a timepiece will be prominent and before which a table is fixed, on which is spread the business of the evening. This is approached by the two young men in an eager manner, and the tea party, numbering three, seat themselves in the meantime on boxes, casks, or what they may most conveniently group.

The fare consists of tea well sugared and whitened with deliciously rich cream, bacon, stewed evaporated apples, and scones. Occasionally a stray mosquito darts about in a meditative humming manner and diverts the appetite, but that is pleasure in comparison to being in the midst of the thousands outside. Shut your eyes and if possible picture this in your mind and you will have an idea of what Spring Creek farm is like. I have not depicted the inhabitants; that however is the easiest done of all—three individuals of the masculine gender garbed in old clothes and wide-awake hats,[5] with well-tanned countenances.

You will be glad to hear that we now have a post office about a mile from us. Our address is now Elton Post Office, Grand Valley, Manitoba, NWT.[6] At the same place also divine service is held every Sunday by a Presbyterian missionary. All this with the railway about three miles from us about harvest time causes us to think that we are very well off.

I promised in my last letter to continue the record of my doings. Unfortunately I was unable to keep a journal but I will do my best to remember. We arrived at Portage la Prairie on the Friday evening, and journeyed up the main street, a perfect sea of water, to our abiding place. We very gladly welcomed the inside of the stable-yard, put up our oxen and entered the hotel quite ready for our supper, as we had very little to eat since morning. The hotel was just crammed with all the visitors to be expected in a western would-be city, and sometimes it was difficult to get a bed—otherwise the place was very comfortable. Everything about the place betokens trade, but that is the most that can be said of it, other than that it was a combination of wooden houses; mud, water and snow struggled about but bearing the marks of a hard struggle to be reunited.

Our goods did not come forward as we expected, and not till Monday evening at six o'clock did we get resuming our journey, leaving some of the goods that had not come forward to come by the steamer up the Assiniboine.

This time we journeyed alone, as the Bryants had gone on before. We travelled nine miles that evening, the greater part of it with the aid of no light. We had very hard work driving the oxen over a not very good trail, but like everything else the journey had an end, and that about eleven o'clock at a place called Rat Creek.[7] When crossing the creek by a frail apology for a bridge we saw an Indian encampment at the edge of the creek—you know the shape of the tent with the bright fires. I that night thought them very comfortable. We had great trouble waking up the landlord of the stopping place

---

5   A soft felt hat with a broad brim and a low crown.
6   At this time the McVicar house was used for mail in Grand Valley.
7   A settlement in the Portage la Prairie area.

because of the intense cold—I do not think he thanked us for our untimely visit.

Next morning the frost was very keen, but the hard snow on the trail was very good for both the waggon and the sleigh. We had for company a large family of Indians, but their dogs were the only ones who intercoursed with us. The men are swarthy, strong, rather fine-looking fellows, but the females—faugh—physic.[8] I have not seen as many of them—that is, the Indians—as I expected. They are more numerous about the towns and none of them are to be seen where we now are.

About mid-day a bitter cold wind began to blow over the prairie and rendered our first camp dinner a failure. The camp stove only commenced to crackle cheerfully when we were ready to start the trimmed bread cousin Agnes kindly provided us with, which was on occasions like these thoroughly appreciated. We heartily welcomed the sight of Cook's Stopping Place after a sore afternoon's driving up a steep trail among deep snow.

The lady of this establishment was a study. She was evidently a well-informed, educated woman, but a tremendous talker. Her tawdry, washed-out appearance gave me the impression that she was thus hermitized far from any neighbours because of drink, but I was agreeably surprised into admitting that she was a good cook. She was provided with an American Organ—I could appreciate it.

Next day we had very unpleasant journeying. The snow was soft, sometimes the sleigh would stick, other times the waggon, causing a continual changing of oxen. At Beaver Creek the waggon had a very dangerous descent. The haul down the bank was very steep and crooked, and many a smash has been occasioned by it. We got down it pretty well, although I must admit I was very nervous over the driving, and would not for a good deal do the same again. The bridge over the creek was out of repair and we had to cross on the half-rotten ice. The hind wheels flumped about midway, but we got over without damage. We arrived by Bryce's Stopping Place just before dark, thoroughly tired out. The only person there was a young German who cooked and attended single-handed to the wants of his guests. This was the roughest night's up-putting we had on the journey.

---

8   Faugh—an expression of disgust. The passage is unclear.

We had a terrible day's travelling next day. At first the road was among water stumps and small hills, but farther on the snow became very deep and wet. Time after time the waggon stuck. We had sleigh runners fastened to axles, and in desperation we took the wheels off. This occasioned the cutting down of our first tree, but still the yoke of oxen were unable to draw it. At last we had unwillingly to leave behind the sleigh and its contents. We had not far proceeded when smash went one of the runners on a tree, and rendered it useless. Again we had to go back for the sleigh, put all the more valuable things on it, clear out the waggon, replace the wheels, draw it aside from the trail, and leave it to the mercy of the wolves and weather. We had a long, tedious, wearisome journey of nine miles through sand hills and snow covered plains to Pine Creek.[9]

Next morning Andrew and I had to retrace our steps for the waggon. It was standing as we left it—the only thing missing was the whipple tree chains. So much for prairie honesty. We had pretty hard work getting the waggon through the snow, which at this time was particularly soft because of the frost being thawed out. Two or three days afterwards the snow would in all likelihood have disappeared.

We had purposed up till this time journeying to Rapid City, but here we were induced to travel to Grand Valley.[10] We started on the Saturday morning again, and had another sore day's work among the snow, only accomplishing twelve miles, arriving at Flewelling's Stopping Place in the evening. Opposite his house the railroad surveyors were encamped, and alas for us all, the stable accommodation was taken up with their horses, so our poor old oxen had to make the best of it all night in the cold.

I think we were quite justified in starting for more suitable lodgings on the Sunday morning[11]—anyhow we did it, and I must say that it has thoroughly cured me of any desire to further make inroads on the day of rest. At first we got along pretty well. By the bye, I forgot to mention that we left the waggon and its contents

---

9   North of Melbourne, Manitoba, flowing through the "great plains" which lie between Edrans and Melbourne.

10   Decisions on where to locate were often made in this casual manner.

11   The Wallaces were as a rule hesitant to "break the Sabbath."

at Pine Creek, so now we only had the sleigh. We crossed another range of sand hills, and the bare places caused the sleigh some troubles, but when we got on to the plains the snow was very deep and soft, and the trail very intricate. When we were about half a mile from our destination the sleigh made a last and determined stop. It had to be dug out—the oxen had even to be dug from out of the snow. All was useless. Again we had to leave a goodly number of our belongings behind; this time all struggled over the snow. Further on in the evening we came back and got them all right.

We were now at Nicol's Stopping Place about seven miles from Grand Valley. He induced us to start next morning and look at land in the neighbourhood. I had the privilege of being the land hunter—no very pleasant work. I started about six in the morning and was without food for twelve hours, and that on the prairie is itself no joke. Hard walking among snow is also very tiresome. A good twenty miles was covered judging and looking for sections of land. Crossing the creeks was particularly dangerous, as the ice was rotten and covered to great depth with soft snow. The usual way is to cross on all fours with the knees well spread out to give as much surface as possible. This I was not particularly good at, and very often I had a severe struggle to get to the surface. When I got home Papa had been strongly advised to the portion of land we are now on. I had been favourably impressed with a section of land, but it was decided to start for Minnedosa where the land office was next day, [and] there learn the terms for the land we have now chosen.

But I must stop my narrative, as it is getting late, and there is a good deal of thunder which causes it to be rather unpleasant to be this silently employed. We are all well and happy, and getting along very well. We have now ploughed fully ten acres of land, got all the potatoes planted—a goodly number—and some corn sown. Now we will get along better, as the oxen are getting into better condition with the new grass. But I will write further particulars in my next letter. We eagerly await letters from you; they must be particularly interesting. You will now have quite a budget of news. I hope you remember to send a weekly Herald, as we now hear nothing of the outside world. I trust—we all trust—you keep strong and well, that you are getting on with your studies. Some of the inhabitants hereaway are getting interested—they vainly imagine you will become schoolmistress. I will write soon again. We all united in sending our love to Cousin Agnes and Henry and yourself.

Your affectionate brother

Willie.

P.S. Should the friends think we are hatching some conspiracy, let them know that I mean next time to write a letter for public perusal where I shall endeavour to recollect grammar—and we are just now very busy, and little time can be spared.

[P.S. from Andrew]
My Dear Maggie,

I suppose you will be wondering what has come over me that I have never written you since we were at Port Huron, but I unluckily got my thumb cut and then frozen, and it has troubled me till lately so I hope you will take this as an excuse for what you would be beginning to consider as forgetfulness. There will be little use for me to say anything about our journey from Winnipeg except that I had a very sore face which was swollen to twice its usual size, was afterward covered by huge scabs, the last of which did not disappear until a few days ago, so you may judge what kind of spectacle I was to be going through the country.

I like the place very much where we have settled and there are large beds of wild strawberries and a great many wildflowers; there are also a great many birds of every shade and colour you could imagine. The only things which trouble us are the mosquitoes which go in for Willie and I on an extensive scale, Papa getting only an occasional nip from them. As it is coming very near bedtime and I am very tired I will now conclude with love from all to all. I am

Your affectionate brother
Andrew

Grand Valley
8 June 1881

My Dear Maggie,

I purposed commencing this letter before this time, but for the last two or three nights I have been very weary and unfit to make much progress at letter writing, so you must excuse this letter being no better than its predecessors.

Tonight I am perhaps worse off, as the wind is in the south. You do not understand what that means, simply this—our stove is not finally fixed up, and the upper outlet of it presents a bold unbroken face in that direction, consequently our humble abode is filled with wood smoke that has a particular and peppery regard for the eyesight.

My last letter concluded with the information that we were bent for Minnedosa. Andrew was left at the stopping place with full charge of our worldly gear. Papa and I very quietly departed on our journey, informing no one of our intention, as this might have resulted in somebody soon being ahead of us. We had not journeyed far when our old friends, the creeks and marshes, troubled us. So far as I can remember, we waded five of them. You soon get accustomed to them and go for them with your boots and trousers in their usual place and without winking or hesitating. These we crossed in this manner but the last attempt failed, as we foresaw the prospect of the water getting over our trouser tips. This snub caused us to retrace our steps two miles to a farm house where we got accommodation and fortunately, the promise of a drive to our destination and back.

Next morning we started at five o'clock and with two horses in a waggon we made good speed through creeks and over prairie. The country we travelled through must be exceedingly attractive in the summer time, dolled all over with groves of trees and innumerable lakelets, quite unfitting it for farming. We occasionally met with Indians in full hunting style, long barreled guns and plenty of knives, all along the trail. About 28 miles from where we started the number of houses could be counted on your five fingers.

We stopped at one to give the horses their midday meal. There was no one about the place. The mud hut was secured but the stable could be entered, and the horses had the advantage of their superiors— they got their dinner. We had not been long prowling around the premises when I espied a portly, middle-aged gentleman making for the house with a gun upon his shoulder. He introduced himself as the owner of the establishment. Fortunately he was peaceably disposed and invited us into the house. The interior was very much nicer than the exterior, but all confusion and bachelor-like.

We gradually learnt from him that he had been a captain in the navy and had for a long time been in Africa—rather a decided difference from Manitoba. Here he and a brother were settled, evidently going in for stock raising. I wonder what his friends in England would have thought had they seen him, especially when he kindly doubled over a decided corporation on his knees and applied his wind organs to the stove fire, warming some tea for us.

After enjoying this luxury we to the trail again and arrived at Minnedosa about three o'clock. This place was at first called Tanners Crossing because of a half-breed who there kept a stopping place. But this did not satisfy the inhabitants of the western city, and it was easily re-christened Prairie City. Again unsatisfied, they less easily termed it Minnedosa, with the result that it may be styled either of the last two names. It is very pleasantly situated in a valley with pretty high land all around, that in the north side is table land, the first of that kind I have yet seen. The river Little Saskatchewan runs down the valley, and the city consists of a sprinkling of wooden huts and houses on both sides. The railway having been altered to our city has blighted the prospects of this city very much.

The land office is at a place two miles up the river called Odina[12] so thither we at once started. The river ice had swept away a part of the bridge and across that we had to go over a single plank. On coming back from the land office I think I really had symptoms of having found the bottom of my stomach, having had nothing since breakfast. About two o'clock a good American supper, the like [of which] is unknown in Scotland, soon put us all right. I was not quite so badly off as a gentleman in the hotel—I think he must have been in government employment. He had just arrived from an 800 mile journey, and for 2 or 3 days he had been unable to stop travelling to cook even pemmican lest he should have been frozen.

---

12 Odanah was surveyed in 1879 as the site of a future city.

Now we are able to look at the Northwest with more peace and pleasure, for really we had secured land there and had an interest in it. I will not here describe the land but will do so later on. I here wrote you a postcard stating our place of settlement and also sent one to Birdtail requesting your letter to be again addressed—it has not yet come to hand, and I fear must have gone astray, so I trust you did not send many sweet things in it.

I was determined to secure a dog, and soon I had the city informed of my intention, with the result that I at last obtained what is called a ducking spaniel, three months old. The man's children were spoiling it, and it them, and he was glad to be rid of it. When all things were ready next morning I provided myself with a string and went for the pup, but unfortunately it detested compulsion and abhorred halters. It no sooner felt the string catch than it committed a series of yells that would have done a frenzied ass credit, and round the locality it went like lightning. Taking advantage of a serene moment, I got it in my arms and to the waggon; there Papa was snugly ensconced in the rear, and he bravely—armed as he was with a pilfered beef bone— volunteered to care for the animal so long as the waggon remained steady. All went peaceably, and the bone had sweetness, but at the first turn of the wheel all animal enjoyments were at an end with the pup. The yelping, biting, howling, dancing it performed around that waggon defies description, and brought every dog in the city to mournfully join in the chorus. However, we did at last manage to dissolve the relationship, and after a time got along quietly.

At that time of the year settlers set fire to the old grass on the prairie to enable them more easily to proceed with the ploughing, and they are quite indifferent as to the proportion these fires may assume on the trail. We saw these fires all around, and really it was a grand sight. Our old friend the navy captain was very energetically either encouraging or protecting his property from one of these, I could not distinguish which.

We slightly changed our route, and this enabled us to arrive at the Fingerboard[13] in time for dinner. This is a well known stopping

13 This was on the Edmonton trail west of the present town of Brookdale. A fingerboard pointed out branches of the trail leading to Brandon, Minnedosa, and Rapid City. There was a stopping house nearby run by the Dodd family.

place, and so named because at that point a directing post was erected on the Minnedosa trail to the newly formed Rapid City. I tenderly carried my doggy into the dining premises and tied it to the chair foot. The clatter of dishes caused at first a slight entanglement but I managed with great tact to appear interested in my own dinner and the conversation, whilst at the same time, with great slight of hand aiding the dog in helping me to consume an extraordinary 25 cents worth. But when the hunks of provision failed, the grand finale came. I had just left my chair when a noise caused the pup to spring it lively. Round the house it went with the chair, and the smashing and yelping that ensued was I am sure never equalled in that house before. But at last the noise was quelled, much to the comfort of an old Newfoundland whose hair was actually standing straight on end, and our journey soon thereafter came to a happy termination.

We saw two deer on a hill a short distance away. Seventeen of them wintered last season a mile or two north or our place, so there is a temptation, Maggie—venison. We remained at the farm house all night, as we heard that the stopping place was filled with travellers unable to cross the creek. We eased Andrew's mind as to our welfare next forenoon.

That night there was no room in the inn, and I tried to sleep first of all on a haystack, but fearing rain and desiring more company I adjourned to the stable and learnt the truth of the adage "better have no company than bad company." That night mine was principally hens and a cock—a cock that regularly crowed the hours at the highest pitch a chronic form of bronchitis would permit. Had it been other than very dark and my surroundings uncertain, my murderous intentions would surely have been fulfilled.

Next morning Andrew and I returned to Pine Creek for the waggon and its contents, and with the oxen did the distance—28 miles—in one day, not very bad work considering the heat. Nothing worthy of note occurred on the journey. I was quite enchanted by the sight of a few blades of green grass in the Sand Hills after the white snow and black mud—it was a pleasant contrast. When we arrived at Pine Creek we found the bridge swept away, so we had rather a damper before we got to our destination.

I here became acquainted with a recently arrived Scotchman named Mr. Grierson. He had before been in the corn trade in

Glasgow and L'pool, but he had lost a great deal of money, and here he was beginning life anew. He was the first real Scotchman I had spoken to since arriving in America. All the people hereaway are Canadians, but more of them afterwards....

We remained at Pine Creek[14] over the Sunday, and the following morning started to return. This was more pleasantly begun, as the bridge was temporarily replaced. But despite our exertions we were forced to remain overnight at a place four miles from our destination. On resuming our journey next morning we got on well, even the Bogey Creek—a regular bogey—until we got stuck in an alkali swamp, and for an hour we had our share of digging out and whipping up of oxen in the rain. But this journey, like the others, had too an end, and this time we continued on and stopped on our own property. I will not further continue in this letter the story of our doings, but will leave some things to help my next one. We all look forward to the mail on Saturday, as we are certain to have a letter from you, and I trust also a Herald. A newspaper will be a novelty as we have not perused one since leaving the Portage, so we are ignorant of the doings of the outside world.

You would I suppose be at some great display on the Queen's birthday. Papa and Andrew drove down to the Valley that day. There the people had a grand display of flags.

We are well and getting along splendidly. We have only yet managed to plough about seven acres, but our oxen are now improving and we are likely to make better progress. Andrew wants me to write you that he has nothing particular to write about, so the sooner you are here to cuff his ears and sharpen up his powers of observation the better....

P.S. Would you kindly obtain and send to me a copy of Isaac Pitman's system of shorthand. The price is, I think, sixpence, and you can get it about Renfield St. sometime when you are passing down.

Your affectionate brother
Willie

---

14 The south branch of the Hudson's Bay trail, after leaving Portage la Prairie, passed Rat Creek, McKinnon's Creek, Pine Creek, Oberon, Moore Park, and Rapid City, then joined the north branch of the trail a few miles east of the Salt Lake, in the neighbourhood of Strathclair.

Grand Valley
23 June 1881

My Dear Maggie,

Glad, glad was I when Papa and Andrew returned from the Valley yesterday bearing a letter from you, a very voluminous letter, so much so that the P[ostal] Officials thought it worth ten cents before delivering. A very interesting letter; I have read it with unabated interest three times, and a little longer meditation over it will cause me to go over it again—and lastly a long-expected letter. We have given the postman a lively time of it, informing him of our expectations and requesting him to do more than he could possibly do. Andrew and I even went the length (now do not let this go further east or west than Partrick) of travelling through myriads of mosquitoes and over flooded creeks for twelve miles Sunday a week ago, after Church service, and great was our chagrin when nothing was the response to our eager inquiry. But now we are so far satisfied, and your succeeding letters will be more easily obtained, as Elton post office is not much more than a mile from here. I was very much pleased to hear of your welfare and all the news regarding our friends. I am truly sorry to hear of Uncle Hugh's decision and its results. I fear he will soon give up preaching. I will write him next week and impress him with the fact that he ought to come out to the prairie for a month or two. The dry bracing atmosphere would do him a world of good. I have as yet written none of my old friends—you have been my only correspondent . . .

You ask me how the barometer is getting along. It was not up since getting here, however it has gone back once. Indeed, it was as far back as it could go. I think the depressing influence is the thunder and wind usually prevailing during this, the rainy season. Next month it will, I trust, recover. You also inquire after the flute. I can with variations blow two or three easy tunes out of it, but the mosquitoes will not permit anyone to employ both hands. For a short time so little progress will be made until they are *non est*[15] . . .

---

15 Non-existent.

I do not think I have in any of my letters described our position from Winnipeg. Grand Valley is considered to be 150 miles west from Winnipeg [via] the trail. If you have a map of the colony showing Portage la Prairie, just follow the River Assiniboine from that place as far again as it is from Winnipeg, and to that add a third or 30 miles and you have the position of Grand Valley. Our locality is six miles north. Minnedosa is farther north, about 25 miles.

In my last letter I left you in suspense on our own property. We purposed that afternoon taking possession, but the goods were not long emptied from the waggon on to the ground when a high wind resolved itself into a perfect gale or blizzard, and we were back to the stopping place in time to escape the rain and snow that followed. Towards evening it cleared away, but it was too late to set up the tent so we abode for the night under cover of wood.

Next day we completed the transfer and before nightfall the tent was completed. But if the season is the rainy one and goods outside liable to be spoiled with any stray showers that might be around, and with strange cattle tethered out on a strange place, my experience is the reverse of pleasant. Hard work is a good nurse, so we all slept well the first night, but in the morning, oh!—the rising that morning I shall never forget. The frost was intensely keen, and all my clothes with working about the creek were as hard as boards—my socks could have carried water. But the sun soon thawed us out.

Two or three nights of the tent was quite sufficient, and Andrew and I set out for the sawmill twelve miles distant for wood to build a shanty. We reached the mill about 12 o'clock, got loaded and purposed getting back that night, but the load of wood was too much for the oxen after a bit, and we had a time of it. Time after time we had to disload the wood, go forward with a portion and come back for the remainder. It was really distressing and disheartening work. We only accomplished half the distance that night.

Next afternoon we reached our place, and speedily house-building was proceeded with. Soon we had some sense of comfort. It is not very large, 12 × 12 feet, but it suits us nicely. We purpose after the proper house is built to turn it into a granary and root house. We spent our first Sunday out on the prairie in it. Since that time we have been getting along very pleasantly.

Our attention was first turned to planting potatoes and getting in some garden seeds. We planted a goodly array of both. Unhappily our first sowing of peas were made away with during the night by the oxen belonging to a neighbour—still, we have five drills left of later-sown. We then ploughed and sowed oats, but the immense number of birds picked up a large amount of the seed, and it consequently is rather thin. Then we sowed barley. The birds did not care so much for it, and we will likely have a good crop, as these were all sown in the sod. It does not get the chance to grow quickly that otherwise it would have, but so far these all promise very well. The potatoes will be ready for use in less than a month. Our time has since been occupied in breaking ground for next year. We are progressing rather slowly, as our oxen were, with the journey and subsequent exposure, in very poor condition—but we have about twenty acres ploughed.

The prairie is all covered with a great variety of flowers, and the number of strawberry blossoms is beyond conception. We are just now experiencing the rainy season, and really the term is an unhappy one. We have not had a really wet day, just occasional thunder showers—they are heavy but do not last long. Next month ushers us into real summer weather, and the possibility is that little or no rain will fall until May next year.

The thunderstorms here are really a grand sight—the lightning is very vivid and flashes over a great tract of sky, forming itself into a wonderful variety of strange devices. Last week I saw one shaped exactly like the outer tracing of a Prince of Wales feather.[16] The thunder roll is particularly heavy and continuous—I have heard only one sharp report, and it was a stunner. We were out ploughing at the time. Papa and Andrew unyoked when the rain became heavy, but I was nearer the end and was not so prudent. When hurriedly unyoking and loosing the inside chains, the rattle came. I do not know what it could be compared to. It made such a terrific noise the oxen were completely scared, and off they went in fright, with a plough and ploughman dangling helplessly behind them. Happily however, their mad career was checked without any damage.

I never tire of watching the sheet lightning. After dark all around the sky will sometimes be covered with dark heavy clouds, and from

---

16 The coat of arms of the Prince of Wales displays ostrich plumes.

each of these the lightning is continually blinking, sometimes so brilliantly that everything can be for an instant distinguished over the prairie. It reminds me very much of the glaring representations of thunderstorms shown by magic lanterns, only more brilliant and vast. You will be thinking I have written plenty of the sulphurous.

We are getting plenty of houses round us now. A fine one is being erected by a neighbour, the saw mill owner. He was recently married, and I suppose will now reside on his farm. But I will write you more of our surroundings next time, meantime I trust you will excuse my short letter. So many of us are writing that I am afraid the postman will fine you also ten cents. By the bye you might impress Mary Miller with the fact that the Northwest has a lovely climate, and is a good country to invest money. By August I expect the mosquitoes hereaway will be pretty well murdered out. I am very glad that Cousin Agnes has got so well over the operation that she had good reason to dread. With kindest love to you all I remain

Your affectionate brother
Willie

Grand Valley
24 June 1881

My Dear Maggie,

We received your first and long-expected letter on Wednesday when Papa and I were at the Valley with a team of oxen and the waggon. As you wanted to know what kind of oxen I have it might interest you if I gave you an account of our journey to the Valley. We started at about half past seven in the morning and got on all right till we came to the first creek, when the oxen took a sudden fit and ran the waggon up on the bank and nearly upset us into the water—as it was, both of us had to jump out, and after a little trouble we got back to the track and crossed all right. The next creek, which was over the hill, was lined with mud on each side, and in it we fared no better. For when we were halfway through the mud one of the traces came off, and the pole of the waggon came out, and I had to get out and wade through the mud to fix it up, and again we proceeded on our way. The next creek we managed to cross without any mishap, but when we came in sight of the Assiniboine we were surprised to see that it had overflowed its banks—a thing which has not occurred for twenty-five years. Before entering the Valley there is a part of the trail very soft and low-lying, and this was completely flooded with water, and was almost as broad as the Assiniboine is at its usual height.

Again bad luck was with us. For when we were in the middle of it, one of the thongs of the oxens' hems broke, and Papa rolled up his trousers and waded forward and mended them, and then led the oxen out. We managed to cross all the creeks safely on the way back, although at the second-last creek I firmly believe we would have stuck had it not been for the fact that we were going home, as the waggon was up to the axles in mud. We got home at about four o'clock. From this you will see what kind of road it is to the Valley. The colour of my oxen are white and brown, and the other is completely white, and Willie's are white and brown and the other brown. We have got a dog, and I get some rare fun out of it, and it is with it that I spar, only it uses both its teeth and its feet. I will give you a description of the rest of the things about here in my next letter. . . . love to you all from

Andrew

Grand Valley
29 June 1881

My Dear Maggie,

This is a confidential letter between you and ourselves to let you know all about our condition, and your prospects of joining us here.

You already know all the particulars of our journey here, but will be curious to learn why we did not proceed farther and secure more land. The reasons were our oxen were unloaded, and this delayed us when travelling, and cause extra expense. When we arrived here our oxen were jaded and our purse very light, rendering it impossible to proceed much farther. The land we did take up is without doubt a good investment. By the end of the next summer season we could sell it and our stock at a sum that would refund the principal and pay our expenses coming here and also, if reckoned desirable, home again with possibly 50 or 100 [pounds] additional. Now all this considered, causes me to think over the fact of whether or not you should join us at the time agreed. I will try to inform you of both sides.

The climate, so far as we have experienced it, is simply unparalleled, but the winter will be, I am afraid, very unpleasant. All admit hereabouts that extraordinary precautions have to be taken, rendering travelling dangerous. Confined thus to the spot, I fear the long dark nights will be very monotonous. The soil is peculiarly and particularly rich, but the country's aspect is not very picturesque. Plain after plain is all that can be seen, with hardly a tree to relieve the scene. In the summertime it is very beautifully arrayed, with gorgeous and many-coloured flowers, but that is only for a comparatively short period. During winter it is just one flat after another of white snow. This, you can imagine, will be very dreary. This all causes the country to be a splendid one for farming, but the beauties of rurality are very so-so.

The farm houses are principally built of long tree-logs with notches at both ends and laid one on the other, mud or lime filling up the intervals, no plaster, seldom even whitewashed inside. The ground floor is one apartment with stove not far from the centre. A trap stair or ladder leads up to the attic, the usual sleeping apartment—this is seldom even provided with curtains. Our prospective house I will write of further on.

The outhouses consist of a stable or byre. This is just a frame or skeleton covered over with piles of straw or hay. The farm steadings therefore have anything but an immense or attractive appearance. Although they may be suitable, all this constitutes a rather bare and dreary scene unless the sun is shining brilliantly, as it usually does during the summer days.

The inhabitants, our neighbours, are our principal cause of dislike. Nearly every one of them came from Lower Canada.[17] The stock question is "what part of Ontario do you come from?" (It is their estimate of the winter I gave you). They as a class are very undesirable society. A good-going Yankee is pleasure compared to them. They are about the greediest, least thankful, unenthusiastic lot

---

17 In fact, they came from Upper Canada.

I could imagine. Their ignorance of everything but surroundings is awful, and renders intercourse wearisome and unentertaining. Boors and clodhoppers is exactly the term they deserve. You would think they imagined that all things were common. Into the house they will march without asking your leave, no matter whether Sunday or Saturday they take an unblushing inventory of everything, spit all around and talk commonplace. No things or articles are safe from their borrowing proclivities. Notwithstanding this horror they are [a] hardy, hardworking, fine-looking, rough-and-ready class of people. Now, how would you like ten years or so at the least of these surroundings and society with sometimes pretty hard work?

But this is not all. We are at present hampered for want of money, and before you come out we must borrow £50 to build a house. It is almost impossible to obtain logs. We will require to build of lumber or sawn boards. After two years we will be sure to have sufficient money, but at first we will be a little scrimped. Now the question before we do this is, will you care about coming out? By coming here you will forego all the exertions you have made for some years, as I fear it will be impossible to procure a suitable or convenient school engagement except at some distance. You will thus in a manner render yourself dependent without your certificate. I myself would . . . [letter unfinished and unsigned]

Grand Valley
1 July 1881

My Dear Maggie,

The River Assiniboine is flooding great tracts of country along its banks and has stopped all ferry communication—such a flood has not been for twenty-five years. It is reported that heavy rains in the west have been the cause, others report that a large lake has burst out, thus are we in doubt of the cause. But sad to state, not so with regard to the effect. The post boy is unable to cross, and your first letter is as yet the only one we have received. I trust we will get it by next week at the latest.

The flood must have caused a terrible amount of damage, as the banks on the river course are low and the well-populated, well-cultivated districts adjoining are very flat. Grand Valley, or Brandon City, as it is to be styled, has been entirely submerged. The inhabitants are all in tents, and passing time as best they can on an elevation. It is very comical to see the storekeepers in very small tents seated or lying down with the wares all piled around within real handy distance. The water has washed away some of the railway embankment. One house was washed away, and the steamer was engaged to bring it back to its former site. Already the flood has lasted fully a week, and it does not yet show much prospect of abating. Curiously enough, the half-breeds last year prophesied a deluge and the drowning of Winnipeg at this time. Just now great teams of them pass down to dispose of the result of their winter's hunting. Nothing can stop them. They cover their carts with skins, and swimming their horses they cross anything in the form of water.

Since writing the last letter we have been getting along in the usual way. The other day we experienced a very heavy thunderstorm. The hail fell as large as marbles and did damage to the potato leaves. Farther east the hailstones were much heavier and damaged houses and crops. Our crops promise very well, growing quickly and strongly. You would think you saw them growing.

We are getting along slowly but surely with the ploughing. One of our oxen, Crookie by name, has been played out with the heat. So we will not work him further, but fatten him for the butcher.

For two or three days back the heat has been great. Then sometimes registering 85 deg. [F] in the shade. Just now it is 84 deg., but the prairie breezes temper this very much. The mosquitoes are sometimes very bad. My face and hands are just a mass of pimples, but their season will soon be at an end. During July they gradually disappear. After nightfall we have in the creek great illuminations. The fireflies are there in myriads, twinkling their bright lights in a pretty show when stationary, or leaving a bright trail when flying. In the Northwest we also see a splendid comet every night. Do you see it or know anything about it? It is inexpressibly grand to view the clear vault studded all around and above with myriads of brilliant stars. I really wish I had a taste for astronomy, as here a splendid opportunity for [studying] it is to be had. The sunrise or setting is also a glorious sight.

So far we have not done much in the way of shooting. All the birds are just now hatching. We have too little around our place to get any great variety. Wild ducks are the most common. Should we however go further west, we will select a woody district and among other advantages we will gain, we will have a great variety of game.[18] I am afraid I must now conclude this letter. I have with this mail written to Uncle Hugh, Jackton, Alex Dykes and Alison Nancy, so I have not been idle. I trust you are remembering to send an occasional weekly Herald. We long dreadfully for news hereaway. I suppose just now you will be having the holidays. Please send a full account of your doings. Have you seen the new opera of Gilbert & Sullivan's?[19] We have sung the Pirates[20] here into shreds. We actually from practice have forgotten the sense of the words. You might at your leisure copy something new and funny, another policeman-like song. . . .

Your most affectionate brother
Willie

Grand Valley
25 July 1881

My Dear Maggie,

I was very much pleased to receive your second letter. It was read and re-read with great interest. I was glad to see from it that you were likely to spend a portion of your holidays at Melrose. I trust you have enjoyed yourself during the holiday time—write all particulars. You ask if we are well off for news—really we are not. Sometimes we get the loan of a Canadian paper, but we have not been long enough in the Territory to be sufficiently interested in

---

18 After only a short time in the district they were already thinking of moving. Apparently their land was too wet.
19 "Patience" was first performed in April 1881.
20 "The Pirates of Penzance," first performed in April 1880.

such news. I trust you will send an occasional Weekly Herald—from it we will learn all general news. Write us only in your letters about yourself and friends.

Since writing my last letter things have been getting along very quietly here. Papa had to start for Winnipeg on Monday about a mower and a rake that should have been forwarded and to do some other necessary business. We expect him back on Saturday.

Tomorrow I will require to spread around among the settlers on this side for subscriptions to defray the expenses of the missionaries. I am afraid I will in some places get a cool reception. The missionary is a regular pharasaical humbug, ardently determined to start the Northwest into the gallop along the right road with doleful visions of the bottomless pit. This is the hardest name he very considerately gives it. But really it is a sight to make your blood creep as he stands behind a table covered with a white cloth, steadfastly gazing at old-looking manuscripts, enforcing with the energetic use of his right hand and tongue his bad logic and worse grammar on the minds of his congregation, while his left is busy murdering a lot of irreverent mosquitoes. I am sure he is only submitted to by the others of his flock because they do not congregate for the sake of the sermon but to get the benefit of all the country news. . . .

The service was first held in Nicol's Stopping House, but unfortunately a horseman stopped for refreshment one Sunday during the service, and perplexed and annoyed our host very much. Since then it has been held in a neighbouring log house, much to Mr. Hyde—the missionary's—disgust, as Nicol could boast a large, family, ministerial-looking Bible among his worldly possessions. Now a small pocket Bible must do the purpose—that, you know, is not quite so impressive. It is astonishing the great scarcity of Bibles here away. Seldom more than one Bible or Testament in a family.

Since I wrote last we have had two magnificent thunderstorms after nightfall. The lightning was dazzlingly brilliant and constant. The thunder rolls were actually deafening. . . . I do not remember anything else I can write about, so I will conclude, as Andrew is anxious to get the desk. I wish you would give him a good nagging. He will neither read, write, learn or play the fiddle. . . .

Your affectionate brother
Willie

P.S. You are not to be scared from coming out because of the missionary. He leaves in September, and likely we shall have a regularly ordained missionary.

Grand Valley
12 August 1881

My Dear Maggie,

We got another of your letters in the beginning of the week and were glad to hear you were enjoying yourself so well at Melrose. We are very busy here just now cutting hay, and have already got up one large stack, but will require to put up another one yet. Next week some of the neighbours intend to commence their grain [harvest], and some of our barley will require to be cut then too, so you see we have got plenty to do.

Two weeks ago a terrific tornado swept across the prairies and we thought our shanty was going to be blown away, but luckily for us it managed to stand the blast. At the railway camp two men were killed with the lightning and five others badly injured; one of our neighbours was also struck with it, but was stunned only about twenty minutes. We had another gale yesterday, but it was not quite so bad as the last one.

We are very badly off here for drinking water as the creek has nearly dried up, and as the well is not yet properly sunk, any water that is in it is very bad, so we have to drink sour milk or some other mixture instead.

Some of the neighbours have a bear roaming about here, and the other night Willie heard some animal smelling the boards of the shanty. Thinking it was some of the cattle broken loose, he got up to look after them, and great was his astonishment to find that the cattle were lying quite snug and what must have been the bear, gone. So you see he very nearly caught it. As this is all I have got to say I will close with love to you all.

Andrew

Grand Valley
12 August 1881

My Dear Maggie,

I am very sorry that I did not get the letter finished I intended for you last mail but I was ill through either bad water or well digging—and in very low spirits because of the amount of work to be done and inability to do my share. But now I am all right.

We have been disappointed in not receiving a mower and horse rake, and consequently we are very much busier, as the hay has all to be mown with a scythe. What the Steamboat C. have done with the implements is still a mystery.

In addition to hay cutting we are building a stable, and today Papa and I were at the bush for an additional supply of wood. We also get firewood at this place, distant about seven miles. So you will in a manner understand the extent of the journeys we occasionally undertake.

In a week or so harvesting will be general, and we will require then to be at our small lot of barley and oats. After that, a cellar will require to be dug, our shanty shifted over to the other side of the ravine and eighteen inches of turf placed around and between the insides and John Frost, and a break ploughed all around the premises to snub prairie fires. After that, the well will get another deepening, the future garden ploughed up and fenced. Then all our spring breaking will be required to be reploughed deeper and harrowed over three times. Now this is our autumn programme, and must be completed in two months before frost sets in decidedly. You can understand from this description that we have abundance of work before us, and I only let you know of it so that you may pardon the short, but I trust sweet, epistles during that time.

The other morning I rose very willingly, but on consideration I remembered that it was the morning of Saturday, and the prospect of the following day's rest spurred me up to the performance of duty. Busy, busy were we drawing hay, when we were interrupted by a neighbour in all the glory of holiday attire: slouch hat, no such thing as a wincey blouse[21] but a long decided tailed coat, no vest, but a blazing flaming red shirt from in front of which the buttons shone forth like pearls, and such a pair of light (not spotless) trousers. This neighbour is quite a notable personage—he rejoices in the name of Billy Wight. He spends sleepless nights over every girl who immigrates to the locality.

Well, this same personage leisurely approaches me, and I quite prepared myself for the usual "will you be using your ... ?" After twice begging his pardon, then studying his whole appearance, carefully endeavouring to make out if his wits had accompanied him, I had frankly to ask him for an intelligible account of his mission. Then I understood his question to be "Don't you know this is Sunday?" "No" I said, and endeavoured to get up on my oxen. But still he would insist, and volunteered to prove he was correct by an Almanac. I quite proof-positively referred him over to Papa and proceeded. However, a second discussion forced me to admit he was correct and we were all wrong. Hay forks were quietly [put] at rest, and soon no one could have imagined that we unintentionally had stolen three hours' work from the day of rest. We had, in some unaccountable manner, doubled our ideas of Wednesday—but this will prove the genuine earnestness of our "labour" (hear, hear). You must excuse the nonsensical manner of describing this awful display of North-western shortcomings.

Do you know a bear has been seen prowling in the neighbourhood with which I am certain I nearly had one night an adventure. Papa was away at Winnipeg, and sometime during the night I was awakened by a heavy sniffing and smelling along the boards just outside where I was lying, and a rattling of some chains hanging at the corner. I thought it would be some cattle loose, and fortunately opened the door in a careless noisy manner. But on looking all around I could see nothing, and again went to bed mystified. But when a neighbour spoke of having seen a bear prowling around his oats, I understood the cause of the midnight disturbance. The animal must have been scared into the ravine or among the corn by the noise of the door. I did not think they would have troubled the plains with their presence, but I shall certainly fortify my courage by

---

21 Wincey—a strong material of wool and cotton, or wool and linen used for shirts.

having my trousers on at the next untimely awakening. The want of them assuredly decreases both strength and courage fifty per cent.

We have been very much pleased to receive your two letters from Melrose, and happy to learn from them that you are there thoroughly enjoying your holidays. We were also truly grateful to receive a Weekly Herald from Henry. We sometimes get a Canadian paper, but still we have a failing for Scotch news. However, do not cause your letters to supply this lack—let us know all about yourself and doings, and all about friends. We will survive the want of general news. We knew of the Lefron business but not of the Garfield assassination— but what is the odds, if we are not miserable. We look forward to getting a letter from you next week. So far we have only received the newspaper before mentioned, so you can judge whether it is prudent to continue sending. You might try the scoundrels' honesty with a Weekly Citizen. Now excuse my stopping—it is late and the letter must be at the P. Officer before six o'clock tomorrow morning. We are all well. We unite in sending fond love to Henry, Agnes, and all other friends whom you may meet during the holidays.

Your affectionate brother,
Willie

Grand Valley
25 August 1881

My Dear Maggie,

I endeavoured to write you after sundown last night, but my hand was with ploughing quite incapable of performing its part. Today the heat has been very great—94 deg. in shade, 129 deg. in sun and hardly a breath of wind. We had to stop outdoor work early in the afternoon. Andrew and I were not long in getting into the pond keeping the fishes company. All the creeks and pond holes so far as we know are dry and hard. The never-freezing spring in our pond fortunately keeps it fully supplied with cool water. We were surprised a week or so ago to find it pretty well stocked with a good-sized fish somewhat like the pike, but we have not had time to have a haul at them. It also attracts to our dinner table a good supply of wild duck. One we had today weighed two pounds.

We were pleasantly surprised Sunday a week ago to receive a letter from you. It had travelled very quickly—it came to Winnipeg [from Scotland] in twelve days....

The Blacklaw friends should come right away to Manitoba. Over and above the Government grants you can get as much land as you like, soil and situation unsurpassed, at [$]2.50 per acre with a rebate of a [$]1.50 for every acre ploughed within three years. John should come out himself and prospect before the family venture. If you decide upon coming out Papa and I propose [going] further west sometime in October. The trail is just thronged with emigrants every day. It will not be long at the present rate till all will be settled to the Rockies.

We expect the railroad cars will be running here in five weeks. A local company have commenced operations for supplying Minnedosa and other places on the previously proposed railway route with a railroad. This the Syndicate have counterchecked by a track leaving the main line at our station, Bogey Creek and passing east from here about three miles. So with these and another projected scheme by the Northern Pacific, an American Company, we will be well supplied with railways. This was my greatest fear at first—the competition will be ruinous, I am certain, to all but the Syndicate and the settlers.

You mentioned in one of your letters that Uncle David has a favourable opinion of the St. Paul's district. So far as we saw, all around there is very hilly and light soil, but a short distance NW is Minneapolis, the great flour milling city, and around north of that are the Minnesota prairies, and for 500 miles the railway runs through them. They're perfectly level with hardly a tree to be seen. The soil is thin and nothing like Manitoba soil for growing wheat. The produce is much inferior in quality and quantity. We made particular inquiry and learned that all the land worth anything was taken up 300 miles from St. Paul. Another drawback is that to get on well you require to be Yankified. Manitoba is certainly far superior in every respect to any American state....

We could not help grinning at your assurance about the mosquitoes—enclosed you have one. The long trunk in front he, with great perseverance, excruciatingly inserts nearly the whole length and then he pumps out the blood until his body is as round as a bullet. There are an endless variety of them, large and small, grey and yellow. The big yellow one's bite is worst, and nothing escapes him. Sometimes they are so thick that they patter on your face like heavy rain. Their first prick is the most painful, and they favour you with it long before you can grab. I met a young lady from Northumberland at a neighbour from Berkshire's house. Her face was literally swollen beyond recognition with the bites. But it is too bad to scare you so. They are only occasionally so bad, and although I have suffered with my tender sensitive skin very badly, I yet do not consider them a serious drawback.

We have a worse and more annoying plague sometimes in the shape of flying ants—they fill the air in clouds and cover you completely. We have three times this year been annoyed with them, but they only last for an hour or two in the afternoon. The last time I was sorely troubled with them we had been at the bush, and when about four miles from home they with hum descended on us, and for two hours I catched it. My shirt neck was unfortunately open, and all my back was quickly covered. Sometimes they completely blinded me. To make matters worse, the oxen scared at them and went off at the gallop. I had been a short distance back slaying millions with my jacket, so I had to get up on them. But no further could I go than the end of the waggon. So catching hold of one of the logs, I had to hang on and follow, sometimes so quickly that I was nearly on my knees. The mad gallop lasted for a good bit over the prairie, and when at last they stopped from sheer exhaustion I was in a pitiable state and quite prepared to start for a more congenial climate at a moment's notice. Their bites have just exactly the pain of a mustard poultice. Try from this and conjure up what my condition was—gasping for breath and pouring with perspiration. But this, like all other things pleasant and disagreeable, have an end, and hard thoughts will be forgotten till next time. . . .

My last letter is sufficient apology for this one. It would not do for you to receive too long letters—I am afraid they would cause you to waste valuable time in two ways. We all unite in sending our fondest love to you all. Andrew has an epistle herewith. I suppose he will be again at that bear. The wonderful musical streams our dog emits at worshiptime are quite too much for his gravity. Papa is not writing, but he superintends—he is keeping very well.

Your affectionate brother
Willie

Grand Valley
25 August 1881

My Dear Maggie,

Since I wrote you last we have been doing a lot of work here; we have got in nearly all our hay and are very busy now with our grain which is all ready for cutting. Both yesterday and today were very hot days, the thermometer standing at 129 degs. in the sun and 94 degs. in the shade. Today we had to stop working for a time and start again in the evening. The mosquitoes have nearly all disappeared but the number of house flies is tremendous—they are continually going into something and even tumbling into your tea while you are drinking it. We are greatly annoyed just now with a neighbour's cattle, which continually insist in taking up their abode with us, and tonight we discovered five of them helping us to cut our corn. One of them seems to think this is his proper home, for whenever he gets an opportunity he comes over our way and keeps clear of his master when he comes to take him away. Last night we were again disturbed by the bear, but as it was a very dark night we did not go out, but when we have good moonlight we intend trying to give him a supper. About a fortnight ago he turned up at a neighbours who fired at him but missed. As this is all I have got to say I will now close with love to you all from

Andrew

Grand Valley
15 September 1881

My Dear Maggie,

I trust you will excuse the long silence since I last wrote. We have been working like blackamoors and experienced [?]. The shanty has been taken down and is being erected on the other side of the ravine. Just now we are residing in the newly built stable. We are all very glad to learn that you enjoyed your holidays so pleasantly.

Last Sunday week we received your important letter, and all of us heartily approve your decision.[22] I think that I in my letter suggested such a course, but did not think favourably of it, as it would occasion long separation—but having reconsidered it as a reality it is without doubt the best plan for all concerned. By two years' time we will here have got all things snug and comfortable. In the meantime we will manage to get along very well as all of us are now expert housekeepers, although a little rough, but this helps the fun. You can imagine the delicious goodie-goodies I am now able to manufacture, so you need not expend any pity on us. I am just afraid your housekeeping abilities will be quite in the shade when you come out, but then certificated talents will help you to snap your fingers at us, and we will sing awful dumb before your independence. It is without doubt a long time to be separated, but we will think more of one another when again united. I trust the time will pass quickly and as pleasantly with you as it in a rough way does with us. Two years makes a vast difference on a colonial farm. You will be, I am sure, quite proud of our joint possession when you see it. Though thus disappointed in seeing you for a time, an occasional photograph will help to fill the void.

Papa will go west prospecting as soon as the shanty and some other things are fixed up. He will, in all likelihood, take up land for the three, and next spring we will sell here and move west to our new settlement.

I will not write any more just now. We have no fire in our present abode—it is cold and getting late. By the end of next week we will be in warmer quarters, and then I will write you a very long letter with

---

22 Presumably a decision not to emigrate for a year or two.

all news. We gratefully received a second Herald from Henry. By the bye you must not write once a week. A letter received certainly once a fortnight will be quite as satisfactory. With kindest love to cousins Henry, Agnes, all other friends and yourself from all of us.

Your most affectionate brother
Willie

Grand Valley
22 September 1881

My Dear Maggie,

We last night had the pleasure of sleeping in the new shanty, but we are not yet so comfortably circumstanced as I anticipated when last I wrote. This filling is not quite completed—things are rather confused. I have little more to say with regard to your decision.[23] We all feel very much the necessity for so long a separation—assuredly it is the wiser course and the only one that will not possibly be regretted after all is over by any of us—least of all by you, as it will render you independent should the new life not come up to your expectations. I can assure you I did not feel at ease after the letter was dispatched and could not muster courage to write again on the subject. I was very much relieved when I read the cheerful brave way you accepted the position. I trust, or rather we all trust, that you may be preserved from down-spiritedness or a sense of loneliness and that a healthy happy frame of mind and body may enable you to continue on and conclude the course in a brilliant and successful manner.

Our consolations are, I think, about equal—you possess all the pleasures and comforts of civilization and association, while we enjoy our own company and find pleasant employment farming. But I expect all this I have written is rubbish and will not bear revisal. I feel I must say something but am not in the mood for doing so as I should—however, you know our feelings on the subject better than I can express them. Remember, however, should you not get

---

23 Likely Maggie's decision to seek a teaching job in London.

on as you anticipate, or weary and become homesick scruple not to let us know—pack up and come right away. You will not in any possible way be a burdance rather than a help. The roughing must be done—be you here or not we shall fail to attain what each and all of us would like.

When we learnt you were not for a time coming out we set about transforming the shanty—this is now completed. The alterations are a large cellar underneath for winter vegetables, an additional six feet to the south end, a wooden floor, a bed and store garret, and a water-tight, weather-tight roof. So now we are no longer at the mercy of tornadoes or thundershowers and are quite above the cold sward. A wooden floor is quite a pleasant change. I wonder how the five months camping out will have affected completed floors and other sundry civilized knick-knacks? Strangely, no doubt.

The houses in America are as a rule poorly furnished—in Manitoba they are not furnished at all. Some boards on four legs form a light useful table, and anything does for a seat. Boxes and forms are the common apologies for chairs. Before you come out we will show an example that will possibly be a silent means of reforming settlers' notions of house-furnishing.

The harvest is now all over. I have already helped at two threshings, strangely enough. We have had a good deal of rain. For three days the sun was clouded and we had cold, heavy showers of rain—enough to bring up visions of Scotland and scare away symptoms of homesickness. The most of the grain was on the field lying, a great deal of it not even bound, but no damage was done, and now all is secured. Crops so far in this district are yielding very well.

At present I am busy ploughing and getting on very well. In about a fortnight I expect to be finished. The frost is making a slight show. The grass is pretty well frozen and the leaves are getting in their Indian Summer shades. Soon I will be able to attempt a description of the glories of the famed season. Again I must beg you to be content with this short letter. All are abed, it is getting late, and even the wooden floor is getting cold.

I trust you will obey my last request—a letter certain once a fortnight. Please send them long. We thankfully received another Herald from Henry. I also got a mail from A. Nivan (more of him in my next). The P.O. scoundrels seem to be scared into their duty by a legal business-looking hand of writing. The Marquis of Lorne[24] would I suppose pass here a short time since. If it is not making too great an inroad on your pocket money you might send one number of illustrated papers, Graphic for instance, if it contains any remarks or sketches of Manitoba. I am very much indebted to you for troubling with the shorthand book—better employed with it than whittling or whistling. With kindest love to cousins, all other friends and yourself from us all.

Your affectionate brother
Willie

Grand Valley
6 October 1881

My Dear Maggie,

I suppose you will be deeply engrossed with school work. This would account for no letter last week. We were just a little bit disappointed. Your two previous letters came together—this ended the disappointment very much, still I think the weekly resolution would be rather much—it would take up too much of your precious time, and we might begin to think rather lightly of the letters if we did not require to look forward a little bit and wish. Possibly it would be more satisfactory if we each numbered our letters and so prevent any misunderstanding should any go a-missing. We truly appreciate the Heralds sent by Henry. They are not long in being cut into four pieces. . . .

The fiddle is at present satisfying my taste for dabbling in music. You should hear me now perform the little lowly band. The lovely quiver on the upstroke would place A.B. Dykes[25] on the Aged Ministers' fund instanter. I had a letter from him. . . . Our missionary has gone back to his studies. I sincerely hope for the sake of Christianity that they will do him more good and that he will at his next appointment be enabled to make a better use of them. The membership at our station was only a dozen, yet seventy-seven

---

24 The Governor-general.
25 A writer of Victorian hymns.

dollars was collected—seventy-five was the stipulated sum for expenses. That beats the old country collections. A neighbouring settler subscribed for the Methodist church twenty dollars.

We are quite cosy and warm in our new shanty, and we are getting on well with our work. Tonight I baked scones two inches thick and a foot in diameter, great puffy luscious ones. I do not think you could beat that. The bread baking has not yet been very successful—the loaves are rather damp, but we must creep before we walk.

Andrew is now installed between the plough stilts and he is big and proud. He can be heard a long way off telling the oxen his ideas of them—"Haw, wo back, how, you stupid, gee back, Brownie, where are you going?" and so on is his constant cry. He has also become quite a sportsman—two ducks and two blackbirds have become prey to his gun.

I am sorry to say that Papa broke two ribs when we were in the bush on Monday. He tripped and fell on a tree stump. He is, however, getting gradually better, and has all the time been able to go about. Just now he is carefully smoothing out the soft brown fur of a muskrat he shot today. If no Atlantic intervened we might be able to provide you with a fur outfit—skunks, badgers, martens, foxes are all prowling about on the locality. A skunk was shot by Papa and skinned but the fur has disappeared—doubtless Casey[26] had a supper from it. They are about the size of a terrier, but a good deal plumper and round with short legs, a pretty black and white fur, a long bushy tail and a horribly atrocious smell. We expect John Frost to make his long last appearance in a week or so, and in this country he puts an end to all work but chopping, smoking, talking, and firing up. Now I must conclude, as we are all ready for the night's rest. In a fortnight or so I will have more time to write respectable letters. We all unite in sending our kindest love to Agnes, Henry, all other friends and yourself.

Your most affectionate brother
Willie

---

26 Their dog.

Grand Valley
20 October 1881

My Dear Maggie,

John Frost has come at last. Yesterday morning at sunrise the thermometer registered zero [F]. In addition to this the ground is covered with six inches of snow, an unusual thing in the Northwest at this time. All this has caused work hereaway to cease meantime. Papa is busy chopping, Andrew skating on the pond, and to kill time like the others I have taken to letter writing. Chopping, skating, scribing—if I had thought in time I might have written a poem on the subject. The NWT is the place for skating. The ice is here long enough to, I suppose, give you a surfeit and strong enough to make it thoroughly safe. You also save six pence and shoe leather and can buckle your skates at the stove. Can you imagine any place more suitable? We expect and sincerely trust that winter has not yet finally set in as we have some ploughing yet to do, and our new places to take up farther west. We have not yet been blessed with the famed Indian Summer, therefore we daily expect a thaw followed by three weeks of fine open weather. . . .

I was down at Winnipeg last week and enjoyed the journey pretty well. I travelled on the cars all the way back and was agreeably surprised to discover that the cars stopped to put down passengers about three and a half miles from here. Doubtless a station house will soon be erected—it is called Charters [Chater]. I propose writing a description of the trip for the MS Magazine and will send it to you for correction. You will from it get all news of the journey.

When at Winnipeg I discovered that our mower and rake were at Brandon on the other side of the Assiniboine. We have been shamefully treated in the matter. Compensation can only be had from the Steamboat Company by law and that, in this country I understand, is risky and in our position impossible. As it is we get the rake on credit for fully a year, and the steamboat manager pays charges and damages, if any. We purpose going tomorrow for them. Next day we will go for firewood and after that, as soon as the snow lifts, Papa and Andrew go out west to look at and possibly take up land about fifty miles from here. We will likely take up 96 acres this fall—we surely will not have land hunger for some time after

43

that. The land in that district, Oak River, is well spoken of and not taken up—but you will hear more definitely our arrangements in a fortnight or so.

I am, in view of Andrew's absence, getting my hand into the milking, and find it a good deal easier than I anticipated. The cow fortunately is exceedingly quiet. All our cattle are shut up in the stable for the winter.

Papa is getting better—he is quite able for work. In fact, the accident has troubled him a great deal less than any of us expected. We are all otherwise well and happy. Now I must conclude this letter, as I have yet one to write Uncle Hugh, and I am miserably deficient of news. We unite in sending our kindest love to cousins and yourself.

Your most affectionate brother
Willie

P.S. Andrew I expected would supplement this letter with another, but he discovers that a sore hand prevents him. He received the injury when boxing the nose of an ox for misbehaviour. He desires you to excuse him, but in the circumstances I hardly think you should. You mention in your last letter that you think we only let you know the best side of things. I really wish you could witness our musical efforts—Papa at one side of the table with the flute and I on the other with the fiddle having a go at "Dunfurmline." I do not think you would recover your [composure?] for a good many days. By the time you come we will have a regular orchestra organized.

Grand Valley
4 November 1881

My Dear Maggie,

Last week Papa and Andrew were away west to Oak River, Arrow River, and Shoal Lake (these you will see marked on the map) land hunting, but they could get nothing to please them. I was left behind, as it was considered that I would be the least disturbed by the uncanny noises during the long nights. So for a week I and the dog were alone on the prairie, tending the stock during the day and trying all we could to forget or drown the discordant harmonies roused by wolves and such-like outside after dark. I proposed to while away the time by writing letters to Uncle Hugh and you— good long ones, but found that a very eerie feeling resulted from a long spell of silent writing. I had recourse to the fiddle, and many a queer echo you may be certain was aroused. Doubtless you will in the circumstance pardon the change.

I think I wrote you before that this district as far west as Fort Ellice has recently been ceded to Manitoba.[27] This has occasioned an election for a member to the Legislative Assembly at Winnipeg in our County of Brandon. Eight candidates were in the field, and caused no little stir. Had it not been for this, I should have been a hermit, having no intercourse with the outside world. One of the would-be members of parliament favoured me with a call, and two days afterwards the postmaster surprised me with a visit and canvassed the claims of another would-be. These are the startling events in my diary last week.

On Sunday, I went over to the post office and got your letter and Henry's paper—above all I got your pictures. My stars, what a ladylike personage you are in your gorgeous pucker braided dress. Really it is enough to stagger the ideas of us simple-minded settlers. We must keep the photos to ourselves else it will stir up the envy of the damsels hereaway.

I hurried home, got my dinner cooked, and set me down to demolish it. Carefully I placed first the one and then the other photo against the salt cellar and scanned them carefully and critically. I discovered two faults. The first objection was you kept your eyes on me, satisfying my hunger, but they had not benevolent gleam in them—nothing but a cold stoical stare. The second fault was that your nose seemed to me to have a slightly cynical expression. Now no fault could be found with my appearance, as I was dressed in my best. I concluded that the quality of the fare was the cause. Taking all with all, you must admit that the first mentioned was very unnatural on your part and the second very unsisterlike. I did

---

27 This refers to the 1881 extension of the boundaries of Manitoba.

not like Mr. Rutherford's treatment of his subjects. He would, after a short covered or muffled gaze at you, come over, poke you up and tell you not to smile, as that looked foolish. Then after another gaze back he would come again, touch you up artistically and ask you not to look too serious over the matter, thereby confusing all your preconceived notions of putting an attractive face on the sensitive paper that was so far and near to bring you in remembrance of friends. Now remember next time to put the operator at defiance and don a right jolly laughing expression. I must admit that you look exceedingly well and very much improved, and the hard work—to judge by your looks—is agreeing with you. I trust the time will soon come when you will have a more natural and sisterly share in our farming operations.

On the Sunday afternoon I witnessed a splendid prairie fire. For some days previously the horizon had been darkened by smoke and at night all the clouds around were gleaming with the reflection of fires, but this fire brought the display closer to home. It began in a south-easterly direction, and in about twenty minutes travelled north out of sight. The wind was pretty high at the time, and it drove smoke and fire before it at a great speed—quicker by far than a railway locomotive. The chain of fire twinkled like glass beads, and when a thicker clump of grass was caught up it would shoot to a great height the great dense clouds of smoke. The sparkling string of fire, the crackling hissing noise hurrying along at railway speed over immense tracts of ground covered with dry yellow grass and instantly leaving behind it nothing but blackness and puffs of smoke, caused a grand sight.

On Monday afternoon when ploughing I was surprised to see Papa and Andrew appear on the top of a slight rise of ground that we call the Sandhill. I did not expect them till the end of the week, but they had been thoroughly disgusted with the amount of scrub and willows in the district they had been, and I was glad, you may be certain, to see them. Next week if the weather holds good Papa will go west to Birdtail Creek and Fort Ellice and see if anything good can be had there—but I will let you know further in my next letter. On Wednesday the prairie grass was burned all around here. We had seen the fire coming, so I went back from the house a bit and started one on our own account. This protected us, and the big one spent itself at our creek. The burnt ground is pleasant walking compared to the long grass, but it has changed the appearance of the country very much, giving it the appearance of a Scotch moor.

The ploughing is now at an end we think. We have the most of ours done, but the most of our neighbours will have a great deal to do next spring. Just now the wind is very cold, but we have not yet had the thermometer below zero, and only once [as low as zero] at that. You ask about our winter clothing—we are very well supplied. The underclothing we got from Uncle Hugh is yet to be in to. We have warm caps, top boots and a pair of moccasins for teaming made of moosehide. Inside them you can put any quantity of socks. We have three pairs of Cousin Agnes' socks not yet worn, so that with plenty of firewood we ought to have a pleasant winter. The Indians prophesy a mild winter as the more provident animals are out this fall putting past a winter supply.

We are daily making progress in the musical way. Papa takes the tenor part with the flute, Andrew the alto with his fife, and I the treble with the fiddle. I can now play two scales, G and C, and play the tunes at sight. My only difficulty is a tendency that the bow has sometimes to slightly grunt and squeak. I wish I had taken Henry's advice and learnt it instead of piano. By the time you come along with your piano we will have a regularly organized orchestra.

I do not think I told you that we got our mower. I learnt its whereabouts when in Winnipeg. We got it at Brandon, a most unlikely place. We had not paid freight or storage, and got the rake on credit until January 1883, so that we are better off than anticipated. Now I must conclude, as Andrew is wearying to get the letter away with him to the post office. We are all keeping well. We unite in sending our love to Cousins and yourself.

Your most affectionate brother
Willie

P.S.

Grand Valley
[4] November 1881

We got the letter containing your photo last Saturday, and we were glad to see you were looking so well over your hard work, and hope you will look as well after your big examination. Today the ground is again white with snow, so Papa and I started out to see if we could shoot some chickens but did not get near any of them. Last week Papa and I went west but could see nothing to please us; at Oak River the land was very scrubby, and at Arrow River it was rather light, so we had to return home without taking up land. Papa intends to look at Moose Mountain soon. We have not eaten the calf—as you suppose, they are rather valuable here. All the work is nearly stopped here and we will have very little to do now but cut wood to keep the cold out. I will now require to stop as I must go to the post office tonight. With much love from

Andrew

Elton, Man.
16 November 1881

My Dear Maggie,

We only received from your quarter a paper last mail—knowing well that your time would be more than fully occupied with your school duties we pardoned you, and more than that generously determined to forgive such conduct until next year. But after that we expect to be exceedingly jealous of our privileges, so you had better not fall into bad habits during this indulgence period.

Our neighbours on the southern half of the township are quickly taking advantage of their newly acquired Manitoba rights. They have appointed a committee and forwarded a petition to the Government for a grant to enable them to build a school and secure a teacher. The school is very much wanted, as there are a great number of children. When at Winnipeg I got acquainted with a young man who had a school appointment at Gladstone, about 18 miles west of Portage la Prairie. He had been there about two years. He was only getting $250 yearly and was, owing to this small salary, about to resign. He intended going to the Qu'Appelle to begin stock raising. You will understand from this instance that teaching is not here a very remunerative occupation. The teaching fraternity down in the lower Provinces are evidently as much in want of elbow room as their brethren in the old country. Before your certificate can be of service here you must have it attested by a J.P. or a clergyman and at Winnipeg undergo an examination that takes place only once a year, in August.

Since I wrote my last letter we have not been doing very much, although somehow always busy. The weather has been very severe and stormy. In fact I have concluded that the climate of Manitoba, so far as its settled character is concerned, is a perfect fraud. Undoubtedly during the summer time we had a long spell of delightful sunny weather but this was no advantage, as it made the ground very dry and unploughable. Later on we had a good many opportune showers, but they were real busters—short storms or tornados. Their severity far exceeded anything I could imagine. However, these and their effects became things of the past, and knowing people characterize the season as a "windy" one.

I had great hopes that the fall would realize the descriptions we heard, and our haystacks were put up to resist wind but not rain. But alas, about harvest times, on came the rains quietly and steadily. At one time it lasted three days. It did our hay no little harm, but our neighbours who were harvesting suffered most. Some had only their crops cut and lying unbound, others had them in stooks very badly set up. No matter, all was soaked. Some of our oats were bound up soaking wet. A spell of dry weather, however, dried them thoroughly, and raised our dampened hopes, not to exalted pitch fortunately. We took the precaution of stacking them with straw and water tight. Many of our neighbours could not, and did not, do that. On came the rain again and consequently a great deal of wet grain has been thrashed. Knowing ones again styled the harvest a most extraordinary wet one.

Now I was disposed to overlook and forgive all this, as another year would most likely enable us to get better accommodation and give us more time to secure things properly—and the rain helped the ploughing very much. Time went on. "Now you will experience real Indian summer, no doubt about that, snow never falls here until the end of December" was what everyone said and I previously understood. Imagine our surprise then at a heavy fall of snow, falling shortly before I left for Winnipeg, and occasional falls during the journey, with the thermometer at zero. "Oh, this is only squaw winter. It will go away in a day or two and then you'll have Indian summer."

Papa and Andrew started out on the faith of this story when the weather appeared to take up, and fortunately they had the summer all the time. But this was a very so-so blessing. With the exception of two days, about noon the thermometer got above freezing point, and the weather was not unlike Scotch March weather. So you may guess our Indian summer was no great treat. The comparatively mild weather hardly lasted a week—since then we have twice had snow falls and succeeding thaws.

One Sabbath however, early in the morning, it began in earnest to blow and snow. We were thoroughly storm-stayed. The heavy drift rendered travelling any distance, however short, dangerous, and it was awful cold. On Monday it cleared up, but hard frost. We started for the bush early in the morning. The thermometer registered 5 degrees below zero—a slight wind blowing made it bitter cold and caused [?] walking all the way, about nine miles.

I always take the future into consideration, and determined to reserve my moccasins for 60 degrees below zero or thereabouts—I had only on my top boots and one pair of socks. During the short time I was standing fixing up my load I felt my feet cold, and then almost immediately had no feeling in the greater part of them. I feared the worst and started home, not feeling very comfortable over the probable result. About sundown the wind began to rise and the cold increased thereby. I actually thought my legs sometimes were frozen completely—I could hardly walk—I seemed to have no feeling in them. The oxen, I thought, would never hurry up sufficiently. As it was, we got home about an hour after dark. Quickly I got off my top boots—the socks went along with them quite white with frost. Andrew got a basin of snow, and into it I put my feet, and with his assistance rubbed the frozen parts for a good long time. I am sure I had my feet on the snow for half an hour. The parts that were not frozen suffered dreadfully from the cold, but when I had the frost all taken out I thought little of this. My left heel was the most seriously affected. I have not yet any feeling in it, and expect the skin will come off. The big toe on my right foot has also been badly nipped, and the nail will come off of it. It is exceedingly painful—for three days I have been a prisoner in the house. I have now learnt the true value of moccasins and will act up to my knowledge hereafter. They are loose and soft—inside them you can put any number of socks. Now after this long freezing story see that you do not accuse me of letting you see the best side of everything.

When we got home we found the thermometer 10 degrees below zero. On Monday night it again became stormy and continued so until Wednesday evening. The wind was all the time exceedingly high, and the snow and drift blinding. Today it has cleared up and the sun is shining brightly. At noon we still had 23 degrees of frost, therefore it is not likely the snow will thaw until next spring. All around there are great deep wreaths—this will cause travelling to be very unpleasant until the surface gets hardened. Now do you not think after all this that I have just cause of complaint against the climate we have adopted? But I suppose that you will conclude that frozen feet have made me lose my temper on the subject.

I was down at our great new city, Brandon, last Friday and was very much surprised at the progress it had made since I was last there before. When the railway route was altered so as to pass through this district, Grand Valley was confidently expected to be the great city of the west, and to that place a great rush was made. My first visit to the place was early in the spring [of 1881] when the ice on the river was breaking up. At that time there were only the post office, the steamboat warehouse, the farmer's house to whom the ground belonged, and three stores—the latter were but small temporary shanties with one exception. But the crowd of people was wonderful, all waiting on the steamers to bring up their merchandise and etc.

The farmer McVicar[28] [who owned most of the land at Grand Valley] had all his place surveyed, and everything betokened him making a fortune by selling his farm in town lots. But his greed ended him. He wanted a goodly price for the lots, and the railway co. could not come to arrangement about ground for the station accommodation. They wished 160 acres and this he for a long time grudged. To crown all, a great flood came down and drowned out

---

28 The story of how McVicar lost his chance at a fortune is a well-known one in the Brandon district. See M. Kavanagh, *The Assiniboine Basin: A Social Study of the Discovery, Exploration and Settlement of Manitoba* (Winnipeg: Public Press, 1946), 110-111.

the place. The steamers were plying amongst the newly erected stores—this caused a good deal of damage to the railway plant and storekeepers' goods. McVicar would after this have gladly let the railway syndicate all they wished before, but he was rather late. They had received from Government six townships on the other side of the river to form a city.

About midsummer [of 1881] tents made their appearance on what was formerly a bare hill. The new city was called Brandon, and to it all the rush was diverted, and thither I journeyed on Friday. On the way I passed Grand Valley, now containing about twenty-five houses, all removed to a higher level than the previous site. It has only one thoroughfare, a very quiet one called Syndicate Avenue, and it wants the great feature of an American city—a railway station. The syndicate refuses to place one there, so the storekeepers require to get their goods via Brandon and ferry them across [the Assiniboine].

I could not get over the river by the ferry boats, as they were stopped owing to the ice, and had to cross by the railway bridge, a temporary erection that will be allowed to go with the ice next spring. It is only composed of piles, across which are laid sleepers to support the rails. Over this I had to cautiously pick my way, as the logs were laid about a foot apart. Underneath you, the river was rushing along in its usual quick way, warning you to be careful. Alongside, a handsome bridge with stone piers is being erected at a high level for railway purposes next summer—I understand that there will also be a traffic one. I got safely over the present one, thereby saving 20 cents, and about a mile farther up entered Brandon. In America there is no such thing as railway trespassing. It's a free country, and the possibility of your being killed is a matter that only concerns yourself, the arrangements and consequences left to yourself.

A nice wooden station with platform has been erected. To the right, northwards, is the river with steamboat landing, four steam mills and one or two stores. To the left, southwards, is the main street. It has at each end a large hotel, and consists principally of stores—one of them has "Bank" marked over it in huge letters. The thoroughfare takes at the west end of this street a turn to the left up the hill. Here there are a number of livery and sale stables with a butcher's tent and a large ironmongery warehouse. Again the thoroughfare turns to the right, and along each side are some very good looking stores and a number of boarding houses, here also is the P.O. Intermixed with, and surrounding all this are a number of nice frame dwelling houses. You can have some idea of the busy city that has in our time here sprung up on the bare prairie. I think there must be fully one hundred buildings, all self-contained, and consequently covering a good deal of ground.

But I discover I have gone beyond the limits of an ordinary letter. I expect my toes will be better next time I write, and I will be in a more amicable mood. Meantime I send herewith a newspaper to take away all bad impressions. We all keep well and unite in sending kindest regards to cousins and yourself.

Your most affectionate brother
Willie

Elton, Man.
2 December 1881

My Dear Maggie,

. . . I am glad to state that we now are getting the Heralds regularly and enjoy the reading of them very much—the Canadian papers are not half so interesting. I trust you received the one I sent, and I suppose [you] would not approve of the jerky slang style of imparting information. I understand Brandon now boasts a newspaper.[29]

Since writing last week we have been getting on very quietly. The weather was at first very severe, but for a week it has been comparatively mild—our principal employment has been hauling firewood. My feet are now happily better—the skin has all come off and new one formed. The others have also undergone their first experience of freezing.

Andrew and I determined the previous evening to start for firewood next morning, and although it turned out to be 30 degrees below zero we harnessed the oxen. But it was cold, no doubt about it—the oxen were squirming and dancing as if they were on hot

---

29 The Brandon *Sun* began publication about this time.

plates. A breeze of wind caused the cold, I daresay, to be more felt. Papa took a run out to the stable to see us getting off, but he had not been many minutes out before the lower part of his nose was as white as marble, and he had quickly to return with a snow poultice. We had not been many minutes started before Andrew's nose had also whitened. I thought it was getting rather too much and that chopping would be almost impossible, so the oxen were "hawed," and you bet they came round at a gallop and made for home as hard as they could, down and up the banks of the creek like lightning. On drawing up, Andrew had both cheeks frozen and had quickly to disappear. This is the hardest frost we have yet experienced, and the wind has helped the cold very much. The ground is covered with snow about a foot deep, so you will understand our wintery looking appearance, going about with moccasins, coats, mufflers, and fur caps.

The creek is filling up at a great rate with ice, owing to the springs. At present we have a great stretch to skate upon. The Assiniboine is now frozen over, and can be crossed anyhow or anywhere.

We are preparing our shanty with strong brown buff paper. We have also partitioned off a part of it for firewood and tools, and now we have a very nicely arranged parlour and bedroom with scullery attached. If lumber were not so dear and money more plentiful I would get an attic boarded, and then we could boast a shanty with four apartments—cellar, scullery, parlour, and attic. I suppose Andrew will be writing that the old clock is again tick-ticking ardently, not concerning itself over the change. We are having long nights now, but they are not yet wearisome, as we now have tea or supper at five, milking and putting the cattle right at seven, and bedtime about nine o'clock.

We are, as soon as we get a text book, going to turn our attention a little to chemistry, as the creek springs deserve attention. The water when boiled has a soft white scum and leaves a white chalky deposit, neither of which we can understand the nature of. The water in the spring has traces of iron, but these we steer clear of when drawing. But the most incomprehensible thing is the great amount of gas that rises in bubbles from the earth to the top. Can you aid us in our investigation? It would be a grand thing if we struck gold, etc., or even iron. As it is, the water in a more civilized district would attract attention from its mineral properties. It is rather sweet-tasting, clear as crystal, and has a slightly purgative effect. May I send you a sample?

But I fear I must conclude this letter. I feel the smell of dinner, and immediately after that meal it must be off to the post office, as it is no easy matter travelling through deep wreaths. Though it will be full moon, it is better to be home before dark. By the time this reaches you I suppose you will be through the trying ordeal of your school experience and enjoying a well-earned holiday.

Should you be thinking of knitting any socks or stockings for bringing out here, Papa wishes you to knit them loose. Otherwise they are of no use for keeping out the cold. You must not conclude that this is a limit—it's merely a suggestion. I sincerely hope you are now fixed for a desirable school. Please give us every particular. We all unite in sending our kindest love, and sincerely wish you a very merry Xmas time and a happy New Year.

Your most affectionate brother
Willie

Elton, Man.
13 December 1881

My Dear Maggie,

We received your last letter by the mail a week ago. We were somewhat alarmed to learn that you were being confined to the house. I trust the trouble turned out to be as temporary and trivial as you at the time expected. . . . You seem to have got over your music examination very creditably. . . . I noticed in the papers that some young ladies had earned public honours for their Fine Arts Exhibits at the Agricultural Show at Birdtail west from this. By the time you come out the settlers will be able to appreciate music and painting, so you will most likely instantly become famous. . . .

Since my last letter we have not been doing anything noteworthy. Andrew and Papa were down at the Valley one day with the sleigh, making purchases. They as usual had some lunch in their pockets, but they did not require them, as Andrew had somehow got the affections of one of the storekeepers, and Papa on returning found him devouring fruit, crackers, butter and cheese. Of course for company's sake he had to join in. Andrew and I went to Brandon yesterday. Our object was to sell an ox but I had, and Andrew I think also had, a wish to again make friends with the storekeeper. But alas, his position was occupied by another partner.

I did not so greatly appreciate the novelty of baker's bread as to pay for it. I bought some currants, and today I successfully attempted to bake a bun. Consequently we expect to fare during Christmas time, as well as more favourably situated friends.

I did not sell the ox—beef here is now a plentiful commodity. Large quantities of it are coming up from Ontario. So much for the blessings of railway communication.

We had a very cold ride in the morning. When we started, the thermometer was 24 degrees below zero, but fortunately no wind. I think I never experienced such a clear brilliant morning. All the surrounding low country was lifted up and exposed by mirage. The higher parts were raised up and cut off from their base, looking like black patches in the sky, giving one the impression that a sea dotted with islands was seen. The whole scene had an unreal, fairy appearance in the brilliant coloured sunshine. The only thing to suggest the necessity for having everything but the eyes wrapped up was the musical crunch of the sleigh runners through the hard frosted snow. The thermometer did not get above zero all day, but nevertheless I was enabled to sit for over three mile stretches at a time.

Today the temperature has been very high, only about 6 degrees of frost. A cloudy day and falling glass causes us to expect another snowfall. The snow is now blown into wreaths around three sides of the house. They are the depth of three feet, and the stable is now protected greatly from the wind by the banks of snow. Andrew is sometimes quite annoyed at the quality of the snow. It is dry and powdery like flour, and he can't make snowballs quick enough—in time enough to pepper one with them when I sometimes take the liberty of punishing questionable obedience by snow rubbing his face. Today we were at it, and soon we were as white as millers. He somehow claims the victory—possibly he will in his letter explain his reason for doing so.

We have sometimes a little skating. Our ice is now something to boast about—Lochburnie would be quite in the shade. The springs have been constantly forming and flooding the whole bottom of the creek, causing a splendid stretch of ice. I tried my inventive genius on an ice machine, but the machine would not move. The other two got some good laughing at me. I got satisfaction—I bundled up my abortive effort and all three of us slid along to the spring where the grand finale happened. The snow the previous night had drifted very much across the springs and to a certain extent getting frozen. We had some discussion as to the whereabouts of one of them. I stepped forward to where I thought it should be and proceeded to argue the matter. In a few seconds I experienced a crackling under my feet and a sinking—I was fairly plumped in. Before I got out I had to plunge three times. The others concluded that nothing could withstand the method I unwillingly took to clinch my argument. When I got to the house my trousers were as hard as boards, and I had to doff them amid roars of laughter.

Papa has for some days back been trying to "ketch" some of the red foxes that are prowling round, but as yet pork skin has failed to lure them to destruction in a bear trap, so I am not the only unsuccessful one.

Just now we are having a very lonely time, seeing or speaking to no one unless when out teaming. Our two nearest neighbours have gone into their winter quarters—the one at the bush and the other to friends. But still we never feel weary or dull. We have just as much work during the day as keeps us from rusting up, and the long dark nights pass quickly with card playing, draught playing, reading, fiddling and flute playing. Just now Andrew is in great glee over getting the better of Papa at draughts, laughing as only he can laugh. From this you will understand the difficulty I have scraping together material for a letter.

We are likely to have neighbours on the other side of the creek next summer. The sawmill proprietor who owns the adjoining lot has let it for the next season. Now you must excuse my ending this rather short letter.... somehow I do not take so readily or satisfactorily to letter writing as I did during my own scribing days.[30] We all sincerely trust that by the time you receive this you will be enjoying the satisfaction of having passed your last great examination in a

---

30 From other hints in the letters it appears that Willie had been a clerk in Scotland.

pleasant and a most likely successful manner, and above all we hope you are now fixed into a very comfortable and desirable situation. We eagerly await tidings from you. Meantime we unite in sending our kindest love to cousins Agnes, Henry and yourself.

Your most affectionate brother
Willie

[P.S. from Andrew]
. . . You remember the new dog we got, well he turned out to be worth nothing, so Willie took him to the bluffs and blew a couple of shots through him and left him for the wolves to feed upon, so you had better give him a solemn lecture for his cruelty. . . .

Elton, Man.
27 December 1881

My Dear Maggie,

We have had for two weeks back an occasional heavy puff of wind. That has caused the dry snow to drift very much, covering the trails with wreaths of snow, and in some places on the railway filling up the track for days, stopping railway communication. We were grievously disappointed by the mail due Saturday a week ago not arriving from this cause. By it we expected to learn the result of your applications for a situation. Last Saturday night was therefore a great Christmas eve, as we then got your two letters and two Heralds. Your deploring the meagre information in the first was quite unnecessary—and so you have resolved and arranged to go to London! Most likely you will receive this letter there. I cannot express to you how delighted I was and we all were to know that you were gladly looking forward to a pleasant and profitable settlement. Sincerely we trust your highest expectations will be realized. . . . should you by any chance become captivated by anything or everything in London, Andrew and I are just going to break away from the glorious liberty of the great Northwest and become excisemen—but we would hope should any such thing present itself that you will in this mood some dark

December day when a ghostly yellow London fog is almost choking you and causing the golden streets to appear as [?] that you will in such a day receive a letter from your friends brimful of the sunshiny life in the glorious clear bright Northwest. That will, we are sure, bring trunks out to the daylight. We are now longing to hear how you fare in your lodging hunt. We trust you will get comfortable lodgings. You mentioned in one of your letters that you expected to be able to help us with money. This you must not think of—get everything to make your life comfortable and enjoyable. You do not mention, but we conclude you will be well enough off for money until you get your first quarter's salary. Let us know every particular.

Since writing you my last we have not been doing or experiencing anything noteworthy. The weather has been exceedingly mild and pleasant on the whole. We have had some pretty strong blows but the thermometer has not been below zero. Today the wind has been very high and the snow drifting so that we saw nothing of the outside world.

We were one day down at a part of the Big Bush ten miles from here for a load of fencing. Next month we propose erecting a shanty there and only teaming one way in a day—this will divide the work and make it pleasanter.

I expect to get some good shooting, and will also become better acquainted with the birds and beasts that are in the bush during the winter. The prairie chickens have all gone—there is not one to be seen on the prairie. When a covey are sitting on a tree they are so stupid that you can, by beginning with the lowest one, shoot them all. They have very pretty grey feathers. Out here you will have quite a wealth of good feathers from them and the ducks.

I the other day got my first view of the woodpeckers. One of them settled on a wood slab against the house and startled me whilst baking with its loud pecking. I really thought some of the supports were giving way. I went to the window and there he was, three feet distant. They are white with a black shade overhead and down wings. A curious little red upright comb gives them quite a military aspect. They are rather larger than blackbirds and made round holes in the trees searching for their food. The little snowbirds are our only other company. They are lively, chirping little birds, all white, with the exception of a slight grey shade on the back.

We spent Xmas very soberly and quietly. Our only extra was, we discarded bread and instead went for sweet cake and bun. We can only allow our energies for such occasions to accumulate until you come out. Plenty of firs here suitable for Xmas. By that time our orchestral abilities will be perfect. How will you get on for a piano now? Most likely you will get one in your lodgings. When at Winnipeg I was pricing them—$300 for a good one. The American pianos have a magnificent round full tone.

You trust we are not wearying ourselves of skating. Well, no. The fact of it is, it is rather a lonely tiresome pastime here. Our present experience is that two at that is no company, three most likely will [be]. Your skates fit me very well, better I expect than mine will fit you.

The frost is evidently having an inebriating effect on Andrew and I here. I have become quite a poet, and tonight at milking time we awakened the echoes and scared the oxen with a song, the burden of which was "There was a man that had two sons and they were very canty,[31] they journeyed out to the Northwest and there they built a shanty," etc., to the tune Goleshell. I do not suppose you will advise me to exert myself to secure an international copyright.

By the bye, we have lately had an addition to our household. On a certain night, as we were returning from the bush, we were not met as is usually the case by our dog "Jess" a good long bit from home. This was a great want, as she enlivens the end of the journey very much with her gambolling, capering, and barking. This night Andrew instead came to meet us, and gravely and pompously imparted the information that Jess' attention was taken up with six wee pups. Fortunately I went to the stable to see them before taking supper, and what do you think? Andrew had allowed the frost to get amongst the litter, and five of them were lying stretched out like the babes of the wood, nearly as stiff as boards. Was he not a fine nurse? Andrew bitterly repented the mishap, and with tears in his eyes carried them to the house in his cap. Happily one of them came around, and now they with their screaming under the stove give one

---

31 Canty means cheerful or sprightly. One of their dogs was given this name.

the impression that a whole menagerie is about. Likely Andrew will tell you the rest.

We are getting on very well with the fiddle and flutes. Tonight we began practicing the March of William Tell. Nothing like ambition. At some leisure opportunity you might copy an easy dance piece, short and sweet.

Since writing last night we have had another fall of snow. Most likely the railway will be again blocked. I trust we will get our letters this Saturday, as they are our only comfort from the outside world. We really look forward with pleasure to the getting of the "Graphic" Henry so kindly purposes to send. Our shanty walls are pretty well decorated already with fans, dishes, clothes, etc., but we will surely manage to somehow make a display. I do not remember anything else interesting. We all unite in sending our kindest love to Henry, Agnes, the Kilmarnock friends and yourself. Sincerely wishing you all a Happy New Year.

Your most affectionate brother
Willie

[P.S. from Andrew]

. . . we have got an addition to our stock, in the shape of two pups. We had six of them but before nine hours passed four of them had been frozen to death. They had all been put out to the stable and as the cattle were all out and the door open, the frost soon finished them.

The two that we have got are getting along splendidly. One of them is called Bossy, and is coloured black except the points of its feet and tail, which are white. The other is called Betty, and is all brown except the feet, which are white. . .

Your affectionate brother
Andrew

P.S. Don't believe what Willie says about me having tears in my eyes, because it was rather dark in the stable for him to see, and I think he had some snow in his eyes which made his rather watery.

1882

Elton, Man.
12 January 1882

My Dear Maggie,

We received with last Saturday's mail the Xmas No. of "Graphic" and a Herald. The last paper still comes regularly and is very much prized—the appearance of the Graphic was of course quite an event. The pictures particularly were attractive, but the stories were sorry stuff. We are particularly grateful to Henry for so kindly remembering our lone and primitive condition. In the meantime we will not adorn our abode with the pictures but will reserve them for our new shanty in the far west. . . . We eagerly await tidings from you. On Monday morning we imagine that we had a clue to your doings. You would be teaching the young cockneys ideas. They most likely would be perversely calculating on the near approach of interval, while we here would be leaving our warm beds and hurrying up for milking and porridge making. That's a contrast for you.

I am again woefully short of material for writing a letter to you, so you must not fret at my making a short story long or filling the letter with mere nothings.

Our expectations of a dreadfully rigorous winter are still being disappointed. The weather is on the whole mild and some days genial. We have had two or three slight falls of snow and now I daresay where it remains, the snow will be two feet deep. A slight fall this morning revealed the extraordinary beautiful character of the snow crystals here. I neglected to use the magnifying glass, but seen by the naked eye they were wonderful. They were all one uniform design and had the appearance of an elaborately ornamented wheel with pearly white stars fixed at equal distance around the rim instead of cogs. The regularly formed, clear crystal framework with the white tips had an exceedingly attractive effect. I particularly remarked the crystals of a former snowfall. They were a little smaller and shaped like stars with ferned rays.

Such a quantity of snow as we have here now is I understand quite unprecedented and is a great drawback to bush work, as the muskegs—that is, soft swampy places—are not being frozen. These are very numerous in the bush in our neighbourhood and unfortunately the valuable timber is isolated by them. In that locality for a week or two back there has been quite a revolution. Before you can take out any wood you must receive a permit from the Crown Timber Agent. But up to this time the most of the settlers ignored that arrangement, as there was no active officials to gainsay them. Now, however, an inspector has turned up. His first action was to fault the sawmill proprietors who, I suppose, resented the interference, and a quarrel resulted. Now they are accused of stealing wood, and some of their belongings have been seized. He next turned his sweeping attention to the settlers, and has effectively introduced a reform. Those who were permitless he, without compunction, gave the "right about"—and that to many was no little hardship, as they would travel ten miles before getting to the bush. One man he caused to unyoke on the spot. I suppose he would go back for his sleigh at some more convenient season. Fortunately we got warning and now we are having an idle time of it until we obtain our permit. We have a good stock of firewood forward and do not require to care much.

I am quite astonished at the rapidity with which time seems to pass here. Just now day follows day although little is really being done. Our attention is constantly engaged, and wearying is an unknown care. Just now the pups afford us endless amusement. They are now able to see and run about, and have entered the funny stage of their existence, but their antics would lose all their value if described.

The cattle are all thriving. The weather is sometimes so mild that they can be allowed some days to roam around and play "tag." As they are very hearty they go for this amusement with great zest. With their heads down and tails erect they gallop along at a great pace, and seem wild enough for a Spanish bull ring. Really they are very quiet, affectionate beasts. One of them, "Brownie" by name, a huge heavy ox, is as quiet and docile as any dog. The calf Billy has a particular regard for leather straps, and if he chances to get a hold of one he will chew the end away quickly. The dog and he have an affectionate regard for one another. He takes great delight in smoothing up the dog's long hair into fantastic shapes. Last night, while milking the cow, I was amused at his vain endeavours to get his teeth at the dog's collar. But I am afraid he will be the means of shortening his own existence, as he has pleasure in using both his horns and heels.

I trust you will have time to copy out for me a piece of dance music. I have got a hold of the song music for the "White Cockade" and will from it try and remember the dance music. We are now quite beyond hymn music. My only difficulty is harmonizing our stock of secular melodies. An occasional bit of Scotch or other nice short piece of song music with the parts would be very acceptable for practicing next winter. I am getting on very well with the violin—my only difficulty is holding the bow. The only easy way I can get is placing my thumb between the hair and the holder and laying my fingers flat on the top, drooping my wrist. If you at any time see a good violinist you might note his style of bowing and let me know.

You have not let me know how you enjoyed "Hamlet." A theatrical company was at Rapid City north of this, but their far-west experiment was not a financial success.

A very tragic affair happened a week or two ago east of this. A young man, a licentiate of the Edinburgh College of Surgeons, came out to Manitoba with his young wife and family to get more scope but he did not succeed in getting an opening. He was under the necessity of taking to [?]. Some influential persons knowing his circumstances secured for him the mastership of a small school, but he seems to have felt his inferior condition acutely. He one day astonished the children by asking those of them who wanted a new teacher to hold up their hands, and immediately after took poison, and before he could stagger to the door he was dead. Subscriptions are being asked to enable his family to go back to the old country.

Another equally sad case has just occurred at the Portage. An Episcopal clergyman stationed in the West Indies was under the necessity of coming to Manitoba for his health. The expense was so great that he only could bring his family to Brooklyn. Arriving here himself, he was soon engaged to officiate at the Portage. But before he had been many weeks there, he suddenly broke down in health again and died, and now his family are absolutely destitute in Brooklyn.

How sad the lot of some contrasted with the many who during this last year made fortunes from the handling of real estate. I noticed one very tantalizing case in the papers last week. A man bought a lot at Winnipeg for $40, and after holding it for a time he last spring sold it to a negro minstrel for $200. Recently the quasi sambo received a dear $2,000 from the same lot. Such instances are very numerous and causing the city people to be almost crazy over real estate—but some time soon there will be a number of burnt fingers.[1] The engineer for the Can. Pac. Railway last month went south with $240,000 he had gained from the reselling of lots in Brandon.[2] If we should squat anywhere near the next new city to be formed out west, Qu'Appelle I think, I will strike out for being owner of a $10 lot. The risk will not be great, and no saying what might result.

Now I must conclude. The clock in your neighbourhood will be somewhere about three o'clock a.m., quite late enough for a farmer to be out of bed. We all long to hear how you are faring in the great capital. The next letter from you will be full of examinations likely. You are not to think hard thoughts of cousins at Broomhill Drive for opening your letter. I address this letter to them as I have the vanity to flatter myself with the idea that they will still like to hear how things are getting on here, and just now am under the necessity of being careful, as this letter deprives me of my fourth last envelope, and I know not how or when the stock will be renewed. We all unite in sending our kindest love to cousins Henry, Agnes, and yourself.

Your most affectionate brother

Willie

---

1   Pierre Berton describes the Manitoba real estate boom of 1881 in *The National Dream.*

2   This referred to Gen. Rosser, after whom Brandon's main street is named. According to *The Assiniboine Basin*, "his pay was augmented by the number of lots he could sell on new town sites" (p. 10).

Elton, Man.
28 January 1882

My Dear Maggie,

I have only one important item of news for you this time, and that is, we have sold our present holding, receiving for it $450. The price is not so great as we might have got had we waited for a month or two. But we got the offer and thought it well to accept, as we could not afford to be going about Brandon waiting on a purchaser, and it leaves us at liberty to think and act freely. A few days afterwards we had a visitor, an implement agent who would have given us $500, but of course we could not foresee this. However, we are now $100 better than when first we arrived, and we have now had a year's experience that will assist us to do wonders this season. We will not require to move from here before the fine weather, as the buyer has only bought it on "spec," and means to sell again. He resides in Grand Valley.

Another redeeming feature to the transaction is that we will not require to team any more wood—in fact we have not been doing so for six weeks. So there is little fear of our being caught by blizzards. They are most frequent next month, although this locality has not had a real genuine one for two years. By a genuine one, I mean a terrific whirlwind with the thermometer 30 or 40 degrees below zero, the sun darkened with the thick whirling drift of snow. We have not yet planned definitely our future course. Most probably the next letter will contain something definite. We last mail received a Herald from Henry. Tonight we expect to receive a letter from you.

The weather since last I wrote has become exceedingly cold. The lowest our thermometer has yet registered was 34 degrees below zero, one morning at sunrise, although the Valley people had it at 40 degrees below. I had the double misfortune to walk to the Valley on the coldest day. I stayed overnight there and was accommodated with the coldest bed imaginable. The whole household, to judge from their talk, must have been nearly frozen up—the house seemed to have become a sieve. Really it was cold comfort. I was glad to start home next day, although an equally cold wind was blowing. How my bones did ache when I got home—fortunately one dose of Chlorodyne put me right. A New Brunswick Mason I spoke to at the Valley, who had been three winters in the country, said he had not before felt it so cold.

Today I think it is equally cold. At sunrise the thermometer marked 30 degrees below out of the wind, and a whole gale blowing with drifting snow. The cattle in the stable were all white with hoar frost, and shivering. After breakfast we went out and boldly faced the chilling blast, and put up a snow bank on the wind side of the stable—it had the desired effect. We were an hour at it. I got my fingertips frozen and had to expend a good deal of time scraping the snow before they resumed their ruddy hue. They nip quite a bit yet. Now all this with Andrew's tale will surely go a good bit to cool the effect of the exceedingly mild weather you had been experiencing.

Fortunately we glean comfort from the fact that in about two months the sun will during the day be warm enough, possibly too much so. You are not to imagine that the cold here is exceedingly disagreeable. Out of the wind you could go about and work in your shirt sleeves, but the wind causes the cold to be extra severe. If you faced it for ten minutes your face would not be particularly cold, but you would not be able to laugh for a $50 bet. Your face would be so stiff, and the nose will be the first to take on the marble hue unless you give it an occasional stroke and pat with your fingers. The frosting is only painful after it is rubbed out. This is the only drawback to the cold here. I have felt it colder in the old country—there it is disagreeably uncomfortable and makes the teeth chatter. I myself think a spell of Manitoban cold is to be preferred. So don't hesitate, but come along when you are ready.

I have been thinking that you would find it an advantage over here if you could work with a sewing machine. Do you think you could get lessons anywhere? A knowledge of pianoforte tuning would also be a great advantage, as it will be almost impossible to get that done many places hereaway, and it will be very expensive every place. I think the extremes of temperature render tuning necessary very frequently. If you like you can see about these. With the first I do not suppose there will be any difficulty, and the result will, I think, amply repay any little time, trouble or expense incurred. The piano tuning will not most likely be practicable, but if you are in the habit of frequenting any music shop it would cost nothing to inquire. What makes me think of it was two of my school companions before going back home to Rangoon went for short time to Graham the music seller in Storby for lessons.

When I am in the way of advising I may as well continue. No doubt you will be thinking of now devoting a little of your spare time to making things for coming away. Our experience is that about two thirds of the things we brought with us were either useless or did not pay the trouble and turmoil they caused us. A number of things here are dearer than they were in the old country owing to the protective tariff, but the difference would not at all pay the trouble of transporting. The only things that need be brought, and that is owing to their being of inferior quality here, are cutlery and anything made of steel, woollen underclothing, handkerchiefs, and a limited number of knick-knack finery and frilling, books and music. There is no occasion for a great number of dresses, and boots ain't worth a kick, so I think you will not require an extra big trunk. If you think of getting one soon, see that it is strong, for the Yankees take great delight in heaving them around. If they were paid to do it, of course, it would not be thought of. But as it is, they consider it good fun to tip them up in the baggage car no matter how large they are, and dexterously give them a heave on to the platform. The fun is rated by the amount of damage done. These well-bound leather trunks, Bullock trunks I think they are called, seem to survive the ordeal best.

Just before sundown Papa went over to the Post Office and brought back our share of the mail—a letter from you, a paper from Henry and another from Winnipeg. All these I have hastily perused—the others you may suppose are deeply engrossed. I am truly glad to see from your letter that you are cheerfully looking forward to your London experience. . . .

Our next move will cause a little expense, and I think of investing in an Indian pony, as we would require legs of iron to do all the walking that should be done. Also, we think of taking a cheap town lot in Brandon. Most likely it will after a season realize well, and neither of two advantages can be said to be risky, as they will at any time realize their first cost.

We have been rather unfortunate with an ox. It is almost useless for work during hot weather. We purposed making beef of him, but that cannot now be thought, as people get cheap meat all the way from Ontario frozen solid. They can get up a very realistic display—they are as solid as a board, and stand on their legs firmly. A butcher store here is quite a scene. Fowl, pork, and beef frozen hard.

However, to resume, our prospects are very good, and if we secure a section of good land a king would envy our place and happiness. We enjoy greatly the prospect of one benefit your London engagement affords, and that is we expect to welcome you about midsummer a year hence. Meantime we are laying great plans for some "tall" work before that time. Now I must conclude you will by this time have entered on your fourth week in London. I trust you will not feel lonely. We unite in sending our kindest love to cousins Agnes, Henry, and yourself.

Your most affectionate brother
Willie

[P.S. from Andrew]

. . . The other day we got a terrible scare. There was a bitter cold wind blowing, and we were all inside the shanty when the stove commenced to roar a great deal, and shortly afterward we heard a crackling noise. We discovered our chimney was afire, and as it was red hot it set fire to the roof of the shanty. Papa got some water and threw about it, and I had to go outside and get on the roof to pile on snow. In two or three minutes I discovered my fingers were all frozen. After we got the fire put out I slipped off the roof and had about fifteen minutes' hard work taking the frost out of them. This is the second time I have been frozen, and I hope it may be the last, as it is very painful . . .

Your affectionate brother
Andrew

Elton, Man.
9 February 1882

My Dear Maggie,

I had only time at the end of my last letter to hurriedly remark on the contents of your letter, but thinking over it since that time I think it better that the money you spoke of should remain on your side of the Atlantic. I had almost written you by last mail to send it on by two P.O. orders, as our prospective arrangements will render it a matter of extreme difficulty to get it at anytime should we think we required it until you came out. But considering the short time at our disposal and the risk of delay I did not do so, so you will still have it for a standby, although I daresay you will consider yourself independent of such a resource.

We have decided to again hitch up and steer westwards to the Qu'Appelle region. We have now a very good knowledge of all western Manitoba, and can find nothing to suit us. The district we purpose going to has the best land throughout the province, with the additional attractions that the climate is a little milder and the country beautifully interspersed with hills and creeks. We intend leaving here on the last Monday of March, and expect the journey will occupy somewhere about a fortnight's time. Our cavalcade will be a very impressive one—two waggons, a sleigh, and a jumper accompanied by a select, though small, assortment of stock. After passing Flat Creek,[3] the present terminus of the railway, where there is a small settlement, we will not likely see anything but Indian wigwams and Half-Breed abodes for about 160 miles. So that we do not anticipate the journey will not be all sunshiney and pleasant, we will require to camp out under canvas—but good land is cheap at that price. We expect to have the benefit of easy teaming to our destination over the snow. After we get there we will be justified in calling ourselves pioneers, as the land will not be on the market, and we will require to "squat" and make improvements to entitle us to a prior claim. The railway will certainly be laid through and past that district before next autumn, and the accompanying rush will not permit us being long lonely.

If you refer to the map you will be able to understand our route. We cross the river at Brandon and from thence journey fully two hundred miles west, passing about twelve miles south of Ft. Ellice. All the maps will have the course of the river marked and the echoing lake that occasioned the French Half-Breed giving it the name of Qu'Appelle (Who calls?). After you get this letter you had better address our letters to Qu'Appelle Post Office, North West

---

3   Now Oak Lake.

Territory, Canada. Mark on the corner of the first one "to be called for," and we will at all hazards get them, although most probably we might be 60 miles from that place.

I am sorry an extra amount of letter writing prevents me writing to Henry by this mail as I would like. I am afraid we are taxing his kindness too much, troubling him with the Herald. We really appreciate and enjoy the receipt of them. Could you not now that you have more time somehow share the work? Possibly it might be better to discontinue them until we get more settled, but you can arrange it as you think fit.

We are in great spirits over the prospects of the change, and already beginning to arrange things. Everything betokens that we will be very prosperous out there. Certainly we will have all things comfortable and pleasant by the succeeding summer, and will all be proud and happy when we understand you have started your journey hither.

I see from the papers that the old country tenant farmers are grumbling a great deal just now. If they could only be persuaded to come here their grievances would vanish—no leases, no rent, and do as you please. . . .

I see that you are taking a sly poke at me about Annie Gebbie's fur set. She must have an extraordinary far-reaching memory, as I cannot think of ever having made such an arrangement.[4] But I do not know what erroneous freaks my memory might have taken . . . just advise the young ladies that the way to come to an arrangement is to at once start out here—they do the choosing, I the shooting and curing, and between us we will somehow get the skins stitched up respectably. Such an arrangement will have one certain and I presume satisfactory result—the young lady or ladies will have no inclination to again face the Atlantic for some time. It is simply marvelous the number of young men etc. who would willingly and gladly get somebody to make their dinners. I should not care if the origins of this paragraph were made acquainted with its contents.

We have just now come in from the stable at 7:30 p.m. On the way I could not but remark on the brilliant display of streamers [the northern lights]. Do you know if it is the case that no satisfactory

---

4   Evidently he had promised a fur coat to a young lady back home.

scientific reason has been given for their presence? I really think there must be some truth in the idea that they are caused by the snow reflecting the sunlight, but before I give my reasons I should like you to let me know if you can what scientists think of them.

For three days now we have had exceedingly mild weather, the thermometer reaching as far up as the freezing point. You will now have quite fallen into the ways of your London life—we expect to have with this mail a long letter giving us a full description of your surroundings and doings. I trust you will have a Presbyterian church at hand, as you will find yourself likely more at home with the members. . .

Your most affectionate brother
Willie

Elton, Man.
23 February 1882

My Dear Maggie,

We duly received Sunday a week ago your first letter from London—heartily do I wish for the time when we shall receive your last—your postscript leads me to think you are also of the same mind. . . . The walking from the school to your lodgings will do you a great deal of good. When you come out here you will be quite an enthusiast over long excursions over the prairie . . .

Our doings here during the last fortnight have, as usual, not been very noteworthy. Last Wednesday we experienced a tremendous storm. All Tuesday the wind was blowing a gale from the NNE with snow. On Wednesday it increased to a perfect hurricane, the snow drifting as thickly as smoke. Our great difficulty was getting to and into the stable, and we are rather proud of the fact that we managed to get into it the three most necessary times. It was groping almost— little could be seen, the wind piercing through like a knife.

I was never so impressed with the easy way you lose your reckoning. Once, on returning alone, Andrew had gone ahead. I for a few seconds lost sight of the house in the drift, but in that time I lost the direction and went dash into the fence almost a right angle off my course. I had immediately after that to go a short distance from the shanty for snow (just now we only use snow water), and to be safe I walked backwards, keeping the house in sight. I think I never saw a grander sight when the drift slacked a little round me. I saw the drift flying over and around the house like sea breakers. The Atlantic Ocean was tame compared to it.

Our worst turnout was at 7 in the evening. We waited for a lull till the last minute, but still it roared and howled. So we had to make up our minds to face it, and I can assure you we had a wrapping up of ourselves—our cap cowls covering our ears, and necks surmounted by huge comforters twisted four times round—nothing but our eyes exposed in a buried manner. The lamp was set on a pail and covered with a cloth. After struggling to the stable we found the door completely blocked to the top with a snow wreath and I for some time had to dig a passageway. A time before I [had] slipped and plunged headlong up to the neck—this time I lost my balance and fell between a post and the wall. It took me a good time, exert myself as I could, before I got to my feet. After digging the door's liberty, we found the inside fully worse wreathed than the outside, and the cattle perfectly white with snow, but warm. The storm went down shortly after midnight.

Next morning was really a gloriously bright one with a good deal of frost—24 degrees below zero, I think. We went out early and gave the cattle the water they had so long wanted, and for a long time we had huge work shovelling the snow away from and out of the stable. This is the worst gale that has been here for a good many winters, and the knowing ones now characterize this as being the worst winter they ever experienced. Last winter was summer compared to this. The extraordinary drift of snow blocked up the railway for a week and made the trails almost impassable. You cannot imagine how searching the snow is here—it would come even through a pinhole. Since this storm, the frost has been very severe—the thermometer generally registering, unless during sunshine, 25 degrees below zero.

But the weather has been very fine. During all the days we have had splendid mirage views, seeing away down to the States. The only objection was the tendency to elongate and thereby distort the reflected object. On Saturday, we had a slight snowfall, and I think the variety of beautiful crystals could not be equalled—stars, diamonds, crosses, roses, etc., all gorgeously fretted in white.

I was at the time returning from the post office, and about a quarter of a mile from the main trail two ox teams with sleighloads of wood were travelling along west, and the appearance they presented impressed my very much. Never before did I feel such a desire to be proficient at landscape drawing. Not a sound to be heard, nothing to be seen but the white snow-covered prairie. No houses, no fences—nothing for a background but a clump of willows and the slightest approach to a knoll, the oxen walking steadily along, the drivers drawing their coats closer about them, preparing for the approaching storm. The whole scene had such a silent solitary weird appearance about it that I, involuntarily for a little, imagined myself the spectator of a panoramic scene.

I trust you are keeping up your proficiency in drawing. There are thousands of such quiet effective scenes to be met with here. If you could depict one of our thunderstorms here it would make your fortune—but enough of the past.

We are getting on well with our arrangements for the great journey west—only a month next Monday till we start. Surely we are justified in anticipating fine weather after all the extraordinary blows and colds we have experienced. You will, I trust, now be addressing your letters to Qu'Appelle P. Office. In a week or two some of us will require to go down to Portage or Winnipeg for pigs and hens. (You are not aesthetic, I hope—possibly I may have misspelt the big word). We also will procure a Winchester repeating rifle. These shoot sixteen times in as many seconds, and during our night sentrying might possibly be found useful—and woe betide any bears, wolves, deer, or Indians that come within its locality. We expect all the time to be favoured with good moonlight. I trust your namesake the cow will stand the exposure, as she is a particularly good one, quiet and giving us plenty of milk even at this time. I think she will stand it all right as she has a good bit of the Montana breed.

We are kept rather busier just now making preparations. We have also great work occasionally excavating the snow—almost everything is blown over with snow.

The people hereaway have become quite crazy over the immense fortunes they are likely to realize from their holding. A place three miles west of Brandon was recently sold to our MPP for $20,000. Were we to come back in two years I do not think we would find one of our present neighbours—they will all have sold out. It is quite a relief to meet with anyone who is satisfied with moderate prospects—the boom seems to be influencing every place in the colony. Three new railways have recently begun making preliminary arrangements. Speculators are already in the rush to Qu'Appelle, all anxious to become first claimants to likely farmsites. The salesman in the store at Grand Valley where we buy the most of our goods had started west with three companions, all proposing to take up ¼ sections that are likely to become towns. The arrangement is that the more fortunate of them will share their fortune with the less fortunate. I understand there are sometimes as many as four squatters or claimants on a single homestead. I do not envy their possible good fortune, considering the cold they will have to experience. Possibly the later ones will be as fortunate as these, and who knows but we may make a fortune without labouring for it. However, I will be quite as happy if we secure a good farming section. . .

Your most affectionate brother
Willie

Elton, Man.
10 March 1882

My Dear Maggie,

Andrew received your letter No. 7 only last Tuesday. It had the misfortune to be delayed a fortnight at the Valley post office owing to the inexperience of a new postmaster and the consequences of a great storm. . . . You can form no conception of our eagerness to get your letters, how carefully they are read and how long and earnestly they are discussed, especially since you have gone to live in a place we know nothing of. Tell us everything about yourself, no matter how trivial—describe your lodgings, all the people you meet in them, the different places you consider peculiar or noteworthy, what kinds of roads you have to school, what is the common like, what different kinds of house do you see and what kind of people do you pass. Do you go to your lodgings for dinner, what kind of children have you in the school, was that Edin. teacher good looking, etc. etc.—these are only a tithe of the questions we are eager to get answered. We hope you will send us a big huge 5 cent letter to Qu'Appelle so that our loneliness may be somewhat enlivened and give us something to think over. Now here goes for showing you a good example.

Since I last wrote our time has been pretty much taken up with preparing and discussing our future journey. Last Thursday [Papa] went down to Brandon to see about oxen. I followed on the Friday with the oxen, and met him at the Valley. The journey from our place to the trail was a caution. The storm I wrote you of had caused great wreaths—in these the oxen had some fearful floundering and wallowing. The trail was pretty good. At the Valley some of the stores were blocked up completely by the snow wreaths. I saw a great number of prairie chickens pecking about the houses like hens—no one seemed to observe them.

We had a rather cold journey home. The wind was very cold and the sky cold and threatening. Sometime after sundown the wind increased to a hurricane, and for two complete days we experienced a storm the equal of which has not been known here before. All Saturday the wind howled in a furious way, and the drift was terrible heavy. Owing to the heavy snowfall, nothing could be seen. On Sunday the snow went off but the drift continued quite as thick, the wind even stronger than the previous day. We had terrible work getting into the stable. Each time we had to dig a hole down from the level of the roof to the door, and every entrance caused the snow to be less easily put away. Andrew and I were completely blinded when trying to dig out some hay. The ice was hanging from my eyelids like ounce weights. We kept up our spirits pretty well the first day, but I was miserable when I awoke on the Sunday morning and heard the gales as fierce as ever.

That Sunday was anything but a day of rest to us. All day we were the greater part of the time battling with the drift. The house was not very comfortable owing to the melting of the snow on our clothes, and we had to melt snow to water the cattle. Fancy us lurching along in an impenetrable drift, leaning ourselves to the sweeping hurricane with a tin boiler filled with six pailfuls of boiling water. This we cooled down with snow in the stable. The cattle appreciated our exertion much, licking us very affectionately. We are the astonishment of the neighbourhood when we boast of our having during the storm regularly supplied our cattle with hay and water. We know of no other one who managed it. The greater number only managed to get to their stock once each day.

The postmaster was the most of Monday digging away the snow before he got his horse out—he did not get for the mail until the Tuesday. One man north of us happened to be down at the bush and was stormsteaded the whole time. His wife could not get to the cattle, and for two days they were without any hay or water. One man happened to be out teaming with oxen when the storm came on; he unhitched the cattle and ran for the station. When he got there it was two hours before they managed to bring him round, and his cattle were found frozen stiff. Another farmer was in his stable and missed his road going to the house. He found a haystack, and in it he had to remain all night. The [railway] cars were stopped directly south of us and the 42 passengers were nearly famished before a relief party brought them food—the traffic was suspended for three days. Fortunately the number of mishaps were few owing to the storm coming on after sundown. Had it, or the previous one, made their appearance during the day the consequences would have been terrible. No such storm had been known here before—the length of time it occupied was particularly unusual.

We are now comforting ourselves with the hope that winter is now over. Since then we have had nice mild weather. The sun is during the day very strong and dazzling. The caps are being laid aside, and we are reverting to wide-awake clerical hats and blue goggles. Were it not for the blouses and top boots, the costume would remind you somewhat of an invalid parson. The Monday succeeding the storm was quite a contrast, clear and bright. We were the most of the day excavating the snow on an extensive scale.

On Tuesday I again went down to Brandon to see about oxen. The deep snow made walking very tiresome. The teamsters from the bush had a rough time. The storm had almost starved them, and they were under the necessity of driving for provisions. You would laugh had you heard Andrew describe the mighty style of a retired minister who was driving home like the rest for hunger's sake with a load consisting of three sticks drawn with great difficulty by a splendid team of horses.

Just before entering the Valley I met with rather an exciting reception. I had happened amongst a covey of prairie chickens. Two of the storekeepers with a breech loader and a rifle were endeavouring to thin their numbers. Of course they considered themselves good shots, would not think it possible that they could by mischance hit me, but I did not relish the salutes.

When I got to Brandon I found cattle had arrived. But such beasts, old and lean. I do not think a summer's idleness and grass would have rendered them capable of working, and the dealers had the effrontery to value each ox at £23.10p.[5] I am heartily sorry for the immigrants who will soon begin to arrive and will be entirely at the dealers' mercy. I bought two slightly used sleighs at about half price, so that my journey was not altogether fruitless. This last snowfall will render sleighing necessary on the journey. I got back home shortly before sundown. I had walked full twenty miles through deep snow and was very tired.

About bed time I was at my nightly occupation, making shavings to kindle the stove. Unfortunately I rather enlivened the process by missing the stick and digging the knife into my knee. I had a miserable hour of it afterwards. The wound did not bleed and as a consequence, I suppose, I sickened. Since that time I have been enjoying the luxury of what Andrew states is a pin leg. The wound is almost closed, and I am getting a little more freedom.

Papa had to start on the Wednesday to the bush after a man that I heard was scarce of money and wished to sell his oxen. He managed to secure them at a comparatively low price—£35 the pair. They are nice young cattle and in good working condition. Andrew is proud of the fact that he is a stockman. Since the new arrivals came he has had quite a busy and interesting time. Likely he will write you about them.

I am now busy stitching. The tents that are for sale are expensive and not commodious. We are making our own one, so I am working at a web of duck[6] like a sailmaker. I have no thimble. Don't you

---

5 The pound was worth about $5 at that time.
6 A kind of canvas.

pity me? We will also have an awning to protect the cattle from the cold—this will cause a good deal of sewing. Soon I will be quite an expert needle-man.

I have also added to my cooking capabilities the making of nice crisp biscuits. What do you think of that? Plenty of butter and sugar among the flour, well-kneaded and well thumped is the secret. Just one other remark to prove that I am a model housekeeper—I have not managed to break a dish since coming here.

Papa started this morning with a roving commission after cattle, pigs and hens. Possibly he may go to Winnipeg. I am sorry this letter was not ready for him to post—forgive the delay. On Saturday we received your second No. 7 letter and it was a great improvement, longer and more interesting.

We are very glad to know that you now consider yourself settled. I am greatly pleased to learn that you are discovering so many really kind friends. What kind of place is the Strand? Is it a public park? I thank you for the music. It is just a shade too difficult I think, but I have not tried it and it does not suit the flutes. The lowest note they can produce is a treble D. They are perfection for both alto and tenor. . . .

We have had a rather stormy day today (Tuesday), a good deal of drift and no sunshine. But it was mild, only 12 degrees of frost. We yoked all our cattle into the waggon yesterday and endeavoured to overcome our isolated appearance by breaking a trail through the snow to the main trail. We managed it after a good deal of wading and digging, but now this drift has undone all our work. However, I am pleased to see it blow and remain unsettled—we may possibly have a better chance of fine weather during our journey.

We have bought an alarm clock, a pretty little business that keeps us in mind of our duty. Every morning its furious ringing rouses us out of our dreams in a shocking manner. The days are now quickly lengthening—the sun rises just now at six and sets about that time.

I think my yarn is about spun. I will again write you before leaving here. After that the letters will be very irregular for a time. . . .

Your most affectionate brother
Willie

[P.S. from Andrew]
... Isn't Willie a fine one to be talking about not having broken any dishes when they are all made of cast metal which he could not break supposing he was willing.

Grand Valley, Man.
10 April 1882

My Dear Maggie,

I am afraid that you will be thinking that we are becoming careless over writing letters to you, but the irregularity has been unavoidable. The principal cause has been the blocking of the railway time after time by snowstorms. March has been an exceptionally stormy month, and this one so far is equal to it.

I started west on what proved to be a wild goose chase after a section of land in Oak River. I was as far as Birtle, near Fort Ellice. The only drawback to the trip was an expenditure of £5 and a week's delay, but I gained an intimate knowledge of our trail to Qu'Appelle and a good deal of valuable information that will I think repay the expense. I got home on Wednesday morning and we at once set to work at the final packing for the flitting. We made the start on Friday morning, but owing to a high wind and the deep snow we only got the length of the main trail. Our tent was [blown] almost over and one sleigh load upset twice. We camped for the night at the side of the creek that passes our old place. We experienced a fearfully stormy night—snow, sleet and rain in succession. Altogether our prospects were dismal-looking—next forenoon was no better. It cleared away a little in the afternoon, and we went back for a load that had been dropped behind. No sooner had we got it back to camp than the storm again raged. Next forenoon the storm rather lulled and we started to the Valley, got there yesterday afternoon. Altogether we have [had] a disagreeable and disheartening beginning—possibly the finish may be all the more pleasant.

We were very much put about the want of a yoke of oxen that had been delayed by the railway blockade. These we have now got, a nice well-matched pair. You will likely become acquainted with them—Diamond and Star are their names. We have been all day getting things fixed up here [with plans to travel] from thence to Qu'Appelle via Ft. Ellice. Our camping apparatus is quite a success, awed by everybody.

We are warm and comfortable but our room is very limited. Letter writing is almost an impossibility. I had a letter written before, but in the disorder it got on the floor and the pups finished it. I managed to save the stamps. I will let you know on every opportunity how we got on.

The country is being deluged with immigrants. Accommodation cannot be got for them—they are being stowed into the churches. This place is a perfect hubbub. Papa suggests that you ought to be applying to the steamboat company to keep a place open for you. The immigrants so far are all mostly from Ontario. Accommodation cannot be had here for less than $1 per day and fight for your bed or do without—I slept one night in a house near Rapid City on the floor with nothing but my wearing clothes. Our tent renders us independent of such an emergency. Numbers are going back scared off by the storms—a great many have been frozen for want of accommodation.

We are glad to hear that you still get on well and pleasantly. I had a letter from Uncle Hugh getting a whole lot of Scotch news. Kindly let him know how you learn we are getting on by your next letter. I trust you will be able to read this one. I must now conclude. We expect a whole waggon load of letters at Qu'Appelle. We unite in sending our kindest love to cousins and yourself.

Your most affectionate brother
Willie

Salt Lake, Man.[7]
13 April 1882

My Dear Maggie,

I have only time to write you that we are all well and getting along pleasantly. We left Grand Valley on Tuesday morning and travelled about sixteen miles, camping about six miles from Rapid City. We had pretty tough work getting over the Little Saskatchewan River, as the valley was all thawed and the river ice quite slushy. We camped that night about nine miles west of Rapid City. Today we have teamed about sixteen miles. When I write this we are camped two miles from Salt Lake. I will post this letter at that place. We are now about fifty miles from Fort Ellice, so that we are making pretty good speed.

I will not write more, as teaming is very tiresome work, and we intend making a very early start in the morning, as the sun is now very warm and distressing. We trust you are getting on well and still comfortable and happy. Our kindest love to cousins and yourself.

Your most affectionate brother
Willie

Birtle, Man.
20 April 1882

My Dear Maggie,

We have now got the length of Birtle, about seventy miles from Brandon, where we have been stopped by the thaw coming on, and will require to wait for about a week. So Willie started out to see the Shell River district yesterday, and it is likely if the land is good we will homestead there, as there will be some difficulty in crossing the Assiniboine to go to Qu'Appelle owing to the river being blocked with ice. The tent on the sleigh has been a perfect success—we are perfectly comfortable in it, and it is the admiration of everyone we meet.

---

7   Near Strathclair.

The first day after leaving the old place we made very slow progress, as we had a bad trail and had only the two teams to draw the three loads, and the second [day] we had only got out to the main trail, a distance of a mile and a half. About midnight it became very stormy, so the next day Papa went with the cattle to the stopping house. The storm did not go down till the middle of the next day, and in the afternoon we started for the Valley and got there about sundown. Next morning Willie went back for the load we had left behind and Papa went over to Brandon to get a third team of oxen, and he came back with a pair of big Ontario cattle.

We did not leave the valley till the following morning, and got to within six miles of Rapid City. We made Rapid City next day in time for dinner, and in the afternoon went eight miles. Rapid City is situated in a valley on the banks of the Little Saskatchewan and has about a hundred houses. Next day we made the Forks [of the trail] and the day following, Shoal Lake where a Sergeant of the Mounted Police examined us to see if we had any whiskey. A number of the people were very anxious to trade a pony for our cow, which we were not anxious to do.

It took us a day and a half to come from Shoal Lake to Birtle where we sold the old ox and the calf. We had to sell the calf because he was perfectly played out and was quite lame. Next morning we started for Fort Ellice, but it took us nearly six hours to go two miles, so we decided to camp and wait till the roads get better. There are now plenty of ducks, geese and turkeys flying about, and last night we had a heavy fall of rain, which had the effect of melting nearly all the snow. I think I will now close with kindest love to cousins Agnes and Henry and yourself, from

Your affectionate brother
Andrew

Birtle, Man.
26 April 1882

My Dear Maggie,

Andrew would write you by the last mail that we had an idea of altering our course to Shell River. I started out for that district

Tuesday a week ago, and was land hunting for two days. Awful hard lonely work it was. However, I selected a section of land 640 acres on the Assiniboine and got back here after being absent eight days. I was glad to find Papa and Andrew comfortable and happy in the tent and the cattle wild with doing nothing. Papa and I went to the Land Office and entered for the land. I will give you a full glowing account of our future abode when we get it up and settled. It is beside the river and Thunder Creek, about 8 miles from Shell River Post Office, where you will now address letters to, about 30 miles north of Ft. Ellice and fully 50 miles from here. Our nearest neighbours at present will be the Bryants, about six miles distant. All the surrounding land is taken up, as a railway will likely pass about three miles distant. The steamboats, of course, will pass on the river during summer. The Bryants, you will remember, travelled last spring with us from Winnipeg to Portage. I will reserve a long description of our journey till we are more settled.

Just now we are busy packing up. Immediately after dinner we will start on our journey to our new place. We will be a long time in getting up, as the trails are bad and the creeks full of water. I will write to you again Saturday a week hence. We will only now have a fortnightly mail. I think we are better suited than we would have been at Qu'Appelle. We will have a good class of neighbours. I will write to Qu'Appelle for any letters you may have sent there. We will now weary very much till we hear from you. Our address will now be Shell River Post Office, Manitoba.[8] Our location is Section 10, Township 22, Range 29. Kindly excuse this short scrappy letter—I expect to be soon able to make amends. We trust you are still getting along well and pleasantly. We are all well and hopeful and unite in sending our kindest love to cousins and yourself.

Your most affectionate brother,
Willie

---

8   The present town of Russell.

Shell River, Man.
18 May 1882

My Dear Maggie,

I quite forgot the regular number of this letter, and think it better to begin numbering anew. It may be as well that you do the same.

We have now got settled down on our land. We had a very rough tedious journey here. I got back to the camp from my land-hunting trip on the Wednesday. Papa and I that afternoon crossed to the land office and entered for our land. The bridge had been swept away the previous evening by the ice, and we had to cross the creek in a small canoe hurriedly built for the occasion. Fortunately the voyage was not a long one, as the canoe let in the water very quickly.

After the land had been secured we went down to the stable where our cattle had been put in. We deliberated a long time whether we should venture to swim them over the creek, but thinking it too risky we decided to let them remain until the next morning. Papa remained in charge of them. Next morning he brought them to the creek for the purpose of seeing what could be done to get them over, but they set all doubt at an end on the matter by plunging into and swimming over the creek like fish. I was very thankful to see them. The usual way is to place a long rope round their necks and pull them over.

During the afternoon a party of Shell River settlers passed. I was acquainted with two of them. Andrew and I started down with them to see them cross the creek. At the crossing all was bustly and excitement. Two canoes were constantly paddling between the two sides with goods and passengers, and a big raft that had been building all forenoon was just about to commence its maiden voyage. It was loaded with a waggon, its owner, and another friend, one of those useful kind ready for anything. It started all proper, but when it got to midstream the current caught and sunk the upper side, shifting the waggon, and two men were up to the waist in water. For a little, everyone thought they would have been drowned, but the waggon got off and the raft righted itself. It was pulled back and condemned—all the freighting was afterwards done by the canoes.

The creek had quite a lively appearance with canoes crossing, and horses and cattle swimming. One amateur canoist got a thorough dousing in the current—fortunately he held on to the tow rope. Another party of novices were carried downstream a long distance and were pretty tired of paddling, I am sure, when they got back.

Next day, Friday, we started on our journey. We had to leave a load behind—I will go back for it next week. We only managed to make four miles that day, as the roads were very bad and we were too heavily loaded. Next day we got to Snake Creek and found it impassable, so we camped at the head of the gully on the open prairie. About sundown an Ontario land hunter called in on us. He was dead beat-up with walking from Ft. Ellice, a distance of seven miles. This is a specimen of Canadian hardihood—we had to give him a bed on the floor of the tent. We remained camped all Sunday. On Monday morning we resolved to venture a crossing—we got over easier than I anticipated. We put the three yoke onto each load. I was up to the waist in water driving them. I now bitterly regret my never having learnt to swim.

On my previous journey going up I managed to get over this creek on the ice. On coming back, however, it was a roaring torrent 100 feet broad. Fortunately I lost my trail and went as far south as the Assiniboine where I got over on a bridge, but even that was very risky, as I walked over it with the rushing muddy water up to my knees. I could not see whether the flooring was still on the bridge or whether it was washed away. The only thing I could see was the wash on the top [of] the current where it met the bridge. I got across all safe—next morning not a vestige of the bridge was remaining. If you have any good opportunity you should learn to swim. I am going on strong for it this summer.

After getting across the creek and drying things a little bit we started, and that night camped in sight of Ft. Ellice on the opposite side of the river. Next morning, to speed our journey a little, we went up to the old trail. We nearly suffered the penalty for being odd—we were almost swamped in an alkali marsh. Fortunately a little judicious digging and driving got us out. I was very thankful to strike the main trail again. We got along pretty well until midday, when we got stuck in a bit of trail pretty badly alkalied. To make matters worse, we camped for dinner and the stove set the prairie on fire. We were kept pretty lively for a time saving our belongings from getting burnt. After disloading the most of our goods and carrying them forward to better ground, we got the waggon out. This is the hardest and most disheartening work connected with teaming in the North West.

Next day we travelled to Silver Creek and found it impassable. The current at the ford was very strong and six feet deep, and showing no signs of abating. There were three camps that had been waiting to get over [for] nearly a fortnight. It was at last decided to build a bridge, and for two days Papa was kept pretty active bossing about a dozen amateur workmen. After it was complete the workers had so little confidence in their work that it was decided to carry over the greater part of the loads. After some little trouble we were thankful to realize that we were on the homeward side of the creek. We started out at once and travelled about four miles that night.

After we had left the bridge, one of the workers at it was almost drowned. He was knocked off by the pole of a waggon they were drawing over. He was jammed between it and the bridge head downwards up to the waist in the current for a minute and a half. It was two hours before they could bring him round to consciousness. Strangers to the structure have more confidence in the bridge as plenty of Indians passed over it with their carts all loaded.

On Saturday we got to within four miles of the Hudson Bay store and eleven of our destination. We remained there all Sunday. On Monday we got to the settlement, the site of the future city. Next day I started out with Papa to the place to show him the beauties of it and to find a feasible trail. After roaming around for a while Papa managed to shoot a partridge, and I saw a rabbit, both very different from the old country varieties. The partridge is the prettiest bird you could imagine, coloured a brownish grey with the feathers shaded like a peacock.

I have endeavoured to give you an outline of the place. A. is Papa's homestead and C. is his pre-emption. B. is my homestead and D. is my pre-emption. E. is Thunder Creek and F. a small creek running into it. Both run through very deep glens, I am sure fully 300 feet deep. The banks are well covered with poplar and birch wood, sufficient to supply us with wood for building fencing and burning for years to come. The point marked G. we call Ben Nevis,[9]

---

9   Ben Nevis is the highest mountain in the British Isles.

and not a grander scene can be seen anywhere than from that point. You see down the gorge to where the creek empties itself into the Assiniboine and down the valley of the river. The point [G] is where we purpose building our house just now, and where we are camped. The part I have dotted round is a flat valley where we purpose putting up our stables and stockyard.

The creek is deep, runs all the year, and could drive a wheel. The water is also good. A finer section for the raising of horses, cattle or sheep could not be imagined. The grass come early and is very heavy. Down in the valley the cattle could graze all the year round without the frost or storms troubling them in the least. The land is good for grass, but it is hardly the soil attributed to Manitoba—it is rather light. In the meantime we think it preferable to heavy black soil—it is easily wrought and will yield five or six good crops. Andrew and I expect to be able to plough sixty acres this summer, and the crop certainly can be harvested three weeks earlier than from the heavy soils. By this means we will be enabled to earn a good deal of money and gradually increase our stock. Before the soil becomes exhausted we will sow it down with finer grasses. By this means we will work into stock farming, the pleasantest and I believe most profitable kind of farming.

The river Assiniboine runs parallel to the section at point H. We have a small part of the valley on our ground. From a bluff of poplars on my homestead you get a splendid view of the Assiniboine valley— the [?] is poor scenery compared to it. I mean to build my house there. The steamers passing in the summertime to Ft. Pelly and the Shell River will make a cheerful site. Papa will build his house on the creek. The law requires each settler to build a house on his homestead.

The surrounding sections are now all taken up on this side of the river, and before the end of the year we will have plenty of neighbours. In the meantime our nearest neighbours are the Bryants, fully six miles away. Two young Scotchmen named Pagan, from Dumfries, have taken up the section cornering this. The settlement is very pretty for two miles. It is dotted over with groves of trees and lakes—after that it is very hilly and well wooded. We are about seven miles from the post office.

Before starting with our loads to this place we parted at a good profit with one yoke of oxen. We received in exchange a yoke one year younger, a good well-made, well-behaved pony, and $35. That is, we got $40 more for the oxen than we paid four months ago and we expect yet to make $80 or $100 off the steers next spring. Andrew will tell you all about the pony—likely next summer you will become better acquainted with it.

We have not got all our garden seeds planted. Next week I will start for Birtle where I will get the seed potatoes and some other things we had to leave behind. I will then go to Ft. Ellice and get a stock of provisions. After I get home we will plant the potatoes and begin our ploughing. Occasionally we will, as opportunity offers, get our log house built—for the present at least we must live in a tent. I have fortunately got a splendid yoke of cattle for ploughing—they walk right out through anything as straight as a needle. I do not require to stop at the ends at all, so that everything betokens our getting on pleasantly and prosperously. The only drawback to our happiness is that nowadays we get neither letters or newspapers. We are now wearying very much to hear from you. Did you send any letters to Qu'Appelle?

Last Sunday after dinner we went out to Ben Nevis point to feast our eyes on the glorious grandeur of the gorge. Away to the east we saw a something travelling on the prairie—gradually as it came nearer we made out five persons walking. At first we concluded they were Indians, then we guessed them to be land hunters. They steered straight for out tent. Who should they turn out to be but Arthur Bryant, the two Pagans, and two young men from Manchester, England, all lost on the prairie—did not know where they were. They had all started in the morning with the intention of seeing the Pagans' section of land and getting back for dinner. They got here about 4 o'clock in the afternoon without making out a section of land at all, tired and hungry. Our bread was all done, so I gave them a cup of tea and a good big plateful of porridge each. You bet they swallowed everything thankfully. It was about the most comical tea party I ever witnessed, but they were all as serious as Turks. I went back a bit and showed them the road. I expect they would get home all right but I do hope some of them got half drowned or burnt on the way back—the stupid beggars quite frankly let us know that they had fired the prairie at a place where they had been smoking.

Next day we saw the fire passing north of us in big swaths, each one coming nearer us. In the afternoon one chain of fire appeared and headed straight for the north of our section. We at once set about firing the prairie round our tent and across between the two creeks. As we rushed to preserve grass for our cattle, we had [an] exciting night's work. Such an amount of flame and smoke I never before witnessed. We cut off the fire pretty well until we came to the edge of the little creek. There the grass did not light readily with me, so I went a little way up the bank. The light started from the match like gunpowder and before we could breathe, the place was in flames. Andrew and I had terribly run before the flames till we got to the top of the hill where we stood, giving up all for lost. The wind, however, reared a little, and the fire slacked, so after some pretty lively work we managed to stamp out the side on which we wished to save the grass. I all along dreaded it would get among the heavy brush in the Thunder Creek. I kept guard on it the greater part of the night, and I for one wished to see no more of the like magnificent displays. At one point where I was beating out the fire, my boots got so hot that I thought my feet would blister in them.

All next day the fire raged on the bank of the little creek, burning a lot of the trees. Two or three showers of rain today [have], however, put all the fires out—we have escaped pretty well. I felt sorry to see the once young grass being scorched up and the groves of young poplar wood being destroyed—it would destroy a large number of birds' nests. At an early date I mean to have a quiet talk with Mr. Bryant. The careless beggar ought to be informed against and fined $50, the penalty for such an action.

I will now conclude. We all trust you are getting on well and happily. We long very much to hear from you. I have broken my fiddle bow and am too busy to even think of the fiddle, so you need not trouble with sending music till wintertime. Could you get any information for our benefit about the making, preserving and using of hop yeast? We have plenty of hop. I trust you will be able to read this letter. The pen feels quite strange and unwieldly in my hand. We unite in sending our fondest love to cousins and yourself.

Your most affectionate brother
Willie

Shell River, Man.
1 June 1882

My Dear Maggie,

I got back yesterday from my journey to Birtle. Today I am resting after the hard work that trip entailed on me, and am taking advantage of part of the holiday to write to you. I wrote last week to Uncle Hugh and posted the letter when at Birtle. Everything has been getting along very quietly here. Spring has performed its work in its usual rapid way—one could almost imagine they saw things growing. The trees especially were covered with leaves remarkably quick. Wild strawberries, raspberries and gooseberries are all bearing promises of a great quantity of fruits. You cannot possibly imagine how pretty the prairies and valleys look when dressed in green. You will be completely charmed with this country when you see it.

Papa and Jess have had a very heroic encounter with a badger when I was away. They came across it one evening near [?] and after a great deal of fighting Papa managed to kill it. The skin is a remarkably pretty one—Papa speaks of selling it. The Hudson's Bay store is about nine miles from here. Likely the skin will be helping to make some monied individual in your part of the world both warm and beautiful very soon. When you come out we will attempt the curing and dressing of furs, so there is another inducement for your coming out as quickly as possible.

Four of our neighbours have settled on their land—we have not spoken to them yet. One of our nearest neighbours will be on his land next Monday, so we will soon have abundance of company. I heard when at Birtle that the railway will most probably cross the section adjoining this one. Who knows but it may bring a small fortune with it for us.

Papa and Andrew, when I was away, were down into our bush felling trees over sixty feet high to make logs for our house. Today they are busy cutting and planting the potatoes I fetched up. I have very little else to write you about. Possibly I might interest you with a description of my journey to Birtle. I started from here last Wednesday morning with the waggon and two yoke of oxen. The one yoke I led behind, putting their harness into the waggon box along with an axe, spade and canvas cover. I made a nice seat for myself with the latter in the waggon. I went across a nice flat bit of prairie where we mean to do our ploughing this year and down into a little ravine or creek that you might suggest a name for. On getting up to the other side of the bank I got to the pins that mark an old railway survey line—these I followed as closly as possible through section 2 and for about a mile in Township 21. This part is nicely dotted on with groves of poplar trees and small lakes. An occasional swamp enlivens matters a little, as the oxen had to be hurried through these very rapidly or they would quickly sink into them beyond redemption. The grass hereabouts is very long—it is a resort for myriads of prairie chickens and ducks.

After getting over this very confusing piece of ground I came across a small creek. On the other side the character of the country was different—large rolling hills with a good deal of wood here and there. Where I crossed the creek the bed was very shallow, but a short distance down it quickly descended between two high banks and formed a considerable gorge till it emptied into Conjuring Creek. I travelled down the direction of the creek some distance until I could get round the shoulder of a hill to my left. I then went a short distance along an Indian trail until I dipped down into another creek. I had not long got over it until still another ravine demanded attention and careful driving. I would now be six miles from home. Away to the left on the other side of Conjuring Creek I saw Rae's house, at present the nearest house to us.

A little distance further on, two men were having hard work, the one ploughing, the other leading the oxen, getting the ground ready for seed—their only dwelling place seemed to be the waggon. A short distance farther on a large lake came in view. When I got almost past it, I struck the trail from what is called the Western Settlement[10] to the post office. After travelling along it a short distance, the side of a hay swamp, I ascended a bit of rising ground along by the side of a fenced field. On the top was a little log house with a turf roof, but the owner was just getting things made better, as he had the walls of a more pretentious house built a little nearer the trail.

10 Russell.

I continued along this trail a small piece farther till it got round the end of a bluff of wood. At the foot of the hill was a nice little cosy-looking house belonging to a Mr. Brown who settled there two years before—he had previously been a clerk in Dundee. At this. point I struck over the prairie and soon got to a trail that led directly to the settlement—it led me downhill to the Conjuring Creek. After some coaxing and whipping I got the oxen over the creek, and passed Mr. DuPre's[11] house, an old resident and married to a Half-Breed. An Indian with a cart started from here and kept me company to the settlement, about a mile.

In due time I arrived there quite hungry for dinner. This part is all surveyed into town lots by a Major Boulton, an Englishman. The city is to be called Russell. He is doing all he can to get a railway station placed here.[12] At present the only houses on the site of the future city are his own and the Hudson's Bay store. So far as beauty is concerned, the situation is not an attractive one. It faces two long, marshy lakes and there are a number of alkali swamps in the locality. I think the City will be in our district.[13] I unhitched the oxen there and let them grass for two hours.

To get dinner I had to go to Mr. Fields'[14] about half a mile distant. He is also an Englishman, had been some years in the Hudson's Bay service, and is married to a Scotch Half-Breed, a very pleasant but not particularly prepossessing lady. After dinner I started again, and had a nice trail along the ridge of a small hill for about two miles. I then got down to the level again, and for some distance had a good deal of swamp to wade through. About four miles from the settlement I passed a nicely sheltered house belonging to Mr. Gardner,[15] a Scotchman who had been for some time in Australia— it is only recently put up.

When I came up the trail first there was no house or living being on this trail from Silver Creek about fifteen miles. I now crossed a range of hills and got down to the Silver Creek district on the

---

11 DuPre homesteaded on 9-21-28.

12 The railway came to Russell in 1886.

13 Meaning the principal settlement. He was wrong—Russell became the leading town of the district.

14 Edward Field homesteaded on 10-21-28, just north of Russell.

15 Homesteaded 16-20-28.

other side. This is all rough ground, a great amount of scrub and swamp, but all now taken up. I here passed a cart and an ox driven by two young men—they are just recently out from England. Their father has taken up a very rough 320 acres on Silver Creek. He has four sons who have completed their education in Germany, no less. From his manner I think he must have been a commercial traveller. His wife and daughter are still in the old country—he expects a gentleman in Melrose will save his daughter the necessity for coming out. Johnstone is their name. Papa happened on their tent at suppertime and they were luxurious and happy over nothing but wheat meal porridge and syrup. That's a western contrast for you— life on the prairie gives you an appetite for anything. They had not long passed when I met a party of land hunters, very anxious to know their distance from the nearest stopping house—about eight miles—and all around huge black rain clouds pouring forth their abundance. They tried to look reconciled. I soon had to buckle up for a slight shower, but very fortunately I escaped all the heavy ones. It was astonishing to notice the oxen darting from the trail towards our old company places. They have very good memories.

In due time I reached the top of the gorge leading down to Silver Creek, a very steep ugly one with an even worse outlet on the other side. The creek is only accessible at these two points—the owner of the ground speaks of erecting a toll bar. The creek is also a dangerous one—a bad bottom with a quick current. I did not venture over the bridge Papa and Co. erected but tried the water and also ventured to keep [to] the waggon—rather a little risk than get one's vest pockets soaked with water. The oxen got to almost the other side when there Brownie, the new ox, saw a ghost or something in the water and shied off as quick as he could. He ran the other ox off the ford up against a willow bush. I had a great deal of trouble getting them out. They had to pull the waggon up the perpendicular bank, and served them right. I got up the other side of the gorge all right and about half a mile farther on I came to Fletcher's stopping house.[16] This concluded my first day's travelling—a distance of 25 miles.

Next morning was a beautiful and clear one. I got up early in case my oxen should rise to stray again, but they kept their bounds. After

---

16 John and Maggie Fletcher kept a stopping house on 16-20-28.

breakfast I started again. The trail was now a good deal better, either up or down a long swinging hill. I passed two houses only till I got to Hamilton's, a distance of ten miles.[17] I travelled close to the valley of the Assiniboine and met no one. At Hamilton's I got dinner, and after the customary two hours' rest I started again, keeping on the ridge above the valley of the Assiniboine.

About three miles distant on the other side I could see Fort Ellice, the oldest place in this part of the country, and likely now to be a very important place. Two steamers were lying moored on the river.[18] The city being formed there is called Colville.[19] I now turned away east, and after travelling about two miles I struck the Birtle and Fort Ellice trail. Here I was kept a little more lively, as a great number of people passed, and I passed down into Snake gully and a very steep hill, and crossed the creek—now a little dub of water—where before Andrew had seen a picturesque sight—namely me wading up to the waist in the creek, driving our two loads over with three yoke of cattle. I suppose it would look pretty. I am sure it was cold, very cold.

I was going along the gully when the oxen and I at the same time espied a horse and cart driving in our direction, the driver wearing a red coat. This was too much for the oxen, and they showed their willingness to pull the waggon back through the creek. I however proved to them the folly of such a course. The cart turned out to be driven by a Mounted Policeman—a comrade was lying behind in his shirtsleeves enjoying a smoke. Immediately behind rode an officer dressed in black, riding a fine horse with any amount of fancy trappings. The whole had a very dashing appearance. After some time a heavy waggon passed filled with a dozen recruits for the service, just arrived from Ontario. They were being taken out to the Saskatchewan district. I did not envy them of their prospects, and they were not looking particularly cheerful. Three of them had been left at Shoal Lake sick.

17　J. Hamilton lived about four miles north of Fort Ellice on sw 6-18-27.

18　The Northwest Navigation Co. steamboat "Marquette" was the first to reach Ft. Ellice. Later boats on the run were "Alpha" and "Manitoba." The round trip from Winnipeg took twelve days.

19　Colville never materialized as a town, though the site was surveyed and lots sold by the Hudson's Bay Company. The nearest present town is St. Lazare.

I had a very lively drive along this trail with so many people passing, all anxious to be informed where to go for good land. I soon arrived by Stoney Creek, my destination, where I found my load lying all right. But I must reserve describing my journey back till another time when I am more stricken for news. You will not likely require to undergo much travelling to get over the prairie next summer to here, as the Steamer "Marquette" will trade all this summer between Winnipeg and Fort Ellice, passing our place.

We have here quite a natural curiosity to find a reason for. When I came acquainted with Thunder Creek first, I concluded that it deserved its name from the rushing sound of the water—but this turns out not to be the reason for the name. When in the gorge you will occasionally hear a slow thumping, gradually increasing in speed, the rate something like the stroke of a hammer on a blacksmith's anvil, ending in a confused dirl.[20] At first you could imagine you heard distant thunder. The noise is heard in a good many places—we are quite perplexed to find a reason. First, it is not an echo. Somehow I think it must be caused by the land slipping, but there is no appearance of land having slipped for five years or thereby? Do you know anything about subterranean noises?[21]

Now I must conclude. We are all happy, healthy and hopeful. . . I hardly think Andrew will manage to write you. The afternoon was wet so Papa and he started off to fish in the Assiniboine. Likely it will be late before they get home, and they will be wet and tired. Tomorrow they go on to the Settlement for seed potatoes, and will then post this letter. We all unite in sending our kindest love to cousins and yourself.

Your most affectionate brother
Willie

P.S. Possibly it may be as well not to trouble with the magazine as the postage may be high if they are not registered for transmission abroad. But really we are badly off for Sunday reading, and I hear no word of church services anywhere in the locality. Use your wise discretion in this great trouble of ours.

---

20 Scots word meaning to vibrate or tingle.
21 Possibly it was the sound made by ruffed grouse.

Shell River, Man.
15 June 1882

My Dear Maggie,

I ought to have been at this letter before now, but at present writing is not very easily managed, as we are working pretty hard, and after work is over I feel very tired, and the mosquitoes are very troublesome. I am afraid that you must pardon the short hasty letters I may send you for some time.

Thursday a week ago Papa and Andrew started over to the settlement to buy potatoes and post your letters, and what do you think? They forgot the letter. This caused Papa to start away on the pony before sunrise next morning to catch the postman. On Sunday I walked over to the post office half-expecting to get some of your Qu'Appelle letters, but alas I was too eager. Possibly they may be with this mail. I went home by way of the Bryants where I had dinner with a large company. The Bryants are very fond of company, and nothing pleases them better than to have a large dinner or supper party. I should think it must be very expensive, but they seem to have plenty of money and are not too anxious to work too hard on their farms. Their three teams last summer only ploughed nineteen acres. I think I wrote you before that they came from London, England. Their father is, or was, in the drapery business. They lived in Balham on some crescent—I forgot the name. You had better be careful how you behave yourself as they have a married sister somewhere in that district yet.

Just as I was going to start home an old friend made his appearance. You will possibly remember my writing to you of Shaw [and] Walker, two young seamen who sailed with us from Glasgow and who afterwards got frozen feet a short distance out from Winnipeg and could not come with us. It seems they got quickly better and came on after the Bryants, sometime later, to Shell River, where they are now settled and likely to get on well. It was Shaw who turned up, and he did give me a regular keelhauling for not calling on them before. We mean to go over soon and see them.

On Monday we began ploughing. During the week we broke up eight acres—exceedingly good work considering that we lost nearly two days. The ground is now very dry and almost impossible to plough. Since Monday we have seen thundershowers occasionally around, but not one came in our direction. This is a most extraordinary spring compared with the last one. Then hardly a day passed without being accompanied by a thunderstorm—this season I have heard only one thunderpeal. I would gladly exchange the bright shiny weather we are constantly having for a spell of the old country rain. Should it continue many days longer the damage to crops will be very severe. At present, work is being greatly hindered. Notwithstanding the drought, our garden is getting on very well. The most of the things are showing a good [?]. All are anxiously hoping for a rain.

Last Monday the ground was so dry that we had to give up ploughing, and we set to work cutting a trail through the scrub and bush in the gorge to the logs. Now we have got twenty logs drawn up to the site of our new house. As occasion offers, we will go on with house-building. The logs are cut to make a house 18 × 24 feet. During the winter we may possibly add a back kitchen. This will give us ample household accommodation. The face of the house will be towards the south—the west side will look down into the creek glen. The back will be in the margin of the valley where we purpose placing the stable, etc. The east side will be the side towards the entrance trail facing the ploughed land. The garden is immediately in front of the house. From the attic windows a magnificent view of all the surrounding country will be had for miles. As soon as the house is up and things more settled, Papa purposes writing you a letter himself.

Last week Papa set to work to make a buggy with the help of the hay rake wheels. He was very successful. Puss the pony was one night harnessed onto it, but she did not go very well. Next morning she was not to be seen. We hunted all around without finding any trace of her. The succeeding day I started out to see if she had gone back to her old quarters, and there I got word she had joined a band of native ponies. I had a long weary unsuccessful hunt after them, but the owner promised to tie her up when he got the chance. Andrew went back again after a day had elapsed and got Puss at the Settlement. Now she is condemned to the hobbles every night. But the cattle and the pony are too much annoyed by mosquitoes and sandfleas to leave the smudge far after sundown. Last night Papa again harnessed Puss, and he and I had a fine drive up the creek. The pony walks and trots quickly and nicely, so I hope to have very little prairie walking after this. One would require legs of brass to do it. Meantime all our harness is home-made.

The cow is now milking exceedingly well, and we are having a superabundance of milk. I ventured a churning two nights ago, but it was not particularly successful as our accommodation just now is not at all suitable for that operation.

Every day I become more and more enchanted with the scenery hereabout. The appearance of the gorge is grand—all the wild fruits are showing a great quantity of blossoms. In a week or two the strawberries will be eatable—after that we will have grand times over the regular succession of wild fruits. The other day we came across a great many wild plums. The ripening of these and the cherries will conclude the fruit season.

I wish sugar was cheaper and we would preserve a good deal, but things in the province have gone up to famine prices, so great is the immigration and so inadequate the means of transport. Sugar is 9 cents a pound, bacon 10 cents a pound, oatmeal 3 cents a pound— and we can't get any and our supply is almost finished. Flour is £1 or 10 cents per sack, so that the cost of living is no joke here.

I think the whole world will soon have flocked into Manitoba. Great numbers of the immigrants have suffered great hardships through the floods consequent in the thaw. I quite believe that if things had been in the condition last year that they are, and have been this year, we would have settled on our land heartbroken with only $500 to buy stock and implements. I do not envy the newcomers' position just now. The best time to come here, if one can afford to do it, is about July or August. Then the weather is certain to be fine, and the weakest could camp out.

It is now almost a settled fact that the railway will cross the Assiniboine scarcely two miles north of us where a city will be formed. That will, I am positive, be the city of the locality because of the river communication and many other advantages. So our fortune is looming. It is not expected that the cars will be running till the summer after next, but even then it will be a welcome sight. If it would only rain now and let us get to the ploughing we would have brilliant money-making prospects. The "wee dog" Canty jumped on my knee just now and was evidently quite well pleased at the prospect of my kindly remembering her to you. She is a droll, determined little [?].

Just now Andrew set up the hallo that a waggon was coming along our trail. I expect it will be our neighbours, the Pagans, making their first appearance, so I will meantime require to stop, as we are without bread, and I must to baking. If I find a chance I will resume again.

16th—I did not get the opportunity to write again last night. The youngest brother Pagan came here last night with his camping apparatus. He had camped it out for two days on his own place, but the loneliness and the howling of the wolves were too much for him, so he has pitched alongside. His other brother is working just now with the Bryants and will do so all summer. We are having delightful spring showers this morning. As soon as Papa gets started to the Post Office, Andrew and I will be at the ploughing—possibly we may manage sixty acres yet.

We weary much for letters from you. Surely we will get some with the mail after this. I must now stop. We trust you are getting on well and keeping strong. With kind love from us all to cousins and yourself.

Your most affectionate brother
Willie

Shell River P.O., Man.
26 June 1882

My Dear Maggie,

We are still without receiving letters from you. We now weary very much to hear how you are getting on. Surely we will receive letters direct by the succeeding one. Since my last we have been getting on somewhat slowly with the work; always getting something to do, but the weather has been altogether too dry to get on with the main thing—ploughing. We have had occasional showers, but the ground is so thirsty that they leave very little impression. It makes one get tired with this everlasting sunshine. The vegetables in the garden are, however, getting on well. In two weeks or so we will be having new potatoes for dinner. The wild strawberries and gooseberries are also well advanced.

Harry Pagan is now camped here. We enjoy the company very much. His brother will remain all summer with the Bryants. They will be both here during the winter—they are building a shanty not far away. I think I wrote you that they came from Dumfries. They have been some years on a place near Toronto where their father is a doctor. Last Sunday the brother came over with Frank Bryant and a Mr. Godley, another newcomer. We had quite a cheery time. In fact, in this isolated situation far removed from human habitations, we have far more visitors than in our old place.

Last Wednesday we had a very noteworthy one in the shape of a black bear. We were ploughing at the time. I would not have noticed it had it not been for the oxen acting peculiarly and staring with all their might in the direction of the creek—at no less a personage than Mr. Bruin. At first I imagined it was Pagan's big black dog, but gradually the short active ears and big clumsy legs informed me of its identity. A huge, pretty dangerous-looking animal it was. It had apparently just come up out of the gorge and was taking a leisurely view of the locality. I tried all I could to attract Andrew's attention to it, but failed to do so until I halloed. When it heard the shout it turned about like a shot and disappeared. It was about the least dangerous, calm, near view of a wild animal anyone could wish to have. I ran to the tent as hard as I could, and along with Harry Pagan, dogs, guns and an axe, we made for the locality. The dogs took the trail readily enough, but I think they took the wrong direction. Anyhow, they could make nothing of it, so we missed bears steaks. The black bears seldom interfere with human beings.

Next day we had a call from a Mr. Teulon[22] who has recently settled about a mile and a half from here. His father is a minister in Montreal. He has been clerking there for about eleven years—consequently he has a lot to learn about farming. He and a companion took up section 20, but unfortunately for him the partnership has

---

22 Henry I. Teulon homesteaded on 20-22-29. He later married Martha Hogg, a minister's daughter, and they had five children.

been abruptly dissolved—now he is leading a lonely life of it. We are his nearest neighbours. He was down to get some of us to go up and break in his oxen.

The day before, he had got an awful scare with a brown, or cinnamon bear. These are dangerous, ferocious brutes. Fortunately for him a gentleman was staying with him whose ostensible object is to look for land, but it is generally supposed that he is connected with the Railway Co., hearing and seeing all he can. They both had got badly frightened with the bear. It seemed to have a regal time knocking everything about in the camp and carrying off some things. Teulon was on his road to the Bryants to get a pistol, and also to leave word with the "Rocky Mountain Sennet"[23] [for] the hunters and trappers in the district.

I went over to his place next day, and really he was lonely-looking. I set his plough right and got him started with the oxen—a whole day's work for which he was exceedingly grateful. I waited rather long after supper before starting—the sun had set. He accompanied me a bit. I was sorry afterwards that I had forgotten about bears and the Thunder Creek. I can tell you I came home like a hurricane going down the creek gorge with a rush and a noise that would have scared even a polar bear. You are not to imagine that the bears will trouble our camp. There are rather too many dogs around to be good for them.

Four landhunters had been here that day making an unsuccessful search for land. Two days ago Papa and Andrew went over to the settlement. Everyone is looking forward to the holiday and Dominion Day at the settlement. They are going to have sports. Everyone is taking an interest in the general elections for the Dominion Parliament to take place on the 4th of July. The general idea is that the Conservatives will be re-elected into Parliament. Their opponents are called Reformers or Grits. I do not think we will have a vote this time.

On the way back they raised two Sandhill Cranes, commonly called Wild Turkeys. After some hunting round, Papa got hold of one of the young ones and brought it home. It is getting on nicely, becoming quite a pet. We think it is about ten days old—already it

---

23 A nickname for a local trapper.

stands sixteen inches high. It is nearly all legs and neck, but very graceful and pretty in its way—it picks about quietly and is quite tame. I expect it will be here to welcome you when you come. The old birds are very wild and suspicious and have somewhat the appearance of an ostrich. I am sure they will be nearly three feet high. Nothing like large poultry. I wish we could get some wild goslings—they are also easily tamed.

I have churned twice within the fortnight, and both times got splendid sweet, rich-looking butter. I think if I had another fourteen cows I could do the work and make money fast, but time no doubt and two good harvests will work wonders in that way. I am also able now to bake the perfection of yeast bread.

We have abandoned the idea of putting up the house till during this winter. We would have some difficulty in getting a number of necessary things, and it will delay the other work very much. We purpose putting up a small log house 16 × 16 feet—we will do so quicker and be earlier into it. Possibly that size will be large enough for us to keep in order in the meantime—afterwards it can be used as a granary. We will get the other house leisurely put up during the winter and finished off next spring before your arrival. I intended writing you a private letter about money matters, but it was thought you might be in Scotland when this letter arrived, spending your holidays. Cousins will therefore excuse and quickly forget the succeeding paragraph.

You wrote some time ago that you had £20, I think, that might be sent here. Have you that still? Bear in mind that you must take care to have a reserve besides—then you will be out a good deal of money preparing for your journey here, and the passage money. I had intended to keep a good reserve of money beside us, but there have been a number of unforeseen and unavoidable items of expenditures that has dwindled it down. Then we got the offer of two young steers that will realize well next spring—meantime it would be folly to sell them. We would like to buy our seed grain before winter, as we shall get it very much cheaper then, and we can store it away to please ourselves. Provisions are also exceedingly high here, and until we can get poultry and pigs our household bills will be large. Possibly we may get both before the winter, but meantime the prospects are that we will be short of money before next spring. Of course the steers can be sold at any time, or we could get credit easily at the stores, but I should prefer keeping ahead of everything. I think that if you could easily spare the money, that would be the simplest way. If you can you might as early as possibly send it either by a bank draft or post office order. It would require two of the latter, either of these I could get cashed at Fort Ellice at the Hudson Bay Store. I should like to get it as early as possible, as I will require soon to go down for a load of lumber, and one trip would do both purposes. . . . But remember, run no hazard of being short, as we could pull through more easily than you could. I will not write anymore at this time. . .

Your most affectionate brother
Willie

Shell River P.O., Man.
12 July 1882

My Dear Maggie,

We were all exceedingly glad to receive with last mail a letter direct from you. It had travelled the distance in a remarkably short time— only three weeks intervened from its leaving you till it arrived at Fort Ellice. . . . You seem to be having quite an insight into London fashionable life. The best and most comfortable way to appear easy on such occasions is to lag a little behind and imitate as closely as your good judgement will permit. You will have quite a surprise when you move here and see the American style. Hereaway variety is liked, not quantity. At [?] especially you will be both alarmed and amused at the number of little dishes set round your plate and solely for your own use. But I will write more of this possibly when I have a greater dearth of news.

Since my last letter the work has been progressing rather slowly. The weather still keeps dry and causes ploughing to be dry, hard work. We will now have thirty-two acres ploughed, exclusive of an acre garden, and for this even we may be grateful, as we are now upsides with the most of the settlers in this settlement, though numbers of them have been ploughing for three years. Now we are ploughing on the other side of the creek in view of the Assiniboine.

On my claim today we laid the foundations of our temporary house, 16 × 16 feet. It appears to promise plenty of room and comfort. The vegetables in the garden are growing at a wonderful rate. I am just afraid our cellar accommodation for the roots during winter will hardly be sufficient. Strawberries are slowly making their appearance. It takes pretty hard searching to get a good feed. I found some hazelnuts today. I suppose you will remember the huntings we used to have for them at Stirling, so that even this far away we will again be able to revive past experiences.

The only casualty during the last fortnight happened today, and Andrew was the unfortunate. I successfully backed my new ox to have a ride home. Andrew essayed to do the same, but after a rather hasty gallop the ox managed to disturb Andrew's exalted position. The story is rather mixed up—the only certain thing is the effects. Andrew is now nursing a swollen thumb, and one of his cheeks appears as if it had undergone a pretty severe scalping operation. Send him a sympathetic letter, do.

Saturday a week ago was a great day with the Shell River and Silver Creek people. It was Dominion Day, and the people hereaway celebrated it by having sports. Andrew and I togged ourselves out in our second best and started out to the Settlement[24] with the intention of having a genuine holiday. The games were advertised to begin at 10:30. We reached the scene about 12 o'clock and were in good time to see the performance of the first item in the programme. An hour or two in the North West is not accounted much—it's a free and independent country. Unfortunately we forgot to take lunch, so our first care was to get some crackers at the HBCO store. After that we made for the ground, and for a time amused ourselves with hunting up old friends, getting introduced to new ones, and critically inspecting all the young ladies the Settlement could boast. I guess you would have been astonished and amused at the gorgeous display of finery. But no more—I don't want my head broken. Letters do sometimes go astray, and all the ladies here are spoken for. Andrew and Shaw resumed some of the [?] fights they had had before on the ss "Prussia[n]." It is somewhat strange that

---

24 At Russell.

four parties here all crossed the Atlantic in that steamer: the Pagans, Lawther and family, Shaw and Walker and ourselves.

Every event passed off successfully, each hardily and creditably contested. I was more taken with the pony and horse races than anything else—the ponies did really well. A ladies' race caused a good deal of fun. Three contested by Miss DuPre, a Halfbreed, went right ahead on a little Montana pony. She had only a gentleman's saddle, but she held on gracefully sitting sideways. Miss Lawther, a Belfast lady (young), followed with Frank Bryant, her adorer, behind, switching up the pony for all he was worth. Miss [?], a Dundee girl, came last, with the assistance also of her young man. A [?] concluded the programme. I was quite astonished at the large turnout—fully two hundred people. The arrangements were very complete, all were provided gratis with lunch and supper, sweet bread ad lib. It certainly did not look well seeing the young bachelors voraciously stuffing themselves full of every delicacy they could grab. But I suppose the most of them will very rarely eat anything but flapjacks, bacon and black tea.

I fell in with an old Glasgow friend, a Mr. Todd.[25] His brother at one time ran the Morrisbank flour mills. There is some talk of him starting a flour mill on the Shell. This brother has been farming here for three years. His companion was for fourteen years clerking in the City of Glasgow Bank. Both came here sometime after the failure.

It was between 8 and 9 o'clock before the games were concluded. It was the intention to have a dance outside afterwards, but a huge black thundercloud warned everyone to scatter home, and soon the rain came on. We ought not to have waited so late, but Arthur Bryant, up till the last, purposed to go home with us, but he had so many delays that we started off ... I did not feel very comfortable on the walk we had before us. We expected to have moonlight, but heavy thunderclouds darkened it out of sight. So we had just to grope our way home, and with the assistance principally of the wind we fortunately struck the tent light about 12 o'clock. I can tell you prairie groping among sloughs and bluffs is no comfortable joke. We got home just in time, as the previous drizzle settled down into a steady thunder rain after we got under cover. Papa and the two

---

25 Thomas Todd homesteaded on 2-22-28, and later moved to Russell.

Pagans had concluded that we were lost and likely to get a night's soaking on the prairie. However, they were glad to see us for the sake of the letters, and Papa especially was happy to get yours.

Sunday forenoon was very wet. It cleared away in the afternoon, and as we were wearying, Harry Pagan started off to see Teulon, who is settled north of us and alone. He was formerly a clerk in Montreal. He is really making a very poor [?] at farming. When we got to his tent we found him gone. We concluded he had lost himself a little when going to the games, and this turns out to be the case, although he will scarcely admit it. The great number of mosquitoes about his place fairly hunted us quickly off—they were in myriads.

Nothing further of any note happened till Wednesday. Shortly after my breakfast when I was out ploughing I saw someone walking towards me from the north. At first I imagined the individual was an Indian, but a closer inspection proved that it was a white man with a huge sombrero hat covering his head and a red handkerchief enclosing it to keep off the mosquitoes. It turned out to be a brother of Haworth[26] who is settled south of us. They both came from Manchester—there my visitor did business as a chemist. The one sailed from England a week earlier than the other in March, and since that time they have not known the whereabouts of each other, hunting round the whole colony after one another. This one had been as far west as Qu'Appelle, where he had received one of his brother's letters. The previous day he arrived at the Bryants, and after dinner he started out for here, where he intended getting directed to his brother's place. But he had gone astray and had to sleep out all night on the prairie without supper or breakfast. When he got here he was pretty much used up and awful hungry. He was glad to know his brother was only ½ mile from here. They are supposed to be worth money. He thought very little of the Qu'Appelle district—the only good land is in the river valley, but all taken up—the rest is light soil. Numbers are returning, and no wonder, as there is not even firewood to be had in sufficient quantity. Were we not mercifully preserved from going there? I find that the only trustworthy thing in this country is your own eyes.

---

26 Haworth settled on 26-21-29.

On Sunday, Will Pagan[27] came over and took away his brother to the Bryants. It seems they had to leave part of their loads at Brandon, and a party similarly circumstanced is being formed to go down and get them. So we will not have the Pagans' pony for three weeks. I don't envy them a trip over soft trails, for three hundred miles will let them see all the peculiarities of Manitoba mud. Will Pagan brought over with him a Mr. Longford to show him the road. He is one of a party of five young gentlemen just out from Ireland. They have taken up the remaining vacant sections on this side of the river—they will be near neighbours. They also get the credit of having money. Certainly they have plenty of firearms. They are strong, wary, gentlemanly fellows—I only hope they are not Roman Catholics.

These are the most noteworthy incidents that have occurred during the last fortnight. We are quite pleased with the quantity of work we are doing. Consequently in good spirits about the future, we all keep well. We are getting a lot of mushrooms—when stewed they make a delicious breakfast dish.... All the stock are thriving, even the little crane. It is nearly as big again, and follows us about like a dog. It does not require any restraint, and finds its way home from long journeys nicely. Its feathers are forming now—soon it will be able to fly. Even then, we understand, it can be allowed unlimited freedom. Hereafter you must know it by the name "Piper." Now I must stop . . .

Your most affectionate brother
Willie

Shell River, Man.
27 July 1882

My Dear Maggie,

. . . Since my last letter we have been getting on very pleasantly. During the last week the only break to the even tenor of our way

---

27 William and Henry Pagan homesteaded on 2-22-29.

was a visit Andrew and I made to the Bryants. They are now a little ahead of their neighbours just now, as they have a female housekeeper, a Mrs. Godly. Her husband came up here with the Pagans in the spring and took up land near the Bryants [and] he stayed with them. He had written his wife not to come out till he had the farm better prepared [for] her and the two children, but she was started from Toronto before the letter got to its destination. He has got somewhat relieved out of his dilemma by the present arrangement.

After dinner we went farther east about a mile and visited Shaw and Walker,[28] the two young sailors who sailed with us on the ss "Prussia[n]" from Glasgow. They have got, I think, a pretty rough farm, but they seem to be getting on well. They were very much put about over one of their oxen that had got badly gored by a bull when tied to the waggon. Shaw has got a team of horses recently, and of course is inclined to be rather proud. He is going back to the old country to see his friends next winter. Alfred Bryant is also going on a like mission. Will I tell him to pay you a visit when in the Balham district? Frank Bryant is soon to get married to Miss Lawther, a young girl who came out here with her parents from Belfast two years ago. The Bryants are all getting houses built, and the partnership is to be dissolved after this summer. Arthur Bryant spoke of giving me for your benefit the address of his sister in London, but I thought you would not care about taking advantage of it. I am going to trade away the brown dog for one of the kittens they are at present the possessors of. You see our stock is extending slowly but surely.

Our work has been principally connected with the building of the house. Already we have the walls up five feet. Before the end of the week we expect to have the frame finished, ready for flooring, roofing, and lining. In about a month I expect we shall be enabled to write you that we shall be proud, happy, and prepared for you to come out at any time and keep our house in order. I think you will be enchanted with its situation. Everyone who has come about, styles it pretty, lovely, and picturesque, etc. In fact, they all deal longingly in qualifying adjectives when speaking of our farm and anything

---

28 George Walker and George Shaw homesteaded on 12-22-28.

connected with it. In everything I believe we are second to none, so that we are getting quite proud and conceited. In the strength of this representation of your new home I really think you would be justified in beginning to throw on "airs" too.

Harry Pagan and Alf Bryant started for Brandon Monday a week ago, and I entrusted them with the getting of a fiddle bow.

Yesterday was the most important day of the last fortnight. We had a constant round of excitement. Papa was the introducer of the first event. I was to stay at home to do the baking—he had gone to cut wood down the gorge. Just before he descended he stopped up, and after a minute he waved me over. On looking down who should I see but his majesty, a huge brown or cinnamon bear, leisurely taking his morning walk on the opposite bank, taking advantage of all the open glades and slowly proceeding up the creek. We all got a splendid view of him, assisted by the opera glass, and he was a huge one. I am sure he must have been nearly four feet high and disproportionately bulky. Andrew's estimation of bears has gone up tremendously. If we only had had a rifle. By a good deal of cautious creeping he would have finished his career there and then. After allowing him to proceed up a bit, Papa started off to tell Langford, one of our neighbours who owns a rifle, whilst I attended to the bear and the baking. But he disappeared in a clump of wood, and I thought he had gone.

After a bit Papa came back with Langford all excitement. He had found them in bed, but when they heard his mission, up they got, Langford (he is a Protestant Irishman, Episcopalian) exclaiming "By my soul!" In a jiffy he hitched on his trousers, boots and a hat, and diving at a chest on which all their eating utensils were laid, he with one arm laid them low with a sweep, and with the other tipped up the lid for his rifle, cartridges, and a revolver. So provided, he declared himself ready. When they made their appearance on the opposite hill, I dived down the gorge to give them the benefit of my advice. I went down part of the gorge smarter than you could wink, flying among bushes down a precipitous bank. We met at the channel of the creek. I fell heir to the six chamber revolver.

On starting out we soon struck the bear track. He had come down the wood to the creek and under cover had proceeded on his journey. His trail, with some little difficulty, was made out from the broken twigs. As hard as we could leg, we followed, jumping fallen trees, creeping below bushes and rushing through willow clumps. It was as exciting as foxhunting.

After proceeding some distance, we came on a place where it had lain down for a nap and evidently been scared away from by the noise we were making. On we went, each step we saw traces that we were nearing him. It was most amusing to see the excited state Langford was in, leading on as if the bear was after him instead of he after the bear. "Look at that" said he, as he handed me back a tuft of brown hair the bear had left stuck on a bush. Thus rushing and crashing, we proceeded up the creek about one mile and a half, and we were congratulating ourselves that the dreamings we had had for bear steaks were about to be realized, as the wood was coming to an end. But alas, the track again crossed the creek and made for a thick heavy clump of wood in which there was no green undergrowth. Consequently we lost all trace of him, and the undergrowth was so thick and tangled that it was impossible to beat over it thoroughly, so we had to give up the chase.

It was really a splendid and very exciting hunt. It occupied fully two hours—we started for home about 11 o'clock. Langford started out pretty smartly to get his breakfast, so you can see our neighbours are pretty go-ahead.

After we got back I got dinner ready. After that had disappeared, Papa and Andrew started down to the gorge to the wood, and I set in dead earnestness to my baking and churning. Yeast baking takes a whole day and requires a good deal of attention. When I got my churn scalded and was about to begin I spied two machines coming towards the tent over the breaking full trot, and soon I was welcoming Major Boulton accompanied by a civil engineer. The other buckboard contained a Mr. Beattie who has taken up a ½ section of land adjoining. He owns a great deal of CP Railway Co. land. This lot is, I think, just a speculation, so he will not be much of a neighbour. They had missed our trail coming from the settlement and had lost themselves a little bit. They were awfully hungry, so I got them some tea etc., and they waited fully an hour to graze their horses, so we had quite a pleasant time of it.

Major Boulton is the leading man in this district.[29] He came here fully three years ago and formed this settlement. He is originally an Englishman, but was for some time in Ontario, where he earned his military title. He was also a member of Parliament. He came to this country before the Red River Rebellion, ten years ago. During that rebellion he was arrested by the insurgents for a Government spy, and was tortured by being hung up by the leg. A companion similarly circumstanced, named Scott, was shot. But he escaped by exerting a good deal of tact.

He is a very pleasant, talkative man, [and] has been the making of this settlement. Continually he drummed the good qualities of the district into the ears of the public, so that now Shell River is well known and well spoken of from Montreal to the Rockies. He has got his land surveyed out into a town called Russell. Recently he was appointed registrar for the district at £300 per annum, so that now he is beginning to reap the reward for his labours. In addition to this he has influenced Mr. Todd, who ruined himself in the Morrisbanks Flour Mills, Glasgow, to come out here. He is now on his way up from Winnipeg to erect a large grist mill on the Shell River.

At this time he was on his way up to land he owns on the Assiniboine where the railway will cross the river and where the big city is to be. We are all perplexed to know for what purpose he is taking up the engineer. After their rest, Papa conveyed them safely through the creek glen. He is the warden, or presiding councillor, for the country, and was quite anxious that the main trail should be here, and wants us to contract to build a bridge.

They had scarcely gone out of sight when the whole sky erupted, we experienced the most severe thunderstorm of the season. It was perfectly deafening and blinding, and lasted till sundown. I was sick of camping during it. Our stove with the oven is outside, and I could not get my bread fired. There was, however, one comfort— there was no wind, so our tent kept out the rain. We were snug and

29 Major Boulton came to Manitoba in 1869 with a survey party. He was involved in the Riel rebellion of 1870, was imprisoned by Riel and sentenced to be shot. However he was released, and returned to eastern Canada. He returned to Manitoba in 1880 and took up a homestead near Russell, which townsite he later established. He commanded the Boulton Scouts during the Rebellion of 1885. Appointed to the Senate in 1889, he died in 1899 at the age of 58.

comfortable compared to many. After the rain stopped, I got at the baking. I had to sit up till morning firing. It was a splendid panorama, the lightning playing and dancing before the heavy banks of clouds. Two or three times I heard the bear grunting in a displeased tone up the creek.

Major Boulton had been on his way to here last night, but they had accidentally come across Teulon's tent and dined with him, as they were afraid to risk the gorge during the storm.

Today we put the mower together, and really it was pleasant and cheerful to hear it whirr. I hope it works well with the oxen. We will begin cutting next week. I trust you were enabled to send in the money I wrote you about—sorry we invested in the young steers, but it was a great temptation, and is likely to realize very well even early in the winter. But I would like to get lumber for the house so that it may get a little time to dry—in any case, however, it will be got in time, I daresay. . . . Don't be alarmed about my bear story—the bears are all cowards. The only dangerous class, I understand, are the "grizzlies" at the Rockies, and the Polars. . .

Your most affectionate brother
Willie

Woodvale, Shell River, Man.
9 August 1882

My Dear Maggie,

With last mail we received the usual very welcome letter, also all the letters you sent to Qu'Appelle, so that now we are fully informed of all your doings during the long silence. . . .

You must excuse my writing at this time a very short hasty letter. Just now we are extra hard at work putting up our winter stock of hay. We are being favoured with very good weather and are of course anxious to take advantage of it. We wish to put up sixty tons, and that will take us a fortnight, work as hard as we may. Both the mower and rake are working well, and the oxen drive like horses—the only instance I know of. We have Harry Pagan working for us just now.

The house building is now at a stand-still till after haytime. We have the bearers fixed for the top floor, so that it has now some appearance of a habitation.

Alf Bryant sent us over last week a little kitten that gives us an unbounded source of amusement. It is coloured brown and white. It bosses all the other pets about, although as yet it is altogether dependent on the cow for its means of sustenance. What name shall we call her? At present we call it "Scud." It has such an absurd way of running with its tail almost on a line with its head, evidently bent on showing its warlike inclination even when engaged in that undignified occupation. But I must now stop—it is late and we are all wearied.... You must take very good care of yourself—do not for inspectors suffer yourself to take cramps. I really wish we had you out here—we would soon make you forget all these dreads of civilization. You would just take a new lease of life and hope, so there is something to cheer you on and put a [?] here in the near future. We all send our kindest love to cousins and the other friends and to yourself.

Your most affectionate brother
Willie

Woodvale, Shell River, Man.
22 August 1882

My Dear Maggie,

I must write you very hurriedly this time. Just now we are working late and early at the hay, and I am just now stealing a moment from sleeping time. This letter is written three days earlier than usual, as Papa is going to the settlement tomorrow to attend a meeting of the Agricultural Society of which he is now a director,[30] and also to offer to build a bridge on Thunder Creek for $76. If we get the

---

30 Peter Wallace was a director of the Russell Agricultural Society.

contract it will be winter's work and all, with the exception of the labour, profit. With last mail we received your welcome letter, also no less than 23 newspapers, the majority of them being the papers Henry so kindly sent to Qu'Appelle . . .

We are getting on very slowly with the hay, as the dry spring has caused a poor crop, but so far we have cut 30 tons. I wish it were now over, as I am anxious to get away for the lumber, so that it may get seasoned a little. The weather just now is very warm and sultry, seldom under 80 degrees in the shade—nice lazy holidaying weather? We all keep well and strong. I trust you will excuse this short, abrupt epistle. I will soon have time to make amends. We unite in sending kindest love to all the friends, to cousins and yourself.

Your most affectionate brother
Willie

P.S. We have named our farm Woodvale. It is no importance whether you address our letters so or not.

Woodvale, Shell River, Man.
7 September 1882

My Dear Maggie,

. . . I do hope that you are getting on well with the piano so that you may cause a sensation among the natives hereaway. At present there is only one piano in the settlement, and the owner of it, Miss Denmark, daughter of the postmaster,[31] is not from all accounts by any means proficient. She regales company with hymn tunes. I would sacrifice a good deal, I think, to get my fingers on a piano or such like again. The violin has too much of the singular number to suit my taste, still it is better than nought. If you have at any time an opportunity you might buy and address to me a book of dance music for the violin. . .

---

31 William Denmark was a storekeeper and the postmaster of the Shell River Post Office, located on 22-21-28. It was later moved to the town of Russell, and in March 1889 the name was changed to the Russell Post Office.

We finished haying this afternoon—all of us are heartily glad to be done with it. We have been a month at it, and have put up five huge big stacks and a smaller one, and now we have some appearance of a farm. Were you along with us we should have had a kind of harvest-home treat; but present circumstances render this impossible, so we must make merry and comfort ourselves with an extra slice of bacon, and most likely your presence will improve on our next like ceremony.

Today an awful experience happened to the kitten. At dinnertime it was having good fun on the top of the stack, and finished up evidently by having a sound nap, thus it had not been noticed. We wondered where it had disappeared to and did not know till we came back with our second load—and then we heard it caterwauling somewhere in the stack. After a good deal of searching we found it covered up with four feet of hay. A good thing it cried out at the time it did—a little later and it should most certainly have been smothered in the stack. We should have been sorry to lose it, as it is now beginning to thin out the mice. I am glad that your household are interested in the pets here. I must endeavour and after this write you some of the scenes that give us a great deal of fun.

Piper the crane is now able to fly about and get in the way either at home or abroad. It is particularly fond of the noise the mower makes, strutting alongside as proud as a soldier. I was in continual dread that it would get its long legs snapped off.

Our whole attention will now be devoted to finishing the house, building a stable, and ploughing. In six weeks' time John Frost will be causing us to pull up our coat collars.

Last Sunday we had a visit from one of our neighbours, Mr. Perrin.[32] He and two companions are on farms north of us. They come from London, but have been farming for some time in Minnesota, U.S. The Thursday previous was election day here for a member to the Provincial Parliament. The whole of the settlers have voted for Mr. Laycock who owns the sawmill in Shell River—likely he will get in.[33] I mean to go up to the mill next Monday for lumber for flooring and roofing.

---

32 Herbert B. Perrin homesteaded on 24-22-29.

33 E.P. Laycock came to Birtle from Winnipeg in 1881 and built an imposing residence on the hill overlooking the town. He was not successful in his first campaign for

Sunday a week ago we had a round of visitors. Arthur Bryant, Will Pagan and the two Haworths, neighbours who came out this spring from Manchester. They did not go away till sundown. We had a great hymn sing-song. A waggon load of us are going over to the Bryant's next Sunday to have a day's seeing and being seen. The only other particularly noteworthy thing I remember was a terrific thunderstorm the other night. How the lightning did flash—and during a cessation outside the night was pitch black—blackness intensified.

The mosquitoes are now almost gone, so that it is a little more enjoyable. All the older settlers are now busy harvesting. The crops have turned out well. You must now excuse my stopping this abruptly—the lamp is not a very good writing light. . . .

I trust that you do not imagine that we desire to keep you short funded, but really it is almost impossible to get on with little money. Everything has to be bought, and provisions are so exorbitantly high in price. Next year will tell a different tale on our expenditure bill. Do not by any means allow yourself to be short of money. That we will never forgive. We could pull through where you could not. You occasionally speak of your money matters, but I can not quite understand them, in fact it would be impossible for us to do so as you are now in a sphere that precludes all possibility of knowing what your wants and expenses have been. If you have been able to send on the £20 it will be a great benefit—however, we could manage quite well with less and even without, so do not allow yourself to get anxious. Next harvest we will, if Providence favours us, have plenty of money, and do not on any account sacrifice either your comfort or your pleasure to save even a penny. I will be grieved deeply if I should ever know that you become miserly on our account. Now I must stop. Send our kindest love to cousins in Glasgow and other friends. We trust you are now back at your work with renewed vigour, pleased and strengthened. With kindest love I am

Your most affectionate brother
Willie

---

the legislature, but was elected later.

Woodvale, Shell River, Man.
19 September 1882

My Dear Maggie,

I cannot this time refer to a last letter to comment upon it. We were greatly disappointed when we did not get a letter from you last mail. The reason, we presume, must have been that you were at the time of its dispatch in some outlandish place—Melrose or Silverwood— or possibly it may have gone amissing. I hope we shall get two next Saturday. A whole month is a great break in the correspondence we value so much.

With last mail I had rather a startling letter from A. Nivan, my old office mate at the Terminus. He had some difficulty getting my address ... He was anxious to let me know that my old employer Mr. D. McArthur had made a crashing failure. When I was with him he latterly began to dabble too much in the Stock Exchange. Often times we prophesied the course would lead to bankruptcy. At that time I am sure he was worth considerably more than £20,000— however, I was quite taken aback to learn that his liabilities were £19,000 and assets only £4,000. He after some trouble arranged with his creditors to pay 4 [shillings] per pound in three instalments, but Nivan writes that he quite expects he will not manage to do that, as he still persists in speculating, although to a much smaller extent. So far the only one in the employ who suffered directly was Archie McArthur, who very sharply and shortly got the order to look out for himself. Nivan is in great distress over the fact that he is a married man and therefore fixed to his situation for lack of a better. The dissimulation and direct lying that prevails in the business, he says, is simply appalling. I congratulate myself on being clear of the catastrophe with nothing worse to trouble me than the occasional wayward fits of oxen.

... The work here is progressing very well. Andrew is wholly occupied with ploughing—already he has got five acres done. Papa and I are busy housebuilding. Just now we are getting the roof put on the stable. The house is now ready for the roof. I have been twice up at the sawmill at Shell River getting boards for the floors and roof. They are now basking in the sun and getting seasoned. In about a fortnight we expect to be ensconced inside walls.

Nothing of great importance has happened since my last [letter]. Last week Andrew and I were over at the Bryants and spent a very enjoyable time. Got a very formal introduction to the future Mrs. F. Bryant. Arthur proudly showed us all over his almost completed house. Before occupying this winter he is going to have a great housewarming dance party. We are all expectation. He is a very upright conscientious young man. The others are little "fast" inclined, particularly Alfred. He left last Wednesday to pay his friends in your region a surprise visit after an absence of five years—possibly you may see or hear about him.

Mr. Dawson, the Episcopalian clergyman at Birtle who occasionally conducted service at the settlement, has also gone back to England, I suppose disgusted with the country. His successor, Mr. Morton, is I understand a great improvement. He proposes conducting service every third Sunday at Arthur Bryant's house. This will be a benefit to us outlandish ones. It is now fully a year since we were at gospel service.

Last Sunday Will Pagan paid us a visit. This week finished his engagement with the Bryants—after that we shall see more of him. In the evening Teulon came along. After hunting his oxen for three days he was very much relieved to find them with us. He was at the English service—possibly he may be meditating a change from Roman Catholicism. Today we had a visit from Walter Gordon[34] also hunting stray cattle, so far unsuccessfully. His father was a farmer in Dumfrieshire, but he and his brother had been clerking in Leith. Their farms adjoin the Bryants.

All our stock are thriving famously. They are the most of the time luxuriating in the glen. It forms a very picturesque scene, seeing them away down up to the necks in grass with a clump of wood in the back high ground. At night the wolves are just now screaming and howling at a great rate, always putting Jess in a great rage by attempting to imitate her barking. Now and then a bear relieves the din with his solemn grunting. The other night two of them carried on a long doleful conversation. All these animals have a wonderful knack of keeping out of sight during the day—where they go is to me a mystery. We never disturb them.

---

34 Walter S. Gordon homesteaded on 2-22-28.

All our domestic pets are getting on well. The kitten particularly is each day getting bigger and funnier, capering round the place at a wonderful pace. There is only one drawback to its being as happy as a king—that is that crane Piper. Between the two there is unceasing enmity. The one caterwauls with its back arched up, its ears laid back, and its tail stiffer and more bushy than nature intended. The other pecks furiously with its head drawn in and low down, its wings swollen out—both apparently in the greatest rage. The crane flies around now and chooses the most startling opportunities to alight almost on top of anyone.

Nature is now decked out in its dying glory. No finer sight can be imagined than is now to be seen in the creek glen. The trees, shrubs etc. painted in every shade from white-yellow to dark brown, relieved by the dark green of the Balm of Gilead[35] leaves. The deep red colour of the faded grass on the opposite hills sets the picture off to advantage. John Frost gives us now occasional reminders of his long confined, hand-binding claim to the earth. In the mornings we quite enjoy the luxury of a fire in the stove inside the tent. I have now written all that I can remember that will be of interest to you . . .

Your most affectionate brother
Willie

Woodvale, Shell River, Man.
4 October 1882

My Dear Maggie,

We received by last mail two letters from you . . . I am sorry that time and circumstances will not permit of me writing a long letter. Winter is now approaching and we are just now "rushing" work. The same cause has prevented my writing to Uncle Hugh. Yesterday we bade farewell to camp life and removed into our log house. For seven months we have been dwellers in tents, and it has really been

---

35 A variety of poplar with heart-shaped leaves.

very enjoyable. The weather has, on the whole, been exceptionally fine, but we are glad to get now more outside freedom.

Just now we are busy plastering. Until the ploughing is over we shall do without glass windows. Then I shall possibly go with the waggon and a team of oxen to Birtle or Moosomin, the nearest station to this place on the CP Railway,[36] and get a stock of provisions, etc. At these [places] they can be bought very much cheaper.

I had almost neglected to write you that we received the bank draft all right. The £10 will in the meantime do our purpose nicely. Mr. Audy, the Hudson Bay factor,[37] will get it cashed for us through the head office of the company. Thank you very much for sending it—we can now hold on till the steers are sold.

We have got our potatoes lifted now—they turned out exceedingly well. Scarcely five bushels were planted, and we dug up thirty-five bushels—this does not include what of them we have demolished during the summer. And although they were planted just under the prairie sod they are of splendid quality. The carrot, turnip, parsley and beet are still in the ground. For a number of days the weather has been very cold, threatening snow—something like squaw winter. Yesterday and today has been milder, but it is too windy for Indian summer. Tuesday was wet all day, the first real wet day we have had this summer. The glen is beginning to lose its gorgeous dress—the leaves are now quickly falling away. In three weeks at the latest, John Frost will begin his long adamantine reign.

This morning the Pagans removed over to their own place. Everyone is just now getting as quickly independent of canvas as possible. Arthur Bryants house-warming will likely be next week. He purposes [?] sixty dancing ad. lib.—won't there be some "guys."

On Monday we had a visit from the land-hunters, gentlemen from Yorkshire, right jolly fellows. They have been roving about but could see nothing to suit them until they came to this district. They like it so much that land they are determined to have, let the cost be what it may. Likely they will take some of the railway sections.[38]

---

36 Moosomin was 115 km distant.
37 James Audy was the first manager of the Hudson's Bay Company store at Russell.
38 The government allocated certain sections of land to the railway companies which could be sold to finance construction of the line.

They went into ecstatic fits of admiration over the scenery in the glen. Now I must conclude this too short letter. . . .

Your most affectionate brother
Willie

Woodvale, Shell River, Man.
19 October 1882

My Dear Maggie,

. . . Since the time my last letter was written we have been getting on very quietly and busily. We are now comfortably ensconced in our new home, enjoying immensely the freedom of going about as we please, and working with plenty of elbow room in lamplight under cover—leisures that some months' tent life helps one to thoroughly appreciate. Now that the tents are removed the hill looks very bare.

Were you now to pay us a surprise visit, you would drive along the trail, after getting up of Skunk Creek, seeing only groves of trees, almost now bared of their leaves, and little lakes (with one specially large one not quite two miles from here) shining like bright mirrors. Were you accompanied by a guide, he would direct your attention to the Haworths' house away south, occasionally displaying itself in gaps among the tree bluffs.

To the west you would see a well-wooded break in the land. This is the broad valley of the Assiniboine. Beyond, the country is a pleasing, well-wooded wilderness where the red man and the wild beast roam with freedom, undisturbed by the white man's presence. Two miles beyond the Assiniboine you step beyond the boundary of Manitoba and provincial government, [to] where law is summarily dispensed by the Mounted Policeman.

Continuing the journey, you would come to a drop of the land towards the river, and at the same time discover the house and stable of the Pagans . . . At this point your surroundings change—the lakes and willow clumps are left behind. The trail no longer winds back to avoid them, but continues straight over nice level land, passing about a stone's throw from the Pagans' house down into what we term the "big slough." A little further down, the marsh is drained into the Thunder Creek by a deep well-wooded gully. In the marsh you would see a great stretch of mowed ground that would make some of our Ayrshire friends stare. This is where we got a large part of our hay. The Pagans style their place "Riverview," as they get a nice glimpse of the river down the aforementioned gully.

A long gradual ascent would bring you to the level again, and after journeying a little bit you would, from the height of the ridge, look down on a very interesting scene. Immediately below are two large stacks of hay. Fenced in and protected by a firebreak is a deep well-wooded glen down which a spring never-failingly sends a clear cold stream of water. On the height above you would see a long, broad stretch of ploughing with a pathway straight through it leading to two other stacks of hay. In front of a number of scattered trees, some machinery and a garden fence complete the signs of life.

Looking north you would distinguish a lumber house belonging to Farrar, a former Cockney. After getting thus far it would be well that you should continue farther. The trail takes a bend and stretches up the valley a good piece to where the banks are less steep. Quickly you will get to the height again and come to the ploughing. At this season, most probably, you would stop and speak for a short time to a tall stalwart ploughman working with a good sleek team of oxen, who answers to "Andrew." By this time a dog would be running towards you barking with a very important air. A kindly use of the word "Jess" would quickly transform the ferocious-looking brute into [a] nice waggish Gordon Setter. Andrew will take care that you do not now turn, because no house is in view, but will take you some distance farther to the edge of the Creek valley. And there to your astonished gaze will be a nice square log house almost under your feet, and a little distance father down the valley, a large stable and a lot of hay.

From this point you will turn to the left and proceed along the edge of the bank among some poplar trees till you come to a track cut down in the bank. At the bottom of that you will find yourself quite at home. The doorway faces the south. There is a window on the west that looks down into the gully and up the opposite bank. The depth of the glen must, I am sure, be 300 feet. Everyone is astonished at their jumping down almost to the front of the house, and at first fear that the snow will drift us up altogether, but there are too many trees about us to render such an event possible. The view of the house from the bank on the other side of the creek is a perfect contrast—there the house seems to be elevated high up on the verge of a sheer precipice.

The cattle are now stabled every night, as the nights are now long, cold and frosty. I think we are now experiencing Indian summer. But an early frost nipped the gloriously coloured foliage that usually bedecks and enhances the beauty of the season. The days are warm and cloudy, quite a change to the cold, dull, squaw-winter days we had last week.

Papa carries the mail for all the neighbours down to the post office about 8 miles from here. This brings us a lot of visitors. A new settler came here last week, a Mr. McDougall, an old highlandman from Prince Edward Island.[39] He took up the half-section cornering us last spring, but it is only now he has come to live upon it. He is just now house-building. Soon the district will look more civilized. Mr. Martin, a former Cockney, one of our neighbours, has made arrangements with Fanny Denmark, the postmaster's daughter, and we expect soon to have that lady a near neighbour. At present there is not a female in the township.

Arthur Bryant was here on Saturday night and gave us an invitation to his "house warming" on Friday night. I will try and interest you next letter with some of the fun that will be sure to be there. Now I must conclude, as it is bed-time. Andrew will likely have told you all about the pups that are just now snarling and growling at one another under the stove. I send you some feathers of the prairie chicken. They are hardly as large as hens. They strut about very proudly and prettily in hundreds on the prairie. Every part of them is well protected by feathers against the cold, as they stay here throughout the winter.

We trust to hear again good news of you by next mail. We all unite in sending you our fondest love.

Your most affectionate brother
Willie

---

39 John A. McDougall homesteaded on 14-22-29.

[P.S. from Andrew]

. . . Last Friday we got quite an addition to our stock in the shape of ten pups, but as four were quite sufficient to supply the demand we drowned six of them. They are real pretty little things . . .

Woodvale, Shell River, Man.
16 November 1882

My Dear Maggie,

We received by the last mail your letter addressed to Willie and the edition of the New Testament. We were glad to hear you were getting on so well with your school work and enjoying yourself in London. You will be surprised to get no letter from Willie, but on Monday a week ago, he and Mr. Teulon started for Moosomin, sixty miles from here, our nearest railway station, to get our winter supplies, and did not get back to Russell till the Monday. He sent on word by W. Pagan for us to go down and get the goods, as they had again started for the Big Bend,[40] sixty miles south of this, for two loads of lumber for the Hudson's Bay Company. So he will not likely be back till Saturday night.

Yesterday Papa went to Russell for the goods Willie had left there and did not get back till after dark. On the way home he killed a splendid muskrat. It is about nine inches long and has a splendid brown coat of hair. They are rather ferocious animals by their way of it, as they attack anything that comes near them, although they don't do much damage.

This morning the ground was again covered with snow and it is not likely this coat will lift again this winter, and all day it has been dark and cloudy. The pups are now ready for going away, and to-day I took one over to the Pagans, and tomorrow I intend going over to the Bryants with the other two—the other one I intend keeping myself. There is a great demand for dogs and cats here, especially the last is almost indispensable, as the mice are here by the dozen.

---

40 Near Minnedosa.

We have got a splendid pony here now. In the spring when we bought her she was almost skin and bone, but now she is sleek and fat and gets the credit of being one of the best going ponies about. So there is an inducement for you to come out. Just now Papa is making a light sleigh for her, so we will not be so long in doing our light errands this winter as we were last winter when we had to take a span of oxen.

We have had splendid shooting for a while now, and have been living on prairie chicken and partridge for a month back. But now they are becoming rather shy, so we will require to turn our attention to the rabbits which we were not aware were about here till a short time ago. I think I will now close as I have exhausted all the news. With kindest love from

Your affectionate brother
Andrew

Woodvale, Shell River, Man.
26 November 1882

My Dear Maggie,

I am sorry that my being from home prevented me writing to you by last mail, but I little doubt that Papa and Andrew made ample amends for the deficiency. I was glad to find when I got home after an absence of nearly three weeks that everything here had been getting on in the usual quiet way, that Papa and Andrew were well, and that the animals were all healthy and hearty. . . .

We have had slight snowfalls every day—now the snow is four inches deep and in good order for sleighing. It is also very dry now, and moccasins can now be worn comfortably—both these features we consider great advantages.

The two Pagans spent the evening here on Thursday, and just as we were about to bid each other good night a knock comes to the door, and who should walk in but Arthur Bryant, hungry and searching about for someone to winter two cows belonging to a Mr.

Godly, who is going to work for them this winter. We could only aid him with the former want. . . .

There is every likelihood I will start from home again next Friday. I have engaged to go up to Big Woods, about twenty-two miles from here, to work this winter. I am to get a pretty good pay at the rate of 30p per week[41] with board and lodging. I guess some of the friends will stare when they remember me as a clerk and now think of me as a "lumberman," but what is the odds! The money will enable me to get a team of horses next spring. The only drawback to the arrangement is that Papa and Andrew may feel a little lonely, but circumstances render this unavoidable. I will be engaged until April.

I must make good use of my present opportunity to write you a long letter. Suppose I do so by a description of my last journey. I arranged to go down to Moosomin, the nearest station to this place on the C.P. Railway, about 70 miles distant, with Teulon, a neighbour settled about 1 ½ miles north of this. He is a very pious, liberal-minded Roman Catholic. His father is of Huguenot descent, and came from London Eng. to Montreal about twenty years ago, where he is now a bank teller. His son, my companion, is about 26 and up till now has been a bookkeeper. He paid a visit to England and France about two years ago. He is a good violinist. So you can imagine he is very gentlemanly—excessively so—and good company. But that is all—he is about as useful as a ten year old boy on the trail. The previous afternoon he paid us a visit and left again two hours before dark to be down with his oxen as early as possible next morning. But Andrew, after supper, when going down with the lantern to the stable, heard someone halloing on the other side of the creek. After a time Teulon appeared, cold and hungry. He had lost his reckoning and had been tramping all the time in the vicinity of my ploughing. I forgot to mention that a slight mist had arisen from the river about sundown, so here he was, ready sure for an early start but minus his oxen. Next morning he started early to his farm, and in due time reappeared with his oxen and waggon.

Together we started and traversed the well-known trail to the settlement of Russell, as it is now termed—there we halted at the

---

41 30p was only about 65 cents—this seems low even for the 1880s. 30 shillings, or $7.50, seems more likely.

Hudson's Bay Co. store. I wanted to bring up a few provisions and supplement my load with freight. This I was successful in getting from Mr. Audy on the condition that I went, on coming back, to the Big Bend on the Little Saskatchewan for lumber.

After a little delay feeding, we started again to make Silver Creek, a distance of 15 miles. We had only gone about three miles when the sun set, and the remainder of the journey had to be performed in darkness. It is dreary, monotonous work travelling with oxen in the dark. The trail was fortunately quite distinct, owing to a slight coating of snow, but the night was cold, dark, and blurry—no houses to be seen, and the only break to the sameness was passing alongside a grove of trees or the edge of one of the lakes. I was very glad to get to the banks of Silver Creek.

We got down the gully all right. At the edge of the creek we found a tent occupied by some wandering ones. After allowing the oxen to drink, we put them through the water to cool their legs. Teulon's balked two or three times with him. On getting to the top again we had to travel a quarter mile where we came to Fletcher's house, where we put up for the night, heartily glad to get into the stove's company and before some supper.

Next morning on awakening, we heard the wind outside blowing furiously, and on going to the stable, we also discovered that it was bitterly cold and cloudy. However, we had to make the most of it and start again, this time overlooking the valley of the Assiniboine. After a time, Fort Ellice[42] appeared in sight before us, perched high up on the opposite bank of the Assiniboine. Slowly and gradually it came nearer. About three miles on this side we saw where the River Qu'Appelle empties, and looked up to a narrow wooded vale. We passed on as if quite oblivious of the presence of the Fort, but soon the long lane showed symptoms of turning, and soon came the tug of war.

Down, down into the valley of the river we went, with waggon wheels tied, and oxen almost on their tails. At last we reached the edge of the winding Assiniboine, and for the small consideration of

---

42 Fort Ellice was established by the Hudson's Bay Co. in 1831 at the junction of Beaver Creek and the Assiniboine River. It became a focal point for trails used by early settlers. It was closed in 1890.

¾¢ we were safely ferried over on a private scow, and began winding among the scrub and brush covering the river banks. We saw fields that had been cropped by the Fort people 50 years ago. Here also I saw the first burial ground I have seen in Manitoba, where the Indians who had been about the Fort lay in their last resting place, a rail frame protecting some of the mounds.

After travelling a mile we came to the four private stores and houses of Fort Ellice, quite ready for dinner. This was in a manner supplied by a rosy-cheeked, snub-nosed, smiling damsel at the modest sum of 1/8[43] each. Thus fortified we climbed the hill, and after some panting and puffing among the oxen we got into the shade of the Union Jack flying from a pole with the initials HB on the crimson corner.

The Forts are now changed from what they once were. The ditches and stockades are gone, and in the place is simply a high strong fence. The buildings are all ranged inside the square. The chief factor lives in a large, double-storey building in the centre, and all around are the low, long buildings for the Company's purposes. A few Indians chopping and plastering complete the scene. We directed our steps to the store. Here we found two or three Indians arrayed in their gorgeous holiday attire, smoking the peaceful pipe, evidently trading their stock of furs. We were a long time delayed here before we got our papers, and it was only after sundown we got away.

We had six miles to travel over an unknown trail—fortunately we made out the forking of the Qu'Appelle trail two miles out. Previous to this we travelled among trees, but now our course led us out on the open plains—not a tree to be seen, the prairie all around white and bare, the stars above twinkling like specks, and the cold wind blowing and whistling furiously. This was my first view of the plains since leaving Brandon, and I tell you I did not think them cheerful-looking. On, on we went, and no signs of a house—the whole prairie as deserted-looking as a desert, and my company wrapped up in an oil cloth and stretched out at the bottom of a waggon.

At last I saw a square light peeping on the horizon, but it disappeared, and I hopelessly concluded my imagination had deceived me. Again however I could make out the form of a house,

---

43   One shilling and eightpence.

and at the same time discovered a creek to be crossed. Soon we got the oxen's comforts attended to, and made for the house. Judging from its internal arrangement we concluded it would be a sorry shelter—this proved to be the case. The logs used in its erection were green and the plaster not matured, consequently the wind whistled through every chink. To break the draught, the proprietor had partitioned off with lumber boards a small corner, inside which he had a stove and the dining table.

Our company was certainly a varied one—an English officer of Afghan experience, now a storekeeper in the neighbourhood, a retired GWR[44] stoker and two Ontarians. These regaled us with tough yarns during supper and up till bed time with their respective experiences—shooting and hanging niggers, wrecking trains, and butchering cattle. Teulon had on his topcoat, mitts and cap, and yet he shivered. Every now and then the stoker would show off his firing powers by pouring into the stove a fearful and dangerous quantity of kerosene oil, causing the stove to shake with agony. Our bed proved cool and quiet.

The very next morning we gladly bade the place adieu. The day was bright and shining but very frosty, and after about five hours travelling we reached what is styled the "halfway house." Here we found the proprietor and his family busy shutting out the daylight between the logs with mud, and his wife at Moosomin. However, he promised to do his best in the way of a meal for us—a very poor best, but he considered it worth 2/1[45] each, stabling additional.

With lighter pockets we started again over the dreary wilderness, taking wide circuits round dry sloughs, and about sundown had the pleasure of seeing the steam from a railway engine, but far, far away on the horizon. Longingly and anxiously did we plod towards our destination, and only arrived there about 8 o'clock. We found it to be a real hopeful pioneer city, aged one month, with about 15 buildings. The accommodation proved very comfortable, but 50¢ for everything, bed and meals, was their demand. You can imagine teaming on your income here is a very expensive "luxury." About two o'clock slumbers were disturbed by the arrival of the [?] by the express train.

---

44 Great Western Railway, in England.
45 Two shillings and a penny.

It had been in a smash—a collision is not an extraordinary affair in America.

Next morning was dark and hazy, and threatening snow. Before we got our loads completed it was three o'clock p.m., so we started with the prospect of more night teaming. An anxious night it proved to be, where about halfway the snow began to fall. I was afraid of it obliterating our track. Had it done so, with a dark sky we could do nothing, but would just have to stop up with no food, wood, or shelter. When anyone loses their reckoning on the prairie they invariably describe a large circle to the left. However, the snow did not fall so deep but that we could make the track out pretty well. We met a man with his wife and son driving in a buggy attached to two nice horses—a stranger he said he was. He was very scared, and his wife was lamenting over the prospect of getting lost.

In time, I suppose it was due time, we came to the post directing to the halfway house. I nearly missed it, and would have done so had I not had an idea of the locality. By stooping I detected it against the sky background. We were very thankful to get back to our old quarters, humble and dirty though they were. The man was a shoemaker, the first of his class I have met farming in Manitoba—I have yet to meet a tailor.

Next morning it was still dark and cloudy. About two inches of snow had fallen, and on we went, beguiled by [the] crunching, howling melody of the wheels on the frosted snow. In due time we got back to Beaver Creek for dinner and entered the Fort shortly after sundown. Next forenoon we were busy rearranging our loads. Fortunately I got the most of my load in the store down in the valley, so that I descended comparatively easy. We were just in time to cross the ferry, as the ferryman was on the point of drawing it up for the winter, the ice along the edges interfering with his progress very much. We had some little difficulty crossing. Each waggon had to cross separately, and we had to double the teams there and all the way up to the top of the banks. After some trouble we got both loads up about sundown. We had then eight miles to make to reach Hamilton's house.

Teulon took the lead, as he had a lighter load. After travelling a good long time, I had an idea we were off the trail, but I could discern no landmarks. However, my suspicions were confirmed when we dipped down into a creek and crossed a bridge. But I could form no idea where we were, or how far from the right trail. However, we could not stand, as I foolishly started with boots, and they were as hard as iron and my feet very cold. After travelling some time we struck a light, and then I learnt that we were on the Gamblers trail to the Indian reserve,[46] three miles beyond Hamiltons and four from that house across the country.

The people offered us shelter for the night, and we gladly took advantage of their kindness. They proved to be the Blighs,[47] two brothers and a sister, the elder one with a wife and family. Formerly they had been wholesale grocers in Halifax, N.S. We had to sleep in our clothes on the floor for a night, otherwise we were well treated.

Next morning, Sunday, we were in duty bound to "get." We travelled across the country till we struck the Shell River trail and reached Fletchers at Silver Creek, six miles distant, in time for dinner. We took the waggons to the foot of the ravine to be ready for an early start, and at the same time watered the oxen. Shortly after dinner a shout brought us all outside, and there we saw about half a dozen wolves, leisurely scampering across the prairie before the house, about 100 yards distant. Cheeky rascals, and no gun suitable to give their valour a salute. We went to bed early and rose next morning at half past twelve, ate some lunch left on the table for us, got our oxen, and descended into the gloom of the ravine. After we watered the oxen and had them hitched up ready to start, the wolves, evidently just alongside of us, suddenly set up a chorus of howls and yells that were reanswered and re-echoed up and down the gorge. After a few minutes their ear-splitting melody just as instantly ceased. I am not ashamed to admit that my heart was pretty near up the height of my mouth, but poor Teulon's terror was most amusing. I never saw one so dreadfully scared. I gave his nerves a turn when I asked him if he had his revolver. Like lightning he darted at the valise in his waggon, and in his desperation to get out the revolver I thought he would have torn the satchel asunder.

---

46 The Gambler Indian reserve.
47 Emerson Bligh and his sister Laura and brother Robert homesteaded on 31-17-28 and 7-18-28. He later became the first reeve of Ellice Municipality.

Nothing else occurred to break the even tenor of our way. We arrived at Russell about sunrise. But if it was quiet on earth, the sky was not so. Such a continued glorious display of Northern lights I could never have imagined possible. The whole sky was one flaming, shooting mass, all converging to one bright point like the sun overhead, the lights dancing at a furious rate. Every now and then the light would intensify at a point, then slowly it would unwind into one long strip, rolling out like ribbon until it circled round a fourth of the heavens. There the lights would begin to wave and play, wavering in brilliant shades all the glorious colours of the rainbow. I am sure that no pen or pencil however able could exaggerate, could not even approach towards a faint description of the display. Towards the dawn the stars began to appear. . . .

Tomorrow morning Papa and I purpose riding down to Russell on the sleigh and it is not likely I shall return with him. This new arrangement will cause me to receive your letters very much later than usual, but I expect to be able to write you as before . . .

Your most affectionate brother
Willie

Woodvale, Shell River, Man.
28 December 1882

My Dear Maggie,

. . . I am afraid this hurried scribbling is having a bad influence on you—your last letter particularly was very short and not particularly sweet where you dash toward a conclusion. Suppose we both turn a new leaf next year and vie with one another as to who writes the longest letters. I was particularly glad to perceive from the tone of the last letter you sent that your mind seemed to be settled on the fact that you would next year join us, and also from the same paragraph that you were a great deal stronger, as you write of "sparring" both Andrew and I—two great big Manitoban ploughmen. Should you come out here and find that we have not fixed up a nice room for you—as we have not so far prepared such an apartment, and I cannot guarantee even when we do so that it will be quite satisfactory—it might possibly be just as well that you go a deal in for gymnastic exercises between this time and that. At the same time I think it quite probable that you will be quite satisfied with our arrangements. Teulon was quite rejoiced for his sister's sake to hear that you were coming and he at once opened a letter he had written to her and added a postscript informing her of the fact. So now you are in duty bound to come. . .

Now, my object in writing this is to ask you if it would be at all possible to reach here about the middle of August. That is, leave the Old Country about the latter end of July. If you could do so it would be a very great advantage to us. At that time a team could easily be spared off the place, and besides your presence here after that time during harvesting time would be a very great advantage to do the housekeeping. I trust you will let us know by the return mail how this could be arranged, as between this time and that we will scarcely have four opportunities of recorresponding. Of course, a great deal depends on the increased railway facilities, but I expect Moosomin will be the nearest and most convenient railway point to this, about 70 miles from here. Please let us know every particular of your plan if you have yet definitely proposed one.

We had a very enjoyable party here on Xmas night. One great feature about it was Teulon's fiddling. He plays high-class music very artistically. His violin is an exceedingly sweet-toned one—mine is a perfect "squawker" compared to it.

I think I mentioned before that we were going to have a wedding in the settlement on Xmas. Unfortunately the prospective bridegroom[48] has been very ill with lung disease for a month. The Birtle doctor says one of his lungs is quite dead. He takes no food now, his only nourishment brandy and beef extract. Nevertheless this sad state of matter, the marriage was celebrated, but the ball and other festivities were postponed. The ceremony should also have been postponed. The main reason for its being carried out was a misunderstanding with the minister at Birtle who came all the way

48 The groom was James Lawther, the bride Agnes Kinnaird. He survived to father four daughters.

up for that alone, and I suppose they did not like to send him away emptyhanded. I must now conclude...

Your most affectionate brother
Willie

[P.S. from Andrew]

... We immediately commenced the festivities of the [Christmas] evening by having supper, and after that we had cards, drafts, music, and speeches till eleven o'clock. We then had refreshments and more speeches and music till four o'clock in the morning ...

1883

Woodvale, Shell River, Man.
23 January 1883

My Dear Maggie,

We received by last mail a letter from you, a newspaper and a book of music. For the latter I am very much obliged to you. . . . Papa and Andrew ably supplied the lack of my share of the correspondence last mail. I had to go from here for a sleigh I left behind at Snake Gully last spring. Teulon for company's sake went along with me. Fortunately we were both enabled to get loads of freight at Fort Ellice, and this paid my expenses, with a dollar extra. The weather unfortunately was very cold and stormy. This delayed us very much and caused our expenses to be very much more than they ought to have been. In fact we were just double the time we ought to have been. Teulon stayed with us the night previous to starting. Tuesday morning was clear and sunny but cold. We got the oxen harnessed and made a start, Teulon's waggon box on top of mine to go on the other sleigh—the one we had at that time I was going to lend him. Thus exalted we drove along like persons of consequence across the ploughing. But a haughty spirit goeth before a fall, and as we were descending into what we term the little creek, the oxen floundered and got pretty much out of sight in a deep snowdrift, and the sleigh followed, but not with the same success. We felt it slowly careening under us, but I kept fixed, thinking it would right itself. But alas, it didn't, and away we went at a pitching pace, I first and consequently underneath and smothered in snow. I had [?] the animals like thunder, and after some difficulty got to my feet and shook the snow off and cast a critical eye around to determine the coast. The sleigh was all right and clear of the drift, but both waggon boxes were on their sides and only half apparent. However, after some rough struggling and cool handling we resumed our seats.

Now, however, the wind rose, and it had the effect of intensifying the frost, enabling it to pierce clothing and sending it right into the bones. After some time we got to Pagan's house, but the only response to our knock was the barking of a dog, so we just had to "jog" on. Poor Teulon had soon to drop off and trudge behind to keep the blood circulating. I can ride famously in the cold, and this quality served me in good stead now, as my moccasins were worn out, and Teulon lent me a pair, but they were badly in want of sewing. I was as comfortable as I could expect all the way.

After an interminably long time we got to DuPre's house, about ten miles distant. There we got off to pay our respects to the stove. Papa was here. He had, with the pony, gone on before to see about seed grain, but had got no satisfaction, and his motto was now "homewards." He got there in the evening with, I understand, frozen nose and ears. After a little warmth we proceeded to the Settlement about a mile distant.

On getting to the Hudson's Bay store [at Russell] I looked at the thermometer and found it 26 below zero. This determined us to go no farther that night. So we watered and fed our oxen and sought the shelter of Mr. Butcher's house for the night.[1]

He came out last summer from Plymstock, Devon, England, where he was a schoolmaster, and he has a family of five boys and two girls, the eldest about 15. Out here he has been appointed schoolmaster with $30 a month. He has taken up a farm, and he adds to his small income the profits of a pioneer hotel. Mr. Butcher has the assistance of a niece, Miss [?], a nice young lady who takes a kindly interest in us. Under such auspices we kindled our pipes by the stove and tried to think ourselves happy, but somehow that idea failed through a variety of causes.

The house was exposed on its most vulnerable point at the front to the wind which had now increased into a gale. The schoolmaster had bought a supply of bad firewood, and do all we could, we could not raise the perspiration. I daresay one fault was the number of stokers. We each and all had a try made and created by the stipulation that

---

1 Anthony G. Butcher homesteaded in 1882 four miles south of Russell on 14-20-28. For some years he kept the Dominion weather records for the district. In 1895 he and his family moved to New Zealand.`

the maker of the best fire would be first married. When in bed, however, I felt quite comfortable, and slept the sleep of the just.

The first thing to attract my attention next morning when I awoke was an uncomfortable stinging in my nose that proved that the cold was as active as ever, and my ears satisfied me that the wind was still as brisk. How I pitied Butcher shivering around lighting the two stoves. But not till I heard the young ladies tripping downstairs did I venture to brave the elements.

And it was cold. Not the chattering, chittering kind of cold known in the old country, but a dry, active, look-lively, nervous cold. After a little we went outside to feed the oxen. And I, proud of a newly purchased pair of mitts, got on top of the stack to cut out some hay. When I got down and into the stable, I thought it advisable to look at my fingers, and just as I might have anticipated, the tops were white, hard and lifeless with frost. I tried outside to rub them into snow, but the extreme cold caused them to get worse, and I had to take the frost out inside. Where the frame of the extremities are bone, the frostbite is very much more painful than on cartilage. My fingers ached, twinged, burned, and stung all day afterwards, and now I am so sensitive that I cannot bear them touching the violin strings. We got back to breakfast and that was a caution. Each hand had to get a turn of being inserted in the trouser pockets, and the coffee was nearly freezing in the cups.

Afterwards we went down to the store, and here Brown was earning fame. A huge stove was dispensing heat around in a blistering manner. During the night the thermometer had sunk to 50 below zero and froze up the HBC store. It marked 39 below zero after sunrise. In these circumstances we decided to defer our journey for some time, at least to see if the wind did not abate. But it was nearly evening before it did so, and another night found us still at the settlement. But Mr. Butcher had got better wood and we had a pleasant evening.

Next morning was cold and clear, but quiet, so we got under way. Poor Teulon got his nose frozen three times and had to trudge all the way. About five miles off we saw a horse frozen stiff and hard at the side of the trail. It had played out with hard work and exposure.

After a long weary fifteen miles we got to Silver Creek and watered our oxen.[2] Soon we climbed the opposite bank and found ourselves at Fletchers. Just before getting there we saw a magnificent circle of sundogs round the sun. Picture a clear circle of white light round the sun like a halo in a blue sky, and at four equal points of the circle, bright lights like greater suns and almost as brilliant, and gorgeously tinted with the colours of the rainbow, and you have an idea of what is termed sundogs. They are particularly frequent in Manitoba, and if they set with the sun, as they did in this instance with undiminished brilliancy, they are a sure precursor of a stormy day. Fletcher's house was rather a cold one, and we very soon drowned our troubles in dream land.

Next morning was cold, dark, snowing and slightly blowing. We had not got a mile away when the snow came on heavier, and the wind blew furiously. Soon the trail was a thing of the past, but knowing the landmarks well I had no dread. On we went, and this time the cold wind caused company for Teulon trudging along. Truly it was a miserable day, a sufficient off-set to the long sunny days of the summer. How we counted the miles to the nearest house and tried to recollect the distance it was from the various landmarks. The oxen and everything were coated as if with wool. We did however at last reach Hamilton's, a distance of nine miles. How cosy and comfortable the inside looked. Home is really a home during the Manitoban winter. How happy the lot of women, I thought, not under the necessity of showing their nose outdoors.

When at dinner, the advisability of proceeding further was discussed. In any case that was out of the question, as I wanted to get to a farm house about seven miles distant. Here Teulon and I had in the meantime to separate—I to go for my sleigh and he to go to Fort Ellice to get and load freight to be in readiness to return when I got there.

The upshot of it was that we did not that day again face the wintry gale. Major Boulton, our Warden and County Registrar, came to the house shortly after us, and he also determined to shelter for the night. So we had a quiet pleasant evening of it, discussing provincial and country politics.

---

2   Presumably by chopping a hole in the ice.

Next morning was clear and bright, 32 degrees below zero, but calm, so I started on my lonely way. The snow was very deep and the long, high drifts troublesome. Many times I had difficulty in making out my direction. Once I was afraid I had missed the usual crossing through Snake Gully, and to satisfy myself I had a fearful long wade to the creek edge, up to the waist often. But there I saw away below me like a map the creek valley and the crossing. After some steep wading I at last got to my destination, Mr. Dutton's house, only to find however that he had my sleigh away for a load of wood. His wife was very apologetic and treated me very well. His parents were from Scotland, and of course she was deeply interested in all pertaining to old Scotia. They come from Woodstock and know John Dunlop. Within the evening Mr. Dutton put in an appearance so that I willingly took up my quarters for the night. Had a great night's fun with the three small children they have.

Next morning was clear, bright as a Sunday morning naturally is. I hitched up my sleigh and started for Fort Ellice seven miles distant. After three hours driving I over-looked the grand, broad, picturesque valley of the Assiniboine about 500 feet deep. The view extended either way many miles, and on the opposite bank the Fort standing solidly and substantially like an old sentinel, the clear white smoke rising from the various chimneys like steam from a high pressure engine. But now my whole attention was occupied in getting down, down, down, till the river bank was reached, then across the swift flowing river all hidden now under thick ice, then a mile's travelling in the valley. And then the experience was changed—now it was up.

Soon I got on the prairie again, passed the Fort gates, and arrived at Bowles' stopping house, there to find Teulon and company looking radiant over a dinner at half past three. I soon got alongside, and though last man, I did not fare worst. Here I got acquainted with a young man, Auckett [?], recently out from Glasgow, where he had been a clerk. Next morning we presented ourselves to the great man, Mr. Maclean, the head Factor in the fort, and had the pleasure of receiving orders to take full loads. These orders we quickly executed, and soon the oxen were drawing the crunching sleighs along the valley towards the river.

This time I took a new trail. The only bad thing about it was a number of "dips" near the river. They are long, narrow ridges or better styled gullies like huge trenches. The oxen take them at the gallop or woe betide their heels. Not being used to them before, the quick run and the sharp jerks sent me spinning along the sleigh tongue between the oxen. After that, I took the precaution of having a good firm grip. After we got over the river, the tug of war began to get up the opposite bank. To do that we had to double the teams to each sleigh, causing two journeys up and down.

When we got to the top we saw Hamilton's—and that meant dinner—like a speck on the hill six miles away. Patience and perseverance got us there at last about 4 o'clock. At five o'clock, sun-setting, we were prepared, renewed, and strengthened to make another start, but we had not got far from the house when the wind rose and worse, the soft snow began to drift. But turn? Never!

On we went, and as the darkness became more intense it was difficult to make out the trail—many places [were] drifted over and completely unrecognizable, and the longer the worse—so that I had simply to watch the oxen, and when I saw one of them flounder up to the shoulder I knew on which side the firm-packed trail had been left.

As we went along past the edge of a large lake the wind blew furiously, making the head quite sore and dizzy. Gradually Teulon fell behind with his load and I had to wait, sometimes a considerable time, before he made up. One time I heard a most heart-rending halloing, so I stopped and went back, picking my way, for I could not see him. When I got there, here was spectacle—oxen up to the shoulders, and load nearly buried. He had lost all idea where the trail was.

I got the whip and just went for them—stupid brutes. If they were not warm, I was. I got them back on the trail, but their exertions had done them up, and get the load on the trail they could not. So I just had to go forward, unhitch my team, bring them back—and loath they were to come—and hitch them in front of the others. I relieved my feelings by giving the rear "stick ups" a side jerk that they will bear in mind for some time. After some delay and advice to Teulon to dust the snow out of his weather eye, we again got started. When about half way, the wind went down, but still it remained very dark. There is a house to the right that a trail led to into which I did not want to get it. So when I got to the place where I thought the two separated, I tried to take the oxen to the left. But not a foot would they budge. Finding coaxing and whipping of no avail, I let them have their own way, and my humility I discovered they were right. After that we got on pretty well, Teulon always lagging behind.

After a few miles more had been traversed I made up my mind to go on ahead, as I did not altogether relish the idea of arriving at a dark, cold house. So I made the hitherto reserved whip swing actively, and after a time arrived at Fletchers just in time to prevent them going to bed, and found that it was 11 o'clock. Six hours it had taken me to go nine miles. Teulon turned up about an hour afterwards, and together we discussed our trials and troubles over a hot supper.

Next morning we discovered a high wind and a good deal of drifts, but we were anxious to get home, so we started. In the valley of the Silver Creek, however, we nearly repented doing so. The drift was so thick that the heads of the oxen could hardly be seen. After we got to the top by doubling teams and saw the drift driving over the prairie I made up my mind that it was everyone for himself—but I must get to the Settlement that night, so I pushed ahead. Poor Teulon's oxen soon began to lag, and it was not long till he was out of sight or sound. I had gone about three miles and got into the shelter of some willow bushes when pity predominated within me and I waited a long time on the laggard, but he did not appear. So I concluded his courage had failed him and he had gone into a house near the trail for shelter. So I continued on, my whole attention directed towards a big, black hill about seven miles ahead that I had to pass, beyond which the settlers considered themselves Shell River people. It was slow, hard, tedious work—the oxen up to the shoulders dragging the load through the drifts while I had to walk alongside, almost all the time in snow up to the knees. Slowly and gradually we neared the hill, and glad was I to get into the shelter of groves of wood about and on the trail. It was like getting into a quiet haven after being pitched and tossed on the stormy ocean. Here I looked back for Teulon but could see no word of him, so I cheered up the oxen with the promise of a fabulously big feed of hay and drink of water if they would do the other five miles before the sun set.

We soon got out of the drift again and soon had the pleasure of seeing the dozen houses composing Russell City. It was fortunate this was so, as the oxen pricked up their ears and went at their collars with renewed energy. Had it not been thus, the little hills we were constantly climbing would have stuck me, as they were quite tired out with their [?] exertions. Oxen are knowing creatures, and well do they know the appearance of a locality where stabling is. Just before sunset I drew up at the Hudson's Bay store, man and beast tired, hungry, and dizzy, having been eight hours toiling over 15 miles without food or rest. Mr. Butcher soon got me a specially huge, attractive supper, and I soon put it out of sight.

About two hours after my arrival, Teulon put in an appearance with his oxen only. He had gone off the trail about two miles back, his load had capsized and he had to leave it behind. Next morning I went back with him and helped him to fix it up again. After dinner we delivered up our freight and made a start home, with light loads and easy hearts. Here misfortune befell me. The thaw of the previous day had melted some salt brine on to the bottom of my sleigh box. Without a suspicion I allowed my feet to get thoroughly soaked with it, and the frost, snow, and it gave me an intensified experience of a "fly blister." How my feet did burn and sting! Next day they were blistered, and I was a lamester, but they soon got better. I was glad to find all at home well after an absence of nine days. The only exception was Andrew, who had frozen his fingers—of that he wrote you.

Since coming home we have been cutting fence poles for a few days back. The weather has again been very cold, and we have kept pretty much at inside work. On Friday it was 48 below zero, Saturday 42 below. The other night I went up to Teulons and stayed overnight with him. At present he lives in his stable with the oxen for company. Next morning we started out to the Irishmen's shanty about three miles from his place. It was a very cold, windy, frosty morning, piercing through every kind of clothing. Teulon's nose froze first, then his ear. When rubbing it out, the other went, and shortly after that his cheeks assumed the marble hue. I guess he is pretty sick of Manitoba.

Now when we got to the place we found quite a crowd, four Irishmen [and] a trapper we style Rocky Mountain Sennet[3] (from

---

3 Alfred Sennet, an old resident of the district, a trapper and prospector, homesteaded on 34-22-29.

his having been there and his never ceasing talk on the journey). He has just trapped a timber wolf—I had the pleasure of inspecting him without danger. A huge animal, with tusks like a finger, and larger than a Newfoundland dog. It was one of them, you will remember, felt welcome to challenge the right of way with me last winter.

Shortly after we got into the house a knock comes to the door, and [we saw] a form enveloped beyond recognition in wraps with a buffalo robe slung like a knapsack and snowshoes in his hand. He introduced himself as the Great Northwest, and begged of them to restrain their curiosity until he had doffed his frosty appearance. The voice was familiar, but who he was I could not think. It turned out to be Mr. Powis,[4] our near settler. So we joined in with quite a large dinner party. We did not start for home till after sundown . . .

Your loving brother
Willie

[Sometime before this next letter was written, Willie has cut his foot. Possibly a letter is missing, because he writes about it as if it was old news, and he says that Andrew wrote the last letter]

Woodvale, Shell River, Man.
23 February 1883

My Dear Maggie,

. . . Last mail Andrew had to do all the writing, as I had to keep my foot straight way from me, and in the position it was almost impossible to attempt writing. The wound is now healing up nicely, but I have no feeling in the outer edge of my foot or my little toe, possibly owing to the shock the nerves got. I may be thankful I possess the foot at all.

This has been a terribly severe winter. The thermometer during this last snap went down as low as 52 degrees below zero, the coldest it has been for 14 years. McDonald, the Chief Factor of the Hudson's Bay Company, says it is the largest and coldest severe frost he ever

---

4   William Powis homesteaded on 20-22-29, two or three miles from the Wallaces.

felt, and he has been in the country 23 years. It would be little if one could get remaining at home, but this travelling long distances with oxen at the rate of two miles per hour is not the thing.

There are a great many mishaps this winter. Martin, one of our neighbours from London, Eng., has had to get two toes amputated—and his intended father-in-law performed the amputation and made a mess of it. He will require to get them operated on anew.

The saddest case of all was a Mr. Currie[5] and another gentleman at Rapid City. The former we knew. He has been a long time in the country and was worth considerable money. He tried to get into parliament last year. The two had been out driving, and the cold had so affected them that when they reached the hotel the reaction of the heat was so great that they both died in about ten minutes.

The newspapers state that a dozen people in Winnipeg will lose limbs—the result of inexperience and carelessness.[6] I hope we may not have such another winter for at least another fourteen years. All over North America the cold has been exceptionally severe. In Montana State, farther south, there was 93 degrees of frost. It causes a little amusement to read the paragraphs in the Old Country papers expressing astonishment at 12 degrees of frost.

Andrew neglected to mention in the last letter that the letter by the previous mail could not be sent, as it was so stormy. Neither are you to be surprised if letters should be a little irregular. We have eleven miles to go to the post office over an almost houseless prairie. And even if that was no difficulty, the mail might be delayed by a snow blockade on the railway. At the present I believe communication is not open through the state of Minnesota. We certainly will not fail to write you every fortnight whether the mail is delayed or not. I am writing a whole pile of letters this mail, as this is the only employment I can take up my time with just now. . . .

Next winter I would desire very much to get an American Organ.[7] I wrote to a firm in Winnipeg, but the lowest-priced instrument

---

5   He operated a ferry at Currie's Crossing, near Rapid City.

6   The *Brandon Daily Mail* for January 27, 1883, gives accounts of dozens of people across the Province severely affected by frostbite while travelling to vote in the federal election held that month. In Minnedosa it was reported that of the 200 people who turned out to vote, four-fifths suffered severe frostbite.

7   That is, a reed or pump-organ, such as many farms had.

they had was £25, and the best terms they could offer was the half payment just now and the balance before six months—just a little more than I could think of spending just now. Musical instruments are very expensive in this province, but never mind, we hope to be rolling in wealth next winter. I have been trying the music in the book you sent me, but find it just a little too difficult and high-class, but soon I expect to be even with it. I read with interest the criticism you sent of the new opera. As soon as the chancellor's song, "Said I to Myself, said I," is published separately, I would like very much to get it.[8] Did you ever send the copy of the opera "Patience?"[9]

There is some talk of starting Penny Readings at Russell, the proceeds to go towards getting a harmonium[10] for the hall in which Church service is held. A Presbyterian minister, Mr. Jones, has come to the settlement. He is an elderly man. Papa met him, but he cannot in the meantime come to our district [since] his district is so wide—40 miles by 20 miles. And there is little inducement to come here, as the most of our neighbours belong to the English Church. A clergyman has been settled at Russell all winter. He is a pleasant, frank gentleman, more intent on farming than preaching, I think. His flock credit him with stumbling and stammering over his sermons.[11]

Andrew would write in the last letter that I had sold my yoke of oxen. I mean instead to get a team of ponies—they will suit our work nicely next summer. They are cheaper, and besides quick runners. This will enable us to go down to church. . . .Do you know it is fully a year and a half since I attended divine service? I expect I would be a little awkward and astonished if I were next Sunday ushered into the church seat beside you.

The good time is coming, though. Next winter we expect to hear the engine whistling over the bridge on our creek, and see it puffing over the hill to the great metropolis of the west.[12] We are likely to

---

8   This is from Gilbert and Sullivan's "Iolanthe," which was first performed in 1882.
9   Also by Gilbert and Sullivan.
10 Another name for an "American Organ." Penny Readings were "entertainments consisting of readings, with music, &c. the price of admission being a penny. They commenced in 1859."
11 Rev. Henry Kenner homesteaded on 16-22-28 in Silver Creek in 1883.
12 The railroad did not come to Shellmouth until 1909.

get another grist mill in the neighbourhood. Logs have been cut to build the foundations to one at Russell this summer.

Since last mail we have been getting on very quietly, no visitors other than neighbours. The Haworths expect a sister out from England next summer to keep house, but I understand she will never again experience the bloom of youth. The Pagans have a brother coming out next spring from Ontario. The Irishmen expect nine companions out from Ireland next summer—they will settle on the other side of the river, likely. Teulon is still fooling about nothing, getting everybody's opinion on this house he has so long been going to begin to build. He is dubious whether his sister will come out or not. She appears to be a very strict Roman Catholic, and objects to the want of a priest. As soon as the snow goes off, Powis is coming to settle on his lot and his family will follow soon after. Then there is Compton and McDougall who will be here with the first of spring, the former with his wife and family, and better, a young lady, his niece. So you better hurry out quickly else I might be smitten.

You will most likely have had a visit from Alf Bryant by this time. He is supposed to leave for here on the first of next month. To continue the budget, Major Boulton has gone to Ottawa, and among other things he is going to get us a post office. But I think he is just a little too hasty to be successful. His family will remove up to our neighbourhood as soon as the snow disappears. A store and hotel will also be put up there at the same time, and next summer will see a ferry boat put on the river. And what else is required to complete our satisfaction in the current affairs but a letter from you definitely stating that you mean to come out next autumn and see it all for yourself. And what is more, unless you purpose doing so, you must send me a stock of this paper if you desire long letters. My supply is well-nigh exhausted, but I may be able to scratch along till mid-summer.

The work is getting along very slowly. It is a drawback my not being able to go out, but in a week or so I expect to be able to do so. The weather is now very pleasant, some days almost thawing outside. Every day now the sun is getting higher and stronger, and it will soon be necessary to protect the eyes with goggles. Two nights successively I heard a bear on the creek trumpeting out his grievances. He must have had his slumber disturbed by the wood cutter further up. The Indians trapped a black one at the mouth of the Shell River. They say that there are a number of Moose Deer there. They killed one, but before much execution can be done the snow must harden more on the top to bear up the snowshoes. It is nearly three feet deep. The upper banks of the creek are a wonderful sight. The snow has been blown over the face and formed into huge, long, white precipices. The prairie chickens are getting very tame now owing to the want of food. They come almost to the door now. I think my stock of news is pretty well nigh exhausted. We are all puzzled to know whether you mean to come out and join us … do not let any consideration for us influence you—keep us out of the question altogether. You must make it a question of self-interest altogether. It would be a life-long regret to you if you gave up a good position and came out here and discovered you did not like the change of scene and employment. Let us know …

Your affectionate brother
Willie

Woodvale, Shell River, Man.
2 March 1883

My Dear Maggie,

… I trust you saw Alf and received a glowing description of our settlement from him. He would not most likely be able to say much about our part of it, as I think he was only once here, and then for a very short time. I was especially glad to have your ideas with regard to coming out, but these have still one fault—they are not conclusive. . . You say that you fear there is no great necessity for you coming out. Well, I must state that there is a very great necessity. For two years now we have been working and cooking. At first, and for some time, I rather liked the housework—now, however, I am heartily sick of it. After one has been working hard outside and then requires to come in, kindle the fire, and prepare the dinner or supper, it takes away all the relish of a keen appetite. It gives one the impression of working continually—even the eating appears labour.

Besides, it takes up a large quantity of valuable time. An hour at least extra at midday and the evening is occupied pretty much with washing dishes and mending garments. Heretofore we have been able to spare the time, but next autumn, even the whole summer, the outside work will hardly have sufficient attention [even] though we should occupy the whole of our time with it. What you write with regard to bad housekeeping is all rubbish—we are all of us qualified, or think we are, to teach.

The other objection you write of—as to being in the way should there be any marital intentions, has also no weight. Should such an event occur, you would neither be in the way or dependent, each of us with farms containing 320 acres. The government insists upon a house and etc. being erected on each of them, to be resided in at least six months in the year, and in view of that Papa would be more independent with you to keep his house—meantime our plan is to flit from one to the other so as to secure each claim.

My great fear in view of this objection is that your independence would quickly manifest itself by being tempted away by some neighbouring pioneer to keep his house. Young ladies are rare here.... . To delay the reunion till the August of next year, I do not approve of it—what with hurried bad cooking, hard work and [?] we would be all invalids by that time and I do not see any great end it would serve. You do not say, but I presume you will be entitled to a full certificate before the holidays in June. After that I would consider you were independent anywhere—even in Manitoba. Here such a good certificate would get you employ, but if at any time should you discover that you did not like the farm work. And so far as you assisting us with money is concerned, we hope to be in possession of as much as will satisfy our wants from the fruits of our next labour, and each year will in the same way, I expect, satisfy our increasing wants. Just now is our worst time, just between the spending period and the earning, so you must set this idea aside from your calculations. The decision however must be come to by yourself.

Andrew and I were differently circumstanced when we proposed coming, where our situation then was not the most lucrative one, besides it was a very dependent and precarious one. Comparing our position then with what it is now there is all the difference in the world. Now we have no limit to our hopes of what we may yet be, so that we have reason to be pleased with the change . . .

Do not for a moment think that by stating this I want to influence your feeling—far from it. I cannot express to you our sorrow at your not joining us last spring. All along, I have since that time been calculating the months that would intervene before you came out, and I think I would for very joy become foolish, outrageously hilarious when you did come. In my imagination I have met you times innumerable and conveyed you to all the picturesque points from which to see our unrivalled scenery, and conjured up your looks of astonishment and words of wonder. But still I would not entice you to do anything you might afterwards regret. . . .

Now bear in mind when deciding, that you are to leave us outside of consideration. We, when we left you in the old country, did what we considered best for ourselves—now you must do the same with regard to yourself. And mark you, if you decide against coming out we will require to debit your account in our books with the wages of an old squaw, or else you may get out of the difficulty by engendering in some nice quiet good-looking accomplished young lady a desire to emigrate to Manitoba and address her to my care and guidance— but joking aside, if you have really a longing to come out that seems to overmaster your desire to remain, just make up your mind.

Next winter our house accommodation will, we expect, be increased. We will then have more money and will get something like civilized furniture. I will get a house put up on my place in which we will all live in the summer time. It will overlook the river where steamboats will be passing next summer. Next winter we shall have a railway passing—in all likelihood this will alter surroundings very much. How would it do to give the change a trial for a year . . .

Since my last letter we have been getting on much in the usual way. We had one pretty severe storm last week that greatly added to the snow banks along the creek. At the house Andrew had to dig a pathway six yards long and five feet high to get up to the prairie. We have now got another pony—Date is its name. It is brown coloured, a little bigger than Puss, but I think the two will make a nice team. I have written to Brandon for harness. When we get that we will be able to hold up our heads a little higher.

We are all well and in good spirits. My foot is about completely better. Today I was down at the bush for the first time and managed to fell 21 trees. After that I had to adjourn, as my tender soles got painful with the cold, but I will have another go tomorrow. I mean to go down with this mail. Won't I astonish the people with my miraculously speedy recovery. . . . Since the last mail there have been two houses burnt in the settlement. The first one was about four miles from Russell, occupied by two brothers and sisters named Simpson. They saved everything, but the house and what things were in the cellar were destroyed. The house was put up last summer and cost $400. The other one was about four miles from here. It was a little shanty occupied by Mr. Godley, his wife and family . . . We unite in sending you our kindest love, and no matter how you decide, I will ever remain

Your affectionate brother
Willie

Woodvale, Shell River, Man.
23 March 1883

My Dear Maggie,

We duly received with last mail a letter from you, and from Alf Bryant [who visited Maggie in England] we have still later tidings of you. We are very glad to know that you are so well and in such good spirits, and furthermore we are extremely pleased to learn that you have really a wish to come out to Manitoba. So we have concluded that you will join us later this year sometime, and are drawing up our summers' programme accordingly. . . .

[The Bryants] had a twelve day sea voyage, very rough and stormy. Miss Bryant was very glad to get on to dry land. The railway journey was no great improvement. They were snowed up two days. They stayed a day or two in Winnipeg where they met Denmark, the postmaster. Together they travelled on the cars to Moosomin. From there Denmark took charge of Miss Bryant and drove her in his cutter sleigh the whole distance to his place, sixty miles in one day. Thursday Alf followed in the rear with the baggage and was met by Frank at Fort Ellice. When passing Denmarks they picked up Miss Bryant and all reached home on Saturday night about 12 o'clock. Miss Bryant has a slight cold but seems otherwise to have stood the journey well.

Andrew and I started out on Sunday morning and spent the day at the Bryants hearing, seeing, and receiving. Miss Bryant had not much to say. She was rather reserved—two or three months in Canada will rub that away. Alf came in shortly after we arrived. His first performance that morning had been to fix on his snowshoes and tramp over to his half-finished house to see really if it were still there. The journey has improved him very much. He brought along with him from England Mr. Pitlow, a cousin, I think. And the same gentleman, before the summer is over, will be I am afraid tired of the N.W. The mosquitoes will make it hot for him—he is just fit for them.

After dinner a whole crowd of neighbours appeared to welcome back Alf and also to sample a "leetle whiskey" Alf smuggled into the west . . .

You should have seen how affectionately Andrew hugged your very kind parcel. The socks are a perfect blessing, and were it not for your school duties I would have the audacity to ask you to knit some more for us and send them by mail. Andrew declares himself the owner of the scarf with the pin. He considers himself with it thoroughly furnished and prepared for the ball next week. I am much obliged to you for the music book. You may be certain it will receive a great deal of attention . . . Spring is now showing symptoms of coming again. The grey owls are now hooting in the river valley, and hawks screaming. I have nothing noteworthy to write about this time. We are all well and getting on well . . .

Your affectionate brother
Willie

Woodvale, Shell River, Man.
2 April 1883

My Dear Maggie,

Papa duly received your last letter, and we read its contents with pleasure. You speak of not receiving our letters as usual, but this may be explained—about that time the weather was very stormy and a journey to the post office on the usual day hazardous. All the letters will however, I trust, reach their destination in time. The like will not for some time happen again . . . The only evil resulting to Miss Bryant from the long journey was at first only supposed to be a slight cold, but that has since resolved itself into rheumatic fever, an attack of which she had previously in the old country. The nearest doctor, forty miles distant, had to be sent for. Today I learnt from two settlers who are not far from them that Miss Bryant was considerably better. It is an unfortunate time to be ill, as the change from cold to heat with the consequent dampness is the most trying of all the seasons. And this is another argument in favour of you coming here in the fall and getting braced up by the clear winter. . . .

We have been enjoying a continued spell of mild, clear weather— the sun glistening on the clear white snow in a dazzling manner, rendering coloured goggles when journeying necessary, and tanning the complexion like an Indian's. Were you here you would be hiding your fair complexion under a monster green veil. Today this has changed—it is a dull dark day and a good deal of smoke falling. It is so mild and damp that we did not go down to the woods. Instead, I am occupying part of the day in this letter.

The only noteworthy [event] in the last fortnight was the Ball— and it was a Ball! Teulon brought down his oxen, and together we had a sleigh-ride to the scene of festitudes. We got to Russell at sundown, stabled the bulls, and adjourned to Mrs. Butcher's for supper. She was very good to us, treating us to a great deal of currant cake and plum duff. The latter's sweetmeat you will soon get acquainted with—every bachelor in Manitoba considers himself an adept at its manufacture. Teulon is a very systematic young man, so he quickly adjourned to the town hall to see the arrangements complete for his violin performances. I indulged in stove heat and small chatter till about 9 o'clock.

When I got to the hall the fun had begun. Fairly owing to the number of causes, the ladies make a very poor turnout—about ten compared to about seventy or eighty gentlemen. Consequently there were a very large number of gentlemen wallflowers. But Major Boulton and all the numerous gentry were there in full force, and the whole assemblage gorgeously arrayed. Dancing occupied a great part of the time. All passed off pleasantly with only one mishap, and that befell Fanny Denmark who is, like yourself, a very tall young lady, and by no means slender. She had been dancing with her father's partner, Mr. Brown. Somehow she got into collision with another couple, tripped on her dress—a long train one as usual—and with a mighty crash she and her partner returned to the dust, the lady, alas, underneath. In a short time she so far recovered that she could be led from the scene with no further injury but a bumped [?] but the affair was too much for many of the irreverent and headlong young men, and at intervals the scene would be rehearsed with a great deal of mock ceremony and superfluous effect.

In addition to dancing, the company were regaled at intervals with songs, recitations, violin solos, biscuits and coffee, and a very amusing character sketch by Messrs. McGibbon and Stewart. The former was master of ceremonies and, last summer came from Leeds where he had been a schoolmaster. (Now that I think of it, we are favoured with three farming old-country schoolmasters in the settlement.) Even I myself gave a recitation, got great credit for it—and it is not my place to comment on the critical powers of the audience. After playing "God Save the Queen" the company dispersed about four o'clock in the morning. I intended starting home, but the moonlight was so hazy and the journey a long, lonely one, that I was not unwillingly shouldered back to Butcher's house, where the fun was renewed. I did not get home till the afternoon. Teulon got back next morning—he had been getting some seed grain.

We are working away getting out fence posts—it is very tedious, laborious work. The snow is quite three feet deep, and it is no joke plunging through it with a heavy rail on your shoulder. The snow will not likely trouble us long now—in two weeks at the most it will be all gone.

On Sunday Andrew and I walked over to my place to the site of the prospective house, and we were quite enchanted with the scenery, even though clothed in its winter garb. To the north of it there is a thick grove of poplar trees that will give good shelter from the Arctic winds. To the west it overlooks the valley of the Assiniboine. The river circles around in fantastic curves, just patches of it seen here and there from among the trees and bushes. The opposite banks of the valley are well-wooded. Beyond, the province of Assiniboia[13] extends away to the horizon, flat as a pancake and dotted over with large and small patches of woodland. To the south, a flat bare plateau extends for two miles, and terminates in a point at the junction of the Thunder Creek and the Assiniboine. Beyond, the course of the river valley is seen turning towards the east. The eye follows the abrupt wooded banks of Skunk Creek and rests on a little square dot on a hill that is the Smithy's house, about two miles from Russell. Farther east, the locality of Alf Bryant's house is seen. That will be [better] seen as soon as he puts the roof on. The high range he is on shuts up a further view but coming nearer, the numberless bluffs of trees are seen scattered about, and just at the creek edge the Pagans' house is seen. A little farther north on the other side of the creek, stacks of hay are seen coming out from the shelter of the wood, and looking north the high bald banks of the Shell River with the Big Woods beyond. At the horizon nearer can be seen Farrar's house[14] peeping up from among the trees. Farther to the west is a large broad tract of prairie without a bush—this is where we will someday put a steam plough. . . . Now could you think of a more attractive scene than this, if dressed in summer colours? On going home we went over the face of the creek banks, sliding, scrambling and tumbling down till we reached a trail we have in the woods, and got harsh welcome from a hawk flying up the creek, screaming out against our intrusion. I was quite astonished to see the great quantity of fine timber we own. We are only just beginning to discover the extent of our wealth in that direction.

We have lately had some additions to the settlement. Mr. Godly has come back from Moosomin where he was meeting his brother-in-law, wife and two children just out from England. They live about three miles from us—and on a section adjoining, a family of the

---

13 The district of Assiniboia was part of the North-West Territories. Saskatchewan was not created for another 22 years.

14 24-22-29, northwest of Wallace's.

name of Stewart—Ontarians—have come on to the land they took up last spring. There are three men and two women so far, yet we have failed to get ladies into our township, but it is a hopeful sign when they settle on the boundaries. I have nothing else interesting to write about . . .

Your most affectionate brother
Willie

Woodvale, Shell River, Man.
12 April 1883

My Dear Maggie,

I have this time to write your letter earlier than usual owing to our now being favoured with a weekly mail. The day on which the mail is dispatched has been altered to Tuesday instead of Friday, as formerly. This change will in every way be a boon to the settlement.

Last Sunday Andrew and I, accompanied by Will Pagan, started out with the ponies to have a drive to Russell. When we got down there after a splendid drive we learnt that there would be no Presbyterian service till three o'clock. We thought that too long to wait, so we got our mail, including your letter. . . . I wrote Uncle Hugh about two months ago. I trust the letter did not go astray—he does not seem to realize that before money can be got we must work for it. So far our home operations have yielded us little—next harvest will, however, mend that, but this, you will understand, rendered it necessary for one to go out and earn a little. Unfortunately I did not get much opportunity of driving;[15] we will, however, manage all right.

After getting our mail we drove north to the Bryants, and when about two miles on our way we met Alf Bryant driving down to the English service. He possesses a nice pure white pony. We got to Bryants and had dinner. All had gone their ways but Frank, his wife, and Mr. Pitlow. Miss Bryant was invisible, but we were told she was greatly better, although confined to her bedroom.

---

15 That is, freighting for the Hudson's Bay Co.

I had bought two pigs from them previously, so I took advantage of the visit to take possession of them. What a squealing there was before we got them into the box! They got home all right and are now thriving and trotting around, filling the air with a new kind of music, and filling the dogs and calf with astonishment. The calf made its appearance fully a week ago—a big strong dark-brown colour, with a few white spots—a bull calf. We are rich and happy with abundance of pure undiluted milk, on which the pigs, calf, dogs, cat and ourselves are thriving and getting fat. The cat has taken on a new lease of life, and is capering around like a lunatic. The black pup, Major, and it fight-play at tag, and have grand fun all day long. We had hard work, or rather the ponies had it, coming home from the Bryants. The thaw set in so rapidly that by sundown large tracts of the prairie were bare. The ponies sank down through the snow on the trail at every step.

Now sleighing is over and gone. Each day since then has been milder than the previous one. The prairie hereabouts is almost bare, and one patch of our ploughing is ready for seeding. This speaks well for the locality. Over towards Russell the prairie and fields are still covered with slushy snow. We will be able to put our seed in a fortnight earlier than almost everyone. Tomorrow I mean to try a little harrowing, but we will not likely put in any seed until next week. Yesterday afternoon it rained more or less heavily till sundown, but tonight it looks more like frost again.

Mrs. Boulton, the first lady to enter the township, went up with the Major on Thursday to reside on the prospective city-site there.[16] The wood for building the ferry boat went up on Friday, so things are beginning to boom there. The steamboat will soon be making its appearance up the river. This will add life to the district, as it will supply the settlers for a good distance east with provisions and etc.

The Russell people are making arrangements for a grand concert and [?] on the 28th, and I am down for a recitation. What do you think of that? My stock of pieces will soon be exhausted. Do you know of any good collections of readings? There are some good ones I think compiled by Carpenter—if they were not too expensive you might send me one of them. Let it be a variety of comic and

---

16 The Boultons lived for a few months at Shellmouth.

serious, if possible. Last time I gave Sergeant Buzzfuzz's speech from the Pickwick Papers. This time I mean to give a sketch from Mark Twain. I discover that all that is necessary to become good at reciting is impudence and a small bit of contempt for the opinion of the audience. I would also like you to send me two first strings for the violin. The ones Teulon gave me seem to be rubbish—each of them slap me in the face before they are many weeks in use. If you send me these I will excuse you sending anything else but long letters for a long time. Now you must excuse my stopping now . . .

Your affectionate brother
Willie

Woodvale, Shell River, Man.
27 April 1883

My Dear Maggie,

Andrew rode down for the mail last Sunday and was amply rewarded by getting a letter from you addressed to him. We were pleased to learn of your welfare and all the other news . . . We have just recently experienced a wonderful transformation scene. A few weeks ago winter truly reigned over the land—and freezing sharply with its icy breath too—and for the last week we have been toiling and sweating over the bare prairie soil. It gives one the feeling they have jumped from Greenland to Florida. A stray snowbank, a monument of what has been, dispels the illusion.

The ducks are back again in myriads with their quack-quack. The geese have passed north to the lakes. Today the turkeys[17] were making their hideous croaking—they are considered to be the latest of the migratory birds. All around, large birds and small birds may be seen sitting on the bare branches proclaiming, each in their peculiar style, the fact that spring has come again. I think everybody sympathizes with their joyous songs.

The winter on the whole has not been a stormy one, but it has been a terribly severe one. I am not likely to forget about it for some

17 Probably Sandhill Cranes.

time—my foot is very sensitive and painful when I walk much. It was only frozen—I had not been previously injured.

We are getting on very well with our spring work—the ponies are working famously. We have fifteen acres of wheat sown—surely the result of that will next winter amply supply us with bannocks entirely of our own manufacture.

Monday a week ago Arthur Bryant paid us a visit. Before that he had been on a trip to Winnipeg. On his journey he invested in a stylish pony and a buggy, so that now he indulges in a little style, which his prospective wife at home no doubt very often shares with him. They are to be married on the 2nd of June. Miss Bryant is now much better.

On Saturday Andrew and I drove down to Russell. We got some provisions but were disappointed in getting the mail—the bad roads and flooded river delayed the carrier. On the way back we had to cross prairie fires twice. Owing to the rapid thaw and no rain these fires have been very sweeping and fierce this spring, keeping the atmosphere in a perfect haze of smoke. One fire this side of the river has raged (and is still raging) for four days—the brilliant glare at night is very pretty. Fortunately we have saved our timber this spring.

On Sunday Papa went down to the Presbyterian services. The congregation was a small one, thirteen only, I think. Just before the service the mail carrier arrived. We had a large number of neighbours eagerly awaiting it. On Wednesday, the Rev. Mr. Jones, the Presbyterian missionary, surprised us with a visit. He seems to be rather a pleasant, sincere individual. Twelve years ago he was settled in Winnipeg, then Ft. Garry. After remaining there two years, he travelled west 1000 miles to Edmonton, where he remained a year. After that he left the country, and for a number of years was stationed in Manitoulin Island. Now he has come back for the sake of his health, to be surprised by the rapid progress the province has made during his absence. His wife has accompanied him on all his wanderings, and I understand she has talk in her for a city. He preaches at four different stations, two each Sunday—Russell and Silver Creek, twelve miles distant from Russell. The succeeding Sunday he preaches at the Scotch Colonization Company farm, ten miles distant—from that to Rossburn, thirty miles distant. I am afraid we will not be able to induce him to at anytime hold service here. At the present we are the only Presbyterians in the district. The great number of our neighbours belong to the Church of England.

We are wearying from [want of] rain now. The ground is getting rather dry. This is an extraordinary fine spring, the finest I think I have ever experienced. Day after day passes without so much as a cloud in the sky. Generally the present time is cold, cloudy, and damp—instead we are experiencing the finest summer weather. . . . I must now halt for want of further news . . .

Your most affectionate brother
Willie

Woodvale, Shell River, Man.
20 May 1883

My Dear Maggie,

I am sorry this letter has been so long delayed, but just now we are so busy getting in the seed during the day, and the want of lamp oil prevents writing after dark. So you must for a time be content with a short hasty acknowledgement of your last two letters and that we are all well and getting on nicely. . . . it is a great disappointment your not coming out, although all things considered it would have been rash to have done otherwise. By next letter I will more fully explain our ideas regarding it.

The country is now beginning to look beautiful. The trees are bursting into leaf. Last Wednesday we had a terrific thunderstorm, blowing and raining fearfully. The rain did an immense amount of good.

Nothing very noteworthy has occurred. Everybody is anxiously awaiting the steamboat, as the whole settlement is nearly out of provisions, almost nothing but flour. Excuse my haste—I will make up for it next time . . .

Your affectionate brother
Willie

Woodvale, Shell River, Man.
1 June 1883

My Dear Maggie,

I am sorry my last letter to you was such a hurried scrawl, but really we have been and are so busy with work that cannot stand over, that you must excuse me and accept hasty letters some time as a necessity. . .

I was very much pleased with the Opera "Iolanthe." Some of the airs are very "catchy" and the words are a very great assistance, but was it not a rather expensive investment for you? The other opera I could not get either sense or music out of. No doubt my musical abilities were at fault.

Your decision to remain where you are, for some time at least, was a great disappointment to all of us. But the reasons you gave satisfied us that you were correct in your choice. I had my doubts whether you would like the change, but thought you would be in a manner independent. We did not understand the insufficiency of your certificate. It is however a cause for satisfaction to us to understand that you are so thoroughly comfortable in every respect, and that your prospects are so good. Surely the dim future will reveal an opportunity for us meeting again before many years elapse.

We now know exactly what we have to do. We will not make any addition to our house accommodation—our present premises are large enough to be comfortable and kept clean. You make some rather decided allusions to us getting married. Unless we get smitten by either half-breed girls or squaws, a very unlikely possibility, it will be hardly worth our while calculating on such an event. That is, provided you do not get some young ladies interested in us. We all sincerely trust you will not weary or have a sense of loneliness, but will find a pride and pleasure in your work, and that you will be very successful. The [?] Inspection turned out better than you anticipated, I hope. In view of the likelihood of us requiring to correspond again for a definite space of time, how would it do for us to give up the formal and hackneyed style of a letter, and instead exchange our news and etc. in journal form, each day's event, no matter how trivial, separate and distinct and written up daily. This style I think would bring to the knowledge of each of us many little items of news that would be interesting, and would be lost sight of or cause a letter to look jerky. Let me know what you think of this plan. I will make an experiment of it in my next letter.

We are getting on famously with our work. The seeding is all over now. The fields are all covered with a splendid beard of young grain—nowhere in the neighbourhood has it an equal for evenness. For a week or so after it was sown the weather was very dry and frosty in the mornings—this retarded the growth very much. Everywhere since that time we have had a good deal of rain—twice, very hard thunderstorms. These gave it a start, and ours seem to have taken an exceptionally full advantage of it.

Our garden promises to turn out well. We planted full half an acre of potatoes, ¼ acres of carrot and parsnip, and the remaining ¼ with onion, turnip, cabbage, lettuce, sugar cane,[18] sweet Indian corn, pop corn, beets and peas. In all we have 1 acre planted. By harvest time we will be reaping the fruits and living like kings.

For some days back we have been busy fencing. We have finished the stock yard and a quarter of the field fencing. It is rather nice work in Canada. They know nothing of hedges. Hawthorne will not grow, instead, wire or rails are used. Poverty causes us to use the latter. It is hard work, the cutting of them. They are built up in zigzag form between supports—this steadies them and makes the fence secure.[19] When all the fencing is done, the beauty of the place will be very much relieved and enhanced. I mean to make a great effort and send you a sketch. But this, no matter how well it might be done, would fail to give you an adequate idea of the splendid scenery. So far as general news, I have not much to relate.

The steamboat, after being long and anxiously expected, made its appearance at last on Sunday evening, a week ago. On that day Papa and Andrew went to church, but owing to the illness of the minister no service was held. Consequently they came home pretty early, just about sundown. I heard a peculiar throbbing noise over towards the

18 Possibly sugar beets?
19 This is the snake fence, which was common in Ontario. It must have been used on the prairies only where there were good stands of trees.

river. It was some little time before I could think what it would be—till the steamboat flashed across my memory. We were watering the cattle in a little pond near the house at the time. We were not long in tying them up. We soon got to the opposite of the creek valley and from that to the edge of the river valley. The steamboat had passed and was a good bit up the river opposite Langford's shanty. We could barely make her out in the dusk. It seemed strange to hear the din and plunging of the paddles so near our abode. Only once before has the river valley been so disturbed, and that was fully three years ago. She only waited a day at Shellmouth and then returned, but she left plenty of provisions, and these are now slightly reduced in price.

Papa and Andrew went up with the team two days afterwards. Denmark has a canvas store there [which] Powis, one of our neighbours, keeps—I expect he has got tired of farming. They have got a large quantity of goods there now. Among other things there is an American Organ that should be sent on to Fort Pelly, but as there is no way of getting there I expect it will open for sale. If I just had the money—what a source of pleasure! But I expect when I can afford that the effect of Miss Campbell's tuition will have departed.

Arthur Bryant is going down tomorrow all the way to Birtle to get married. Miss Bryant is, I hear, quite better now, getting fair and rosy. A younger brother of the Pagans has joined them here. He has brought with him a nice team of horses, two cows and two pigs, so they are getting rather uppish. I went up to Teulons last Sunday. He has got aunts in London who seem to be interested in the fact that they live not far from you. I gave him your address, as they seem desirous of making your acquaintance ... I wish I could transfer our beautiful place to your view. Everything is brilliant with the freshness of spring. We unite in sending you our kindest love, and remain ever

Your most affectionate brother
Willie

P.S. . . . I am sorry to trouble you again about money matters, but we are getting rather short, and I am afraid we will be more so before harvest. I was unfortunate getting laid up at the best money earning time with my sore foot, then followed the fact that we sold so little hay owing to the early departure of the snow. I hardly know how you may be situated, but you speak of saving £2 per month. I understand you will have a good deal of expense in the way of clothing and holidaying, and I sincerely hope you may not form an erroneous opinion of our position and scrimp yourself—you must on no account do that, but if it were possible to send even £5 it would help us to tide over till harvest time when I hope to be earning money in earnest. If you think you see a possibility of doing that kindly get a money order made payable at Brandon Man. post office for the amount. After harvest time we will cease to spend, spend, and will be earning, but meantime we are at the critical period. We are having gloriously brilliant summertime weather now. . . .

Woodvale, Shell River, Man.
8 June 1883

My Dear Maggie,

I purposed in my last letter to write this in journal form. I trust the experiment will prove satisfactory.

Friday—a cold showery day. We tried to do some work in the morning, and found it very cold on the fingers sharpening posts. A shower drove us indoors, and as it was likely to continue, I donned my jacket and went out prospecting for pickets. I crossed the creek and was pleased to find the oats there promising well. The showers were flying down the river valley like mist, the opposite banks owing to the dampness appeared so close the tufts of grass could be distinguished. I discovered what I wanted and then retraced my steps to the creek valley [and] crossed it at the mark line where the surveyors had cut a track through the wood and scrub in the valley. Looking up I saw the point standing out prominently like its namesake Ben Nevis. The fencing along one edge could be seen, and gave the scenery a civilized appearance. On gaining the opposite bank I discovered the Pagans' shanty quite near, so I crossed over and found Will alone, his two brothers having gone to Moosomin. After talking and inspecting the horses and the pigs I started for home, and got there in time for dinner. In the evening it got milder and Andrew and I hauled out some fencing.

Saturday was a beautiful sunny day, a great number of the bushes were in full blossom. I was baking and we were all fencing. We finished a good piece. In the evening Andrew and I went to the Pagans, found them all at home. We had a good night's time getting all the news from the south, and a feast of Canadian apples. The people are going west by the railroad in hundreds. At Moosomin eight houses had been built within a fortnight, and everything booming.

We got home late, ready for bed, and awoke Sunday to find the sun shining brilliantly. After dinner we hitched up the ponies, and Papa and I drove down to church, 10 miles distant. McDougall, a neighbour, accompanied us. We had a most enjoyable drive. The service was poorly attended, about seventeen—I led the singing. We got back home about six o'clock.

Monday during the forenoon was warm and clear. We did a good bit of fencing. In the afternoon a thunderstorm drove us inside, and it continued wet till sundown. Tuesday morning was very misty— after we had been working two hours the mist cleared, but it came on rain and continued wet all day. Papa and I fixed up our fishing tackle and went over to the river. We used frogs for bait. We were fairly successful, catching ten pounds weight of fish. We got home for dinner wet and tired. I forgot to mention that Andrew saw a bear on the other side of the creek yesterday. He had been out fetching in the ponies and noticed the bear first at a small pile of rails, smelling them. It then struck off towards the river. This is the second seen in the neighbourhood this spring. Wednesday was a clear brilliant day. We got on very well with our fencing till in the afternoon, when a thunderstorm caused us to shelter.

Thursday was wet almost the whole day—we got a little work done between times at peeling rails. Henry Pagan paid us a visit during the day. Arthur Bryant, he heard, had not returned from his marriage tour to Birtle. He had lost an ox, and I do not suppose he will be well able to afford it just now. It seems he lent the team to a neighbour named Godly to go down to Birtle with. On the way back, at Silver Creek, Godly let the oxen and load slip over the bank. This injured one of them so severely that it will require to be killed, and even then it is little use for beef, as it is as lean as a harrow.

This Godly is a most unfortunate fellow. On the way up, first he left some of his goods behind, and when he went back for them he found a lot stolen. Then, through scarcity of money he failed to get a house up, and wrote his wife and family not to come, but the letter miscarried and they duly arrived. The Bryants offered them accommodation in their house. He then bought two cows, and one of them turns out to be almost worthless. He did get a shanty up at last, but during the winter it got burnt down, and some of his children got frostbite during the scrimmage. They then sheltered for the remainder of the winter in a half-completed house hardly capable of keeping out the cold. Andrew and I paid them a visit there. I pitied the sight his wife presented cowering and shivering at the stove. She was brought up in the West Indies.

Previous to this he had written to a brother in England to come out and take up a half-section near them, but it was taken up by another, and his brother arrived with a wife, two children and no money, and could get no land. Godly got all his hay burnt by a prairie fire in the spring. At this time he was down at Birtle with some wheat he had bought to make flour, but it was not fit for that, so he got it made into meal for porridge—and this mishap happened to him on the way back. Everything he sets his hand to seems to bring misfortune. How they expect to get along I cannot imagine, as they are not worth a cent, and [have] only three acres broken. Such are some of the afflictions of pioneers.

Friday was slightly chilly and cloudy during the early part, but cleared away nicely in the afternoon. We were fencing all day and I was baking. Nothing very important occurred. Saturday—a very pleasant warm day. During the forenoon we were peeling rails. After dinner I saddled Puss and rode down to Russell. On the way I passed a skunk. They have a pretty black and white fur, a tremendously large bushy tail, and when angry, a bad, bad smell. At Russell I got your letter to Andrew . . . . I afterwards attended a meeting of the committee to arrange for the sports on the last day of this month, Dominion Day this year falling on a Sunday. Everything betokens a success and is to be concluded by a grand entertainment in the evening. Admission ten cents, so fetch your purse with you if you desire to hear any recitations.

I had the pleasure of congratulating Arthur Bryant on his new character, a married man. Miss Bryant was, he said, keeping very well and annoying them very much by insisting on doing what they considered overmuch work. The brothers are now living on their own places. Miss Bryant resides in the meantime with Arthur till Alf gets his house more thoroughly finished. I had a pleasant ride home.

Sunday was warm but with heavy showers occasionally. During the night I had been a martyr to toothache so I napped during the forenoon. Andrew and I went over to the Pagans after dinner and waited till after supper. Teulon joined us. He was a picture. Last spring he used to tramp around with a white collar and fine clothing, but, ah, how changed today! He was evidently sans shirt, sans socks, and a face that was innocent of water for at least two days. Pray don't tell his lady-friends if they should call. I am sorry a variety of circumstances caused me to allow the diary to fall behind.

Monday and Tuesday were shower days, the last one particularly. On that morning I started out fishing alone. I was not very successful, only catching one jackfish weighing 3 lbs. On both days we were busy fencing. Wednesday was a very warm day with occasional thunderstorms. Andrew started out in the morning with his dinner in his pocket to plough on my claim. He got on very well—the prairie is damp and easily wrought. Papa and I were fencing when at dinner we were surprised by a visit from Brown and Fields of Russell. The former is storekeeper there, and the latter a mail-carrier. They were on their way to the city at Shellmouth. They had great trouble getting their horse to go through the creek—it had to be hauled over by a rope and the machine afterwards. Thursday a nice quiet day—Andrew was ploughing, and we were peeling rails and digging out a lime kiln.

Friday was voting day, so we had a holiday. It was a beautiful warm day. Teulon accompanied us down to Russell in the waggon. We had a pleasant drive, registered our votes, saw and spoke to lots of people, and enjoyed the novelty of a justice court on a settler who had been attempting to shoot his wife. We could not wait to the finish, but I expect he will get a trip to Winnipeg jail. Major Boulton was the justice. I think Henry would have had fits if he had been present to hear him examining the witness—such a bungling was a discredit to common sense, let alone legal. We got home about dark well pleased with our day's outing.

Saturday found us working with renewed energy hoeing potatoes, ploughing, cutting pickets in the bush, baking and churning. About five o'clock I saddled Puss and started out to Shellmouth for subscriptions for the sports. The site for the future city is certainly a lovely spot. The ferry boat will be launched next week. Denmark's store and Boulton's house are at present the only buildings. I collected fully twenty-four subscriptions. I had a ride home in the dark. I was charmed by the fireflies flying around like stars. This concludes the fortnight's events ...

Your most affectionate brother
Willie

Woodvale, Shell River, Man.
10 July 1883

My Dear Maggie,

We duly received two letters from you, one addressed to Andrew, the other to Papa. We are sorry to learn that you have been disappointed in not getting your parchment—time will however put that matter all right. Can you excuse my long silence? I am very ashamed of it, but circumstances would not permit my writing earlier. I had the extreme honour to be selected for a committee man to further the interest of the meeting held on Saturday, 30 June, Dominion Day. [20] This took me away from home very much in the evening [as] I could not spare the time during the day.

Since that time my time has been wholly occupied with the priming of lime. Night and day the kiln had to be kept going for a fortnight. Andrew has been staying with Teulon and ploughing. During that time he earned £6. The kiln will, we expect, be worth £8. We will require a large quantity ourselves, the remainder we will sell. Owing to these engagements I have not been able to find time

---

20 Dominion Day, now Canada Day, is July 1st, but the celebrations would not be held on a Sunday.

to write till now, and even now I can only snatch a few minutes at breakfast time.

Dominion Day was a great success here. We drove down with the ponies early. The first part of the programme was the sports—running, jumping, throwing, etc. The champion for running in North England has taken up land in the neighbourhood and was present, he however was successful in only one race—I do not think he was exerting himself. At midday the company was treated to dinner provided by the ladies of whom there are quite a large number in the settlement.

In the afternoon the games were renewed. The only items I really enjoyed were the ox, pony and horse races. The ponies particularly ran well. Wimpie Fields, a little half-breed, ran Puss, but she was out of order far too far, and no preparation, and I think the jockey was rather diminutive. However, Puss came in 5th in two heats. The third heat I did not let her run. We now adjourned for supper, also provided by the ladies.

Then came the great event of the day, the concert. It was a grand success. The Town Hall was just crammed at a [?] a head. The orchestra was composed of two violins and flute, and played remarkably well. The comic element was presented by three negroes with calico trousers, red shirts, unmistakable handkerchiefs and peaked hats. The Hallelujah Band, their songs, conundrums, speeches and dancing afforded a great deal of laughing. One of the niggers was Cribben,[21] who was formerly schoolmaster in Leeds. Two recitations I gave were highly appreciated. The performance was concluded by singing the National Anthem at twelve o'clock.

Then came the scatter. Many would not get home till daylight. We thought it better to camp till daylight—Mr. Ross, the English clergyman, was very kind, gave us liberty to sleep in the town hall. He resides in the upper part. Brought us down some Be-aw[22] to get us asleep, I expect, then supplied us with rugs. With these and the curtain we slept very comfortably—Teulon, E. Pagan, Andrew and I. It was really an enjoyable day—rather warm possibly.

The greater part of that week had been very hot, the thermometer once registering 132 degrees. Day after day for nearly two months

---

21 Or possibly McGibbon.
22 Imitation of upper-class English pronunciation of "beer."

back the sun has been glaring down on us uninterruptedly all day long, with hardly a drop of rain. We are hoping every day to get rain. The crops want it badly now. The garden is getting on famously, the potatoes and Indian corn particularly. Next Sunday we expect to have new potatoes.

I forgot to mention that I saw Miss Bryant at the games and concert, but I did not get an opportunity of speaking to her—she seems to be very diffident. She is looking very strong and well. Her brother Arthur was standing around with his newly married wife. Alf Bryant was over here on Sunday. His house is rapidly approaching completion. He insisted on us going over there next Sunday after church. Now I must conclude.

By the bye I am glad your exchequer is getting so full. I should be very glad if you could send the money here, but be sure you can spare it. I am anxious to work into stock raising as quickly as possible—it is the most profitable and at the same time the most to be depended upon. Besides, our farm has advantages that are unequalled for stock. In two months I expect that we will be self-supporting, and all the money we can get or earn will be invested in machinery or animals that will yield good returns, but remember you must pay attention to your own interests—we cannot know how you are situated. . . .

Andrew is very sorry that he has incurred the displeasure of the young lady in your household with regard to the puppies. I daresay Andrew is less to blame than I am. Should a like necessity occur again I wonder if cremation would be a more merciful and humane plan. My next letter I trust to make longer and more readable. . .

Your affectionate brother
Willie

Woodvale, Shell River, Man.
18 July 1883

My Dear Maggie,

We duly received your last letter, and we were very glad to learn from it that despite your well-founded fear you were still to get your parchment. We congratulate you in the result of your long hard course. . . In my last letter I apologized for its brevity and promised to make amends this time, but circumstances will not permit of this. We are just now busy hay-cutting, and the days seem too short to perform the amount of work we would like to do. The work will now, till frost appears, flow in on us fast and furious, and it must be done—and I know you will excuse my short letter. Letter writing is to me becoming like a lost art. Each time I seem to be getting slower, less satisfied with it. . . .

Andrew is now home from ploughing for Teulon. He earned £6 in two weeks. So far we have only sold £8 worth of lime, but in every way we are getting on well and hopefully. Yesterday we commenced haycutting—today has not been very favourable for that work, occasional showers troubling us.

Last night I camped out on my place alone with the ponies. This I require to do to satisfy the government, who insist on each settler sleeping and eating a portion of his time on his claim. The mosquitoes were very troublesome. I was continually under the necessity of getting up and putting fuel on the "smoodge" (a heavy smoke fire to drive away the pests).

This year the hay cutting will be a pleasure compared to last. The ponies work exceptionally well in both the mower and sulky rake. We are cutting in the river valley, a picturesque spot. The crops are looking remarkably well after the rains we were blessed with last week. The garden particularly is the admiration of everyone who visits us. We are under the necessity of adding to our cellar accommodations to store the produce of it away against the winter.

Last Sunday we drove over to the service now held at Johnstone's house, quite close to Arthur Bryant's house where Miss Bryant resides, but we discovered we were an hour late, so we did not intrude. We met Alf Bryant, the one you met in London. We went to his house, where we had dinner. Towards supper time it began to rain, and we also had supper. When we did get home we were wet, wet.

On Monday I rode up to Teulon's and visited Mr. Powis, our new settler, a little gentleman. He wanted to see me about doing some ploughing for him, but we could not come to an agreement owing to him not knowing the boundaries of his claims. On the way back I called on the Langfords and met their father, an army captain just out from Dublin, paying his sons a visit and prospecting. He has been too long among Hindoos and Irishmen to appreciate our independent ways. How he did declaim against the outspokenness of the countrymen and the want of respect shown to the representatives of the best blood in Ireland. Altogether he is a very free and easy gentleman, but still too much of the gentleman to live long happy here. How scandalized he was to find the house his sons built for themselves nothing better than a miserable hencoop. He was at our place today. They are devoting their whole time to sporting. I am set with the duty of cutting 10 tons of hay for the boys at [?] per ton, and something will be very far wrong if I do not manage it in two days. They haul and stack it themselves.

Last mail I received my appointment as Agricultural Correspondent for the district to the Government Board of Agriculture. No salary, but I consider the honour and the great privilege of a special admission ticket to the Provincial Show[23] which, if I cannot use, I can at least frame and exhibit. Andrew went down for the mail on Tuesday and came home sick, but he is all right now. I think he has been a victim to the craving for new potatoes. Last Sunday Papa and I were down looking at the hay meadows on the river, and we started a deer, the first we have really seen. We see their tracks occasionally, but they are very shy. On Tuesday I surprised a large timber wolf feasting his eyes on our calf. They are big fierce brutes. The calf is better looked after now. Now I must stop. We are well and in good spirits . . .

Your affectionate brother
Willie

Woodvale, Shell River, Man.
18 August 1883

My Dear Maggie,

. . . Since my last letter Father and I have been from home a fortnight. We started out for Brandon Thursday two weeks ago, and got down there with the ponies, 130 miles in two days and a half!

---

23 At Portage la Prairie.

We were quite astonished at the progress Brandon has made. When we knew the place at first it was a bare bleak hill facing the river, only one little shanty upon it. Now it is all covered with houses, with a population of 4,000, nicely graded streets and modern paveways, two traffic bridges and a railway bridge cross the Assiniboine, immense structures, a number of fine buildings and churches. You see what a railway can do.

We remained in Brandon four days. We could ill afford the time, but it was unavoidable—we had to wait on some money from Portage. We went to see our old neighbours—they are all happy and prosperous. Our old place was just as we left it, with the exception of a little extra ploughing. We got some poultry to take home, and now we are favoured with chanticleer's alarm in the morning. We bought another team of horses. Very quiet, easily wrought animals they are, both a chestnut colour and are really a splendid looking team. We are very much pleased with our bargain.

On Thursday we started homewards, returning along the C.P.R. track to Moosomin, 110 miles distant, where we got delivery of a binder. We then turned our faces northward, and after travelling 70 miles we reached home to find Andrew well.

It was a long wearisome journey. Along the plains to Moosomin there are very few houses and nothing but bad water, and that always makes me ill. The day after I got home I was very sick. I am all right now. We camped out all the time. I only had my clothes off once during the whole time, and owing to scarcity of space in the waggon I had to sleep on the prairie.

Yesterday we were busy building up the binder. They are a most extraordinary invention. Our one binds the grain with cord. They do not leave a single straw on the field, and they bind the grain neatly and firmly. This afternoon I expect to be cutting barley with it. Next week we will be at harvest in earnest. Andrew is getting ready to start for Russell, so I must stop. Surely the time will soon come when I can write you long letters—meantime the days seem too short to do all the work we would like. Wishing you all a very pleasant holiday, we unite in sending you our kindest love.

Your most affectionate brother
Willie

Woodvale, Shell River, Man.
24 August 1883

Dear Maggie,

I am sure you would be astonished when you received the empty envelope with last mail. The mistake happened very simply—I addressed the envelope while the others were reading the letter, and Andrew, in the hurry of starting, overlooked the want of the letter, and I did not notice he was without it till sometime afterwards. You must excuse the mistake, and above all things do not follow the example—it would be a great disappointment.

Now we are in the midst of the harvest, and very busy. The binder works very well. I feel quite immense elevated on top of it, with a nice team of horses in front, laying low the golden grain. It falls on a canvas immediately behind the knives. This canvas is constantly revolving, and it carries the grain in between another two elevator canvasses. These in turn put it on a platform, on which two packing arms work. These pack it up against a trip, and when the sheaf is the proper size it presses the trip away. This sets the binding appliance to work in the shape of a large, semi-circle needle that clasps the sheaf round and inserts the cord into the knotter where the string is fixed. After this is done, two boards fall away and the sheaf is thrown off, completed by three revolving arms. Altogether it is a wonderful invention. It does not leave a loose straw on the field, makes a neat sheaf and ties it firmly so that it cannot be unloosened—it must be cut. Surely the farmers in the old country will be turning their attention to them. What an immense amount of labour it would save them. They cost here about £70. We will finish our harvest in four days or so, after that I mean to hire out to do cutting for other people.

I have no news of any importance. We are all well and in great spirits. Tomorrow I purpose riding down to Russell. By the bye, I have been grievously disappointed. We had a Captain Langford from Dublin in the neighbourhood visiting his son. He is an enthusiastic amateur photographer, and I was indulging in the hope of giving you a genuine surprise. Our being away from home was to blame in the first instance, but the cause was an urgent letter desiring him to start home at once. This he did faithfully, and I was disappointed of my photograph of our place.

We have had now good news and decided about the railway. On our way home from Brandon we met with one of the railway "bigwigs" on his way to Shellmouth en route for Prince Albert. He promises us the railway [for] certain next fall, and if this was not sufficient to cheer one up, he was followed by an official from another railway company. And it is reported this railway is also to traverse our neighbourhood forming a junction hereabout. So we shall soon be in the midst of business and civilization. . . . I fear my short letter must now close. Have patience with me, and I will soon satisfy you with longer letters. I am getting quite ashamed of my arrears of correspondence . . .

Your most affectionate brother
Willie

Woodvale, Shell River, Man.
22 September 1883

My Dear Maggie

I am sorry I had to disappoint you without a letter last time. I was so busy, and had to write both Uncle Hugh and Henry. I am quite ashamed of the way I am treating you just now with letters, but really at night I feel so tired and jaded that I cannot think to open my desk. The nights are getting longer, and probably this may help me to amend my ways. . .

Since my last letter, or rather since Andrew's, nothing of great importance has occurred. I took the binder over to Frank Bryant's, but after cutting a day or so it broke down and I had to come home. On Tuesday we went back for it, and on the way father shot nine chickens. I got the binder home all right and found the agent waiting to get a settlement for it. We gave him to understand he might take it away with him—certainly we would not pay for it this year, and not till it was set in thorough working order again.

You will be surprised I daresay to hear that Miss Bryant is engaged to be married to Glover,[24] a gentleman who came out from Bradford, England last year. He is not a great farmer, but he seems to have plenty of money. I saw Miss Bryant at Russell a week or two ago—she seems very shy and distant. I took the liberty of introducing myself, but the conversation was very one-sided. She had heard of your calling at her sister's. She is quite well now and looking a great deal better. It is reported that Alf Bryant is engaged to marry a Half-breed girl, a sister-in-law of DuPre's.

Teulon has met with a sad mishap. He passed our home some time ago to go to Russell. It was near sundown so I advised him to stop with us, but he would go on. He camped about four miles distant, and evidently got cold during the night. Next morning when he got to Russell and was doing some business in a house there, he swung around and fell on the floor in an epileptic fit. After a time he was all right again, with the exception of his arm. It was thought to be sprained, but it appears to be out of joint. He was home for about a week, but the pain decided him to go to Birtle. Last Sunday he passed here with Ross, the English clergyman. Since then a week has elapsed. We have heard nothing of him and we are just afraid he has to go to Winnipeg for medical treatment. It is a great pity for him. He has a lot of sisters at home doing nothing, yet he cannot persuade any of them to join him. Certainly his liability to these fits makes it dangerous for him to be alone.

Owing to my going to the Bryants I missed a treat—Ian Langford shot two geese down on the river. They measure from tip to tip of wings 5 feet and weigh 40 lbs. With the usual generosity and recklessness of Irishmen, he and some friends demolished them in one night. They are very plentiful around here just now on their migratory tour down south. But they are so wary that it is not everyone who has the time to circumvent them. The wolves are very plentiful, making a dreadful din with the howlings at night.

We have now got all our harvest completed and are now busy ploughing. On Monday we will set to work and build a granary. We

24 The Glovers lived two miles from the Wallaces, but by 1891 were living in Winnipeg. The bride died of cancer in 1892.

are anxious to get as much done now as possible, as I would like to have time before winter to hunt up a homestead for Andrew.

I am not doing much at the violin just now, but anytime you have an opportunity you might buy me, say, two books of music, one country dances, the other operatic pieces or lively airs. . . . So hurried and confused have I been lately that I have not informed you how we stand financially. I think we will now manage to get along pretty well, although we have some heavy payment to meet soon. I will try to get employment in the bush this winter. If I get that we will be all right. Do not put yourself about over sending money unless you can do so easily. Your holidays would be very expensive I know, and may have interfered with your intention of sending £10. If you think you can send us that easily soon I shall be glad, but do not sacrifice your own interests. I must now conclude—the others are hurrying me . . .

Your most affectionate brother
Willie

Woodvale, Shell River, Man.
4 October 1883

My Dear Maggie,

. . . Since my last letter there has been at least two events to break the monotony of a prairie existence. Previous to these we had been busy getting the fruits of our garden stored away in the cellar. The garden has yielded exceedingly well. Of potatoes alone we have laid past 180 bushels. And previous to the final taking up, we, with the help of the "grumphies,"[25] must have consumed over 20 bushels. We only planted seven bushels of seed. We have 30 bushels of carrots and two bushels of beets, besides turnips, parsnips, cabbage, onions, leeks, peas and beans. Can you imagine how we can utilize all these during the winter? Surely you must feel tempted to come and help us cook them. The horses and cow are getting as frisky as lambs on turnip food. The sweet corn, popping corn and sugar cane all got frosted.

---

25 A Scottish word for pig.

After we got the garden ground cleared up Andrew set to the ploughing and Father and I dodged around doing necessary odd work. While doing this I met with a misfortune. One of the oxen got lamed by a stick piercing his hoof, and consequently I had to fetch in a load of hay with the ponies. These do well enough so long as the load is not too big or the road too steep. They cannot abide holding a load back before going down the hill to the stable. With this load I fastened a chain on one of the wheels to make it drag somehow. After I had started, the chain slipped and let the load go with a rush, then it caught and jerked up, only to let it slip again. This shook me off the load, over the front, and behind the ponies. To clear the wheels I just managed to jump on to the double tree. After that it took me all I was able to cling on, so that I could not shorten the reins and check the ponies from a trot. They broke into a gallop and passed the stable like a shot, right down into the valley. When we got near the bottom they dashed into the young wood. The saplings thrashed my legs most unmercifully, the stronger ones battering them up against the wheel. At the bottom there is a short but very steep bank. In going over it the whole business upset and came to a standstill. After collecting my thoughts for a second or two I crawled out from the ruin, and was considerably relieved to find my legs were not broken. Wonderful to relate, the only injuries I had received were a pair of cudgelled legs, a knock on the head, a scratched cheek, a tender shoulder and thigh, a big rent in my shirt, my new trousers split at the knees, a bruised heel and a heelless boot. The final pitch was to blame for these latter items. The hay, the hay frame, waggon box and waggon were lying in separate and distinct heaps, but nothing was seriously damaged. Since that day, Tuesday, till today, Saturday, I have been first hopping then hobbling around, very sensitive to external influences. By Monday I expect to be quite able for active outdoor work. The ponies were none the worse, rather proud of the feat. The cute little monkeys had dodged the stumps very well in their own interest, and by doing so saved the waggon from being wrecked.

This little catastrophe cost me a treat—I could not go down to the Agricultural Show next day. It proved to be a wonderful success. We got first prizes for carrots and onions, and second for beets. Had our seed been prime and our grain threshed we would have got more. We did not show any of our stock, although Andrew thinks Puss, the gray pony, would have had a first chance. There was a great turn of people, and from reports I imagine it could not have been more successful.

You may remember my mentioning Shaw and Walker in my former letters. They crossed the Atlantic in the same steamboat and are settled about eight miles from us. Shaw has got married to a Glasgow girl who came all the way alone to Winnipeg, where he met and married her. Her name was Miss Berta Latta. Shaw's people belong to the better grade—his father is an army officer. Walker has recently fallen heir to £700. He is quite a wealthy man now, buying land, etc. Both were formerly sailors.

The directors of the railway company are to meet the settlers on the 19th to make proposals, so we expect the iron horse will soon be in our midst. Three railways are reported coming this direction— this has caused a stir. Building is going ahead at both Russell and Shellmouth, and they are beginning to look more like towns.

Andrew is now eighteen years old, and as soon as an opportunity offers he will go down to Birtle (the land office is there) and take up the east half of section 4. This corners on my claim and is in the river valley. It is very rich, heavy land. We cut our hay on part of it this year. The only drawback to it is that when the river rises part of it is covered with still water. When we come to utilize the land for cultivation we expect to be able, by the aid of drains, to carry off this water at once.

This idea has decided us to change residence. Just now we are living on Father's claim. We purpose removing over to the valley and putting up a permanent and substantial house on the line between my claim and his. This diagram will explain better. I just got this diagram down so that you may know how we are situated. This addition will give us 960 acres of land. We will begin building the new farm-steading next summer.

The change will give us a great many advantages. We will not have so far to dig for water, as we will be down in the valley. The cattle will get better pasture with water and we will always see them. We will be nearer Shellmouth by a mile, near the river where we can get plenty of ducks and fish, and near abundance of hayland, and we will get wood also handy on Andrew's lot. These are all great advantages.

I wish you could see the proposed location. The opposite banks of the valley are thickly covered with wood, just now clothed in the gorgeous autumn hues common only to Canada. Below that is the broad, swift-flowing Assiniboine. Between that and the house are two large lakes, and still nearer a long belt of timber. The valley here is pretty much north and south. To the north the view extends to Langford's shanty only, but to the south the view is extensive, the headlands jutting into the river valley giving it quite a highland appearance. Now I must close. Andrew will not write this time—I am afraid he is very busy making up for my absence in part in the field and in the stable. . . .

Your most affectionate brother
Willie

Woodvale, Shell River, Man.
18 October 1883

My Dear Maggie,

I trust you are not paying me back in my own coin. How disappointed we were when the last mail bag contained no letter from you—unfortunately my past conduct causes me to forbear from expatiating on the enormity of your omission. Probably next Tuesday my wounded feelings will be soothed over when I discover that Her Majesty's service has been at fault, or you have transmitted a long letter containing a sufficient excuse.

Since my last letter I have got to my feet again and we are all getting along as brisk as ever. Andrew has been the most of the time ploughing and our cultivated land is nearly all blackened again. Father and I have been in the bush cutting logs, hauling them up to the house and placing them in shape for a granary.

The weather has been very disagreeable—cold and cloudy for the last three days, raining—more or less recalling uncomfortable recollections of the old country in its worst humours. Tonight the stars are peeping out, and Jack Frost is hardening up the "mushrooms" each night. Now he will be making his power more distinctly felt. Clouds prevented us seeing the eclipse of the moon.

For some weeks back we have given the pigs the full run of the place, and they have been causing amusement. For a day or two after they got out of the pen they scampered about like mad ones conjuring up imaginary ghosts. They give a great "bouf" and scatter as hard as their little legs would carry them till their imagination would get the upper hand again. They have the whole geography of the place off by heart. They quite understand ploughing. If no other amusement is to be had they presently plod up and down the furrow. At one time they will graze with the ponies, at another with the cattle, and there is no escaping their company to the hay slough about a mile distant. And they show their displeasure if the horses run too hard by grunting viciously. They will smell the oxen out down the bush trail, and such an injured attitude they strike when the log bumps in too close proximity to their legs. But their crowning delight is to see you unoccupied, when they will come to you squeaking in a high, and to their idea, conciliatory tone, give your boot a prod with their nose, and then stretch out full length. A nice scratching stick, well applied, is to them the essence of extravagance and pleasure, so much so that they will lie over on their side and appear oblivious to all earthly things. They have only two affections. The cow and the dog are at constant enmity with them, the dog particularly so, if they dare to come near the house about dinner time when bones are plentiful. Now after this long tale would you not be tempted to come and help us to kill and eat such amusing pets?

Inside the house the kitten keeps things lively all day long. It is jumping around putting on warlike attitudes at the dog ... If it can induce the cat to come near it when it is elevated on a box, the spitting and defiant attitudes are something to laugh at, and no matter who or what it is, it distinctly resents liberties with its tail.

All the other animals are getting on well. The horses and ponies are getting fat. The horses can plough 1 acre with a twelve-inch plowshare in a day. The prairie chickens are exceedingly plentiful and tame just now. Often over fifty will be quite near the house. Yesterday four or five of them came down and began picking at the side of the house. Their presence affords us bountiful dinners— just now they are splendid eating. Wolves are also getting more numerous. The other morning about sunrise they awoke us by their dreadful howling. They seemed to be quite close to the house. We discovered one sable rascal spying out the position of things from the bank behind the stable. Henry Pagan was over here for his mail on Tuesday night. When riding home, one got ahead of him and snarled so that the horse was terrified out of its judgement.

On Sunday afternoon Andrew and I took a walk over to the Pagans, and when we got back we found Father entertaining Teulon, Powis, and Langford. Teulon is all right now, but he had to go to Winnipeg. We had great fun at Langford's expense over a pair of trousers he wanted us to bring him from Russell. Powis now has his house up. Langford has given up farming in favour of hunting. He had about an acre of wheat he left standing uncut to serve as a lure for geese. But so far the temptation has not succeeded and he has lost as much as would have kept him supplied with flour.

We are going down to Russell tomorrow to attend a railway meeting there. We are certain to have a railway next summer. No one in the old country can fully understand what this change will do for us. Already Russell presents quite the appearance of a town. I have not seen it for sometime, but I understand it boasts now of twenty buildings. A well is being sunk to supply water to a grist mill to be built immediately, and lumber is being drawn for a hotel. Shellmouth is also progressing. Everywhere bears token that the railway is coming. A land broker, no less, has started business in Russell. I hope in a few months to make you realize that London after all is a poor place. The posting of this letter and the going to Russell tomorrow did not till tonight strike us as having any connection, so you must excuse Andrew writing this time. Father says he will try and write you soon. We trust you are well and on good terms with your work. Remember us to the ladies with whom you reside. With the kindest love from us all, I am

Your most affectionate brother
Willie

Woodvale, Shell River, Man.
9 November 1883

My Dear Maggie,

I am almost ashamed to calculate how long a time since I wrote you. Last mail I fully intended writing you, but a long business letter caused me to break my resolution. Kindly forgive my omission this time . . . Andrew and I wonder very much if you purpose crushing all the knowledge of the age in your head—if you do you will soon be such a learned lady that we will be desiring an interval of half a year or a year wherein we can concoct suitable epistles for your critical inspection . . . Can you not stifle your over-powering ambition? Your long journeys to the Shrine of Art cannot be good for you. By all means keep it to the dull—it may come useful to you should you think of emigrating to Manitoba. A married lady in the other township has been gaining fame by ploughing. Another sister assisted her brother by plastering, and she could do that effectually, as she is somewhere about six feet tall. And still another aided her father, a retired army major, by building hay loads. And yet you and others will actually pay less to woman for the privilege of exerting yourselves. Can you explain this strange anomaly?

Notwithstanding this, however, we were glad to know that you are in such good spirits. Henry was quite right with regards to your money matters. Should you however discover £10 or £20 burning your pockets, please remember that ten per cent is a common rate in Manitoba, and that money and that only buys cows, and the possession of cows means the sale of butter and bacon.

We all congratulate you on your 22nd experience of a birthday, and trust each year will bring you increasing happiness and a never-failing supply of good health. I am afraid your card congratulating me on my birthday will be late in arriving, but no matter, I know your feelings regarding that event. I am glad to know that the increase of your years are not burdening you with a sense of dignity. Certainly they are not doing so in my case. Do you know that Andrew actually, and notwithstanding my nearly completing 25 years' experience of this world, deliberately lifted some mud (frozen, mark you) in his hand, aimed at me, and defiled me therewith. And would you believe it, I had so little dignity that I actually returned the compliment. This system of give and take was repeated frequently and greatly to the retardment of that noble pursuit, plastering. But I think my superior eye assisted me to direct the mud best of all, as Andrew had a bad five minutes discussing the taste, the smell and the feeling of mud in the eyes. This will give you some insight on the high state refinement has reached in this much talked of part of the world.

Andrew had so far left himself last week as to ride down to Birtle, 42 miles distant, and entered himself a landed proprietor in this land of frost and snow. And now our responsibilities are secured by a farm of 960 acres, 600 acres of which is arable, 100 covered by more or less valuable timber, 60 acres of a hay meadow in which a five foot man would at the end of the year be lost sight of. The remainder is hopelessly at present ruined by a covering of either willows, stumps, or shaking bog. The bog is a great feature of Andrew's claim. It is like a sponge and springs under you, elastic, swinging for a great distance. Possibly the day will come when the purely vegetable turf of which it is composed will be utilized for living.

For some time back all our energies have been spent on the building of a log granary 18 × 24 feet. We are now putting the finishing touches on it. Yesterday we finished the plastering of it inside. Today we were all over at the Assiniboine for hay with the sleighs. The first snowfall came on two days ago, but is so thin that the animals had hard work pulling the sleighs. Tonight it is snowing and blowing furiously—the wind whistling and howling in a way that makes us feel comfortable inside.

For two days this week I have been "climbing the walls" with a full-fledged toothache. It was awfully painful. How I did wish myself back in Glasgow in the merciful neighbourhood of a dentist. I incurred the trouble while away at Brandon through sleeping out, I think, and it is more the form of neuralgia. Have you any nostrum? This has been a painful autumn to me, but never mind, where there is life there is hope.

We hope to get our threshing done next week and then we will better know how our profit and loss accounts will stand.

Last Monday Papa and I drove up to the Assissippi[26] Saw Mill for lumber boards for the granary. I have been near but never at the place before. It is a pretty but a perilous looking hole. The Shell River flows down from the north to this point, after which it turns a right angle and flows west, and the town is situated on the point. You see it almost directly underneath when driving along the banks—the descent is very steep. The town itself is not much, but promises well. It boasts a store, a gristmill, nearly finished, a sawmill working, a smithy, and a "Hotel." The place is about nine miles from here.

We were accompanied by Henry Pagan but, poor fellow, his horses bolted from him, and after capering around for some time, left the waggon in a bluff of trees, and shortly afterwards were themselves brought up by a tree. But his waggon and harness were so badly damaged that he had to go back empty.

We got 400 feet of lumber for which we had to pay £2 10s. This will show you how the money goes. We got home about sundown.

The prairie fires have been very fierce and brilliant on the other side of the river. They must have done fearful destruction. Over 200 tons of hay was burned on this side this fall—our district, however, escaped. I cannot imagine how settlers can so carelessly leave their stack unprotected.

The wolves, chickens, and rabbits are very numerous. Just now the first mentioned make the night hideous with their howlings. They seem to hold parliamentary meetings on Andrew's farm. Ted Pagan shot a large eagle last week. It is quite black and measures six feet from tip to tip of wings, with huge talons and beak. It was calmly anatomizing a rabbit when it met its fate. I am baking now so must conclude... remember us kindly to your friends—the young lady who so promptly expounded the cause of the defunct pups in the last letter can have a beautiful black and tan puppy dog on making personal application as reward for compassionate indignation. With kindest love from us all and every good wish for your happiness I still am

Your affectionate brother
Willie

---

26 Assissippi, now a ghost town, began to decline when it was learned that the railroad would pass it by.

Woodvale, Shell River, Man.
24 November 1883

My Dear Maggie,

Father received your letter last night, and we were glad to learn from it of your welfare. I have been so busy that I have not left time to write you a long letter. All this week and part of last we have been busy threshing, and this entails on us arranging to help neighbours in return for their help. Last week we—Andrew and I—were down at the Haworths. We waited a whole day, but the steam-thresher did not turn up till the evening. On Monday, the mill broke down and we did not finish what ought to have been done in three hours till late on Tuesday evening. On Wednesday we were at the Pagans' and there the mill again broke down, and again a half-day's work extended itself into a day. These poor fellows were nearly ruined providing for the threshers the extra length of time. On Thursday they came here, and wonderful to relate, they finished us in one day. At their former rate working it should have taken three. We had fourteen extra hands to provide for all day, and we were thankful to see them take their departure that evening. Another day, yesterday, was lost at Teulons, as the threshers lost their trail, and it was evening before they finished. Today I will drive down to Russell to post this letter and give three of our neighbours a sleigh drive as a reward for them helping us.

The crops have yielded very poor, only half a crop, but still that is not bad for an exceptional bad season. We will only have 500 bushels of grain, and will most likely realize £10, but I will explain this further in my next letter. I cannot write any more as our sleigh-riding neighbours are here and it is all talk, and one can't think under such circumstances. We are all well and in good spirits. Next time I write we will be more settled and have more time. With kindest love from us all I am

Your most affectionate brother
Willie

Woodvale, Shell River, Man.
4 December 1883

My Dear Maggie,

I fully purposed writing you a long letter this, but circumstances which I will explain further on prevented me. We have now got over the mess we were in after the threshing and had just settled into our usual routine when we were again disturbed on Sunday night. After we had all gone to bed I heard a halloo outside. Wondering who was out so late, particularly as it had been a very stormy cold day, I made haste to entertain visitors. In short time a stranger, who eventually turned out to be the Shellmouth schoolmaster[27] and Methodist local preacher, stumbled in quite done out with exhaustion. He had, while out travelling, lost himself, and had been wandering hopelessly over the prairie seven hours till he found our house. Another hour, I believe, would have finished him. The foolish man, a stranger to this country, had on only a pair of boots, and when after some trouble we got these off, I found his feet badly frozen. We got them thawed out, but during the whole night he moaned and groaned with pain.

Next morning he was helpless, and I had to hitch the horses and drive him up to Shellmouth. Last Sunday Andrew and I drove up to ask after his welfare. There he was, calmly permitting his feet to mortify. Yesterday I had to drive over and inform his brother-in-law and wife of his condition and get them to look after him. My Samaritan intentions led me into a long drive—28 miles.

Today I went up to Teulons and from there to Shellmouth to hunt up some money owing us. And there I found the poor man's friends getting ready to take him away. He is now on his way to Winnipeg, and the probabilities are he will lose the half of both his feet. It is a pity of the poor man, as he only came out from Manchester, England, last spring with no money, and a wife and two little boys depending on him. But he is a stamp of man who ought never to have left the old country.

---

27 A Mr. Hardy was the first teacher at Shellmouth.

When I was at Shellmouth today I made our first prominent attempt at selling our produce, and I did so to advantage—I sold nearly £3 worth—so much for the advantage of being in the neighbourhood of a city.

Yesterday I saw Frank Bryant's family—a new arrival in the form of a boy, a bright, intelligent little baby, and his parents are proud, proud and careful.[28]

Mrs. Shaw has had to travel all the way back to Glasgow owing to the death of four near relatives.

I am very much hurried for time as I purpose starting tomorrow for Moosomin station on the C.P.R., 70 miles from here. I am going down for a fanning mill and some provisions. I shall be away five days at least. This explains my haste, but I promise to make ample amends when I come back and we are settled into our winter routine.

There is to be a grand concert at Russell Saturday week, and I was pressed to allow my name to appear on the programme. Do you envy me? We are all well and in good spirits. . . . Excuse my haste, as I must now set to and sew some of my garments. With kindest love from us all,

Your most affectionate brother
Willie

Woodvale, Shell River, Man.
22 December 1883

My Dear Maggie,

. . . Willie was down at Moosomin last week for a fanning mill. He did the journey in four days and a half. If he had had oxen it would have taken him over a week, so you see one benefit in having horses. This week it has been very cold, the thermometer being as low as

---

28 The baby's name was Fred; his nickname was "Freddie the Songster." He died aged 20. The first white child born in the Russell district was George C. Boulton, born October 26, 1881.

forty below zero. We have all escaped being frozen this turn, but one of our hens got frozen still.

Papa and Willie were up at Assissippi with a load of wheat yesterday. They got a dollar a bushel for it, so we will perhaps realize more from our crops than we think. Willie has been very much troubled with toothache this week. He may perhaps write something yet, but at the present time he feels too bad to do anything....

Your affectionate brother
Andrew

1884

Woodvale, Shell River, Man.
4 January 1884

My Dear Maggie,

Andrew last week received your letter with the very pretty and appropriate Xmas card... I do not think I wrote you that Miss Bryant was married. Nobody but the family were at the ceremony, and for some time outsiders thought they were being joked when told. Mr. Glover, her husband, is a nice frank fellow and seems to have plenty of money. Just now they are at Winnipeg. A neighbour with his men are busy housebuilding and fencing on his place some distance from here, on the other side of the river.

You ask if I am capable of making a Xmas pudding. I have already proved myself quite capable, unfortunately the stores hereaway had not the materials in stock this time, but it did not matter much, as Andrew and I were enticed away to help to eat our neighbours'. We both proposed going to the Pagans, but in the afternoon when fanning out grain Langford came over and insisted on my accompanying him and I had to submit. We were in a very select crowd—four Irishmen, a French Canadian, Teulon, and a Scotchman. We were treated to roast beef and plum pudding ... and Irish songs, speeches and jokes to no end. One would shout out "Hooray for Tipperary," but his cry would be mixed up with another's "Hooray for Donegal." The fun began when they got to the dancing in the small confined shanty. It ended when a couple tripped up and in their fall broke away the front platform of the stove, nearly setting the shanty on fire. The frost was pretty severe, and not relishing a freezing the company broke up. I had a splendid walk home down the Assiniboine valley—no moon, but the stars twinkling and glistening in a manner quite different from the old country.

When I got home I found Andrew still absent, and as I did not feel sleepy I set out to meet him and keep him company, but I found him at the Pagans' all quite comfortable, but miserably dull. After tasting their plum pudding and smoking some cigars we got the fun started. A Mr. Williams from England and said to have plenty of money has come to live with the Pagans and see the country—he got acquainted with their father in Ontario. He is a pleasant youth and has brought up an amount of fancy rubbish and plenty of fine cigars. An organ costing $190 was to accompany him, but owing to a strike on the railway he had to leave it behind at Winnipeg. He expects it shortly.

We got home about four o'clock. We got up again about five o'clock when Father and I prepared to go to Assissippi with wheat to be made into flour. We had a very cold ride.

We spent New Year's day very quietly, going to bed early, as I had to get up early. It was election day, and I was Returning Officer at Shellmouth. After a hard walk I got up there, but I had nothing to do for a long time, as the ward[1] is only newly formed—the most of the voters were absent and the greater number of the settlers had not been settled the requisite time. Not till about four o'clock in the evening did the votes come, and then all in a drove. The polling hours were nine to five. Next election will be a busier one.

About six o'clock the whole crowd of us had supper. Father and Andrew had come with the crowd. After supper the seats were arranged, and about seven the residents flocked in and we had a concert. Father was chairman and we had songs, recitations, speeches, violin solos and etc. until 10:30. Ladies, I am sorry to say, were not a conspicuous part of the assemblage. Mrs. and Misses (2) Jackson, Miss Plaskett, and the two Misses Whaley[2] could not be induced to come or we might have had some dancing. Their father was [away] from home, and a Methodist local preacher or some such thing who lives with them warned and scared them into staying at home by telling them that meetings like these were poor preparation for "Heaven." What do you think of that for enlightened Manitoba?

---

1 The polling district.
2 Daughters of Matthew Whaley, first postmaster at Shellmouth.

After the meeting we hitched up the team and started for home, and whough, but it was cold! The cold had been very intense all day, and a bitter wind made it worse. The trail was all blown up, and we lost it, and the poor horses had terrible work getting through some of the drifts. When we got home in the morning we found the animals all right, but what howls and yells proceeded from the cats and dogs! They were feeling the cold very much. Everything in the house was frozen solid. I froze both my thumbs unhooking the snaps on the harness—they were frozen, and I had to take my bare hands.

Next morning I had to start out about sunrise for Assissippi and give in my returns, Andrew following with the horses. Later on I had a nice smart walk of about eight miles, unconsciously sweating myself. When I got to the village I learnt that the thermometer had gone down to 58 degrees below zero, the coldest we have yet had it. After giving in my returns I loitered about till Andrew came. They have got an organ in the town hall, but I resisted the temptation of spoiling my credit. I am afraid by the time I am able to buy an organ I will have forgotten all about it.

We did not get away till about sundown, and then my damp clothes bore bitter fruit. I had to run or walk the whole way home—the cold was so intense that on the exposed part of the face it felt as if it were being roasted before a fire. I was glad to get into the house with my nose frozen, my fingertips and my heels touched. Just when we had finished supper Langford rushed in, out of breath, muffled up beyond recognition. He had been over to the Pagans' for the mail—two postcards were our share. Haworth, who had brought it up, had dropped the papers on the trail, and we did not get them till next evening. Before Haworth left Russell the thermometer was marking 56 degrees below zero, and I should not wonder if it went down to 60 the next morning.

We got the papers and with them the Xmas Graphic, which Henry so kindly remembered in connection with us. We enjoy the pictures very much. Could you not send us some occasionally? I enclose an adv[ertisement] I have looked at longingly. We would like it very much Maggie if you would send us sometimes some readable matter. Do not send books, they seem to go astray, but magazines, pamphlets and such will, I am sure, come all right and be prized highly. We have no Sunday literature now at all, and it is impossible for us to go to church now. Can you not pity us?

Yesterday I had great baking—a batch of bread from our own flour, and it tasted good, good. If I were sending you a sample of it, do you think you could bake it? Newcomers, but more particularly shanty-men make flapjacks first of all. To provide themselves with a meal they cut three or four generous slices of bacon, parboil these in a saucepan and then frizzle fry it till it is like toast. During this process they mix up a mess of flour, salt, and water—if they have plenty of money, a little baking powder is mixed. The greater portion of the bacon fat will go into the mass, a little being left in the pan. The batter then takes the place of the bacon, and when it is sufficiently done on one side, the more expert ones will give the pan a toss, and catch the pancake when falling on the other side, and when this is sufficiently done the meal is ready. A good appetite supplies the rest. The dessert usually is a huge grid of black strap or black sweetened tobacco.

By the way, this explains the [unappetizing?] habits of the Americans. It is a hereditary complaint, and attributable to the flapjack-blackstrap propensities of their forebears. I have often indulged in such a meal, but when I did I was always hungry enough to enjoy anything . . .

Your affectionate brother
Willie

Woodvale, Shell River, Man.
22 January 1884

My Dear Maggie

Your last letter must I think have gone astray. We have not heard from you for a month. We trust you are well. Please carefully notice that you get a letter a fortnight previous to this one. I sent them down by a neighbour who was going anyhow, and somehow I don't think him very trustworthy. I sent a letter to Broomhill Drive at the same time—let me know if they got it. I could have kicked myself after sending them away, but I expect my suspicions are unfounded. . . .

Andrew, I see, is entertaining you with the hardships of hauling logs. My trouble is the cutting them. Fancy getting through the snow, tripping over snow-hidden obstacles till you get alongside a mighty tree about a foot through at the bottom and soaring away up, probably sixty feet. You cut down the surrounding willows and things till you get a clean sweep for the axe. Cold or hot, the jacket is a nuisance and is dispensed with. Careful aim is taken, and with a great swing the axe buries itself about an inch in the tree. Again and again this is done, then you strike further down and make the chips fly. Thus notching and nicking you continue till you get rather more than half through, then round to the other side and repeat the operation till the tree begins to creak, and giving it a final slap, off it goes by the [?] at a tangent, crashing down among the surrounding trees, and then with a great thud it lies motionless in a horizontal position. The branches have to be trimmed off—disagreeable work, as one has to battle and hit everyway because of the undergrowth. Then the tree is measured, cut at a length, and the top next demands your attention—it has to be cut and piled up so that the sticks may not annoy in the future lying loose around.

When engaged in this, Andrew will be heard crying "get up, Brownie," "what are you doing, Spottie?" Soon he appears, the logging chain is fixed round the log and off he goes, and I look around for more executionary work. Just now bush work is pleasant—no mosquitoes or foliage to annoy, and it takes a fearful lot of work to raise a shade of perspiration. The last fortnight has been actually devoid of any news worth relating. We have hardly been off the place. The weather has been exceedingly mild and pleasant.

The two ponies are now grazing on the prairie. Their natural instinct leads them to paw away the snow till they get at the grass. Puss—and she is the leader—pays the house a visit two or three times daily, and Kate follows her cautiously. Up they come to the door, and Puss will quietly but very meaningly open the door with her nose and take stock. With a little encouragement she would come in and take a seat by the stove, but we do not appreciate her movements in that way, as she is very quick—and should she get a hot carrot instead of a cold one or have any such impression which amounts to the same thing, she would just as soon back out through the window as the door. The former would be a more significant protest against treating poor beggars so. Should the door be snubbed they—the ponies—have a great fund of patience. They can wait. They are generally blessed with half a dozen carrots, and how slowly and joyfully and carefully they crunch them up. The other day while we were dining and the ponies lunching on carrot we heard a scream, and turning to the window we saw Puss' heels appearing and disappearing like lightning flashes. Puss had evidently been annoyed by a stick at her hindquarters, and it served her jealous purpose to blame Kate and give her a display of pugilism. Sometimes when trying to catch her I have seen her swoop in towards me, square her heels round on me and draw up her kicking muscles, but it never got any further than showing what would be done if she liked. Meg the mare and she have sometimes great duels. Altogether Puss is an oddity, but as wise and docile in harness as could be wished.

The pigs are another begging nuisance. They possess no patience, and they come to the door growling like a menagerie, and on arriving there you cannot think what heart-rending nerve-splitting screams they can emit, but that is not the worst—they get their snouts at the bottom of the door and give it a probe that you would think would either break the lock or door. They won't be gainsaid, and will only be bribed to silence by something to eat or drink. Two tacks were put at the door bottom, and it would have caused you to forget all your sorrows had you heard the fierce probe and then the silent meditative grunt afterwards—only for a minute, however—back at the nails it came to repeat the sensation.

The cow is another begging pet—at midday she gets a pailful of food. Her memory is short and notions of time crude. No matter what time a pail appears you may calculate Maggie is making at you with the speed of a hare from some point of the compass— with a sniff at the pail she wheels round in front and demands satisfaction or another chase. A calf called Curley also loafs around with his hands in his pockets and a straw generally in his mouth. He generally considers himself pretty badly off—but to run after anyone and beg, not he! That style of thing is above him. He is a thief, and an accomplished one too—no fence or barrier too high for him. If the jump is too high and he gets straddled halfway over, that don't matter—his forelegs will draw his hind ones over. [?] He makes the little puppy dogs mad, contrary to the general rule. He has a high intellectual forehead, surmounted by a plume of white hair standing upright and barely allowing two little white horns to show. He has long ears on either side and when the mess of pups appear he lowers his head to his knees and nervously twitches his ears forwards—this makes the dogs mad—a forbidden pleasure, the twitching ears—how they would dearly love to seize them, chew them, and rend them. Now I must stop. Andrew is off asleep, Papa is anxious to get him wakened so that we may all go off in the orthodox manner. Pardon my dearth of news and hurried scrawl. We hope your holiday was enjoyably spent—eagerly awaiting an account and news of you, we all unite in sending you our kindest love.

Your most affectionate brother
Willie

Woodvale, Shell River, Man.
4 February 1884

My Dear Maggie,

We duly received your last letter from Scotland a fortnight ago . . . Now the fact is, we are going to "strike" for longer letters, letters that will be more highly prized than the newspapers—and do not disappoint us! With the same mail I received two books of music— one of them I am particularly well pleased with, the other seems a little too advanced, but instead of German waltzes I wish you would have sent Country dances or something more popular. Probably my grumbling disposition tonight will get me that too. For a time the want of new music gave me a distaste for the violin, but the new books gave me a quiet recovery. I am very grateful to you for them.

We were sorry you could not send the socks—they are a very appreciable gift hereaway. Probably you did not leave the parcel open at the ends or you might have gotten them away cheaper in separate parcels. Out here socks cost 2/6[3] per pair, and sometimes a poor article at that. The ones you sent with the Bryants are still to the fore, although there is a lot of needlework about them now. During

---

3   Two shillings sixpence, or about sixty cents.

the winter when moccasins are worn, socks wear a long time, as many as three or four pairs being worn at one time—but we would prefer long letters to socks any day.

Since my last letter we have been getting on very quietly. I have no startling or noteworthy events to record. Our work has principally been hewing and skidding logs, and afterwards putting them on the sleighs and drawing them over to our new farm site in the valley. On Friday we were so employed when it came on a blizzard about midday. We got two loads over all right and were down in the creek valley loading again when we heard it blowing on the heights above, but not knowing the real extent of the gale we started uphill. When near the summit the snow blowing off the prairie above blinded us, but when we were so far we thought we would continue, and at the top we catched it badly. I thought the skin would have been roasted off my face, so intense was the cold and biting fierce the particles of drifting snow. After we got the logs off we were not long in galloping back, horses and oxen trotting as if for life, but the horses of course had the best of it, and I was home sometime before Andrew.

That night we discovered a swindle. We are so far advanced here that we do not use gas light—we burn a commodity styled coal oil in the lamps. When at Brandon we got a tin of this, and that night two or three inches of water at the bottom caused us to miscalculate our supply, so the light dropped out and we were in darkness. I went over to the Pagans and borrowed some. The opportunity for a quick chat caused me to get home late.

On the Saturday Andrew drove over to the Bryants and I trudged up to Shellmouth and had a day about town enjoying myself and trying to do business. On the way back Teulon intercepted me and forced me to keep him company all night. He is fond of the company, as he leads a solitary life. He expects a very near relative out to keep him company soon—a cousin of his fifth cousin. I never imagined Cockneys were so clannish or such good genealogists. This young man purposes getting an insight into the ways of the country under Teulon's direction.

I got back home on the Sunday in time for dinner, so you see I have been enjoying myself in a very questionable way. On Sunday Harry Pagan and his gentleman boarder helped me to reform by paying us a visit and getting supper. Yesterday I was housebound all day baking and churning. I baked twelve loaves, huge ones—what do you think of that? I think I am ahead of you in housely accomplishments. Now do you not feel small and humble?

When Canadians meet they are always anxious to have a trade on the barter system, and so deep-rooted is the failing that they will do it for fun. They will "swap" teams or anything for no earthly reason, and when an article is of more value than its opposite, the holder of the more valuable article will demand a margin in cash or its equivalent, and this is termed the "boot." Now, will you trade occupations with me? And how much will you give me to boot . . . The want of having something to write has led me into writing nonsense. With the exception of Father we are all well. He has had a bad cold for some time and is kept pretty much in the house.

The bachelors are going to give the settlement a grand Ball and Supper next week. It will most likely be a grand affair. As I have not the moderate sum of 8/4[4] to spare for such a thing, they will have my room but not my company, although I did receive a most pressing invitation to aid the management. I do not see the fun in feasting a lot of well-to-do farmers and their wives. The young ladies alone are, I think, sufficient, and alone worth the attention. I can think of nothing more to write about. Remember us to the friends and your household companions, and with best love from us all I remain

Your affectionate brother
Willie

Woodvale, Shellmouth, Man.
19 February 1884

My Dear Maggie,

We received your last letter rather early last week. The mail arrives at Russell twice a week instead of once as formerly. Two of our neighbours happened to be there when the second mail came in and they kindly brought along our installment of it that night. . . . I

---

4   About $2.05.

studied the Misses Pounds' more than kind message, and blushed, and cursed the distance that so much interfered with its full significance. The "fat, fair and forty" I cannot quite understand. The two former qualifications might do provided they were accompanied by the knowledge of milking cows and the manufacture of apple pie, a commodity all true Canadians really love. The "forty" will not, I fear, attract—all the local squires hereaway age from twenty to thirty, so I did not advertise the offer until you put me in possession of fuller particulars. English housekeepers are highly thought of in this settlement, so your household companions need have no fear of the result of the venture.

Last Wednesday Andrew drove down for the mail. This interfered with the work at home, so I took a holiday, and started out on a legstretcher of a walk. First I walked to the town of Assissippi and did a little business. From that to Willington Place—the name Adams[5] gives his farm. A dog gave the alarm and Mrs. Adams rushed out with anxiety depicted on her countenance. This anxiety quickly allayed when she discovered it was only me, and when I got to the door I discovered the cause was Mr. Adams' deshabille condition, owing to his wife repairing his nether garment—his trousers. I found him getting back from his hiding place in his pants—this will show you the rural character of our farms, and this one only a mile from town.

After getting my dinner and a talk I started again. Among other things he told me something about Ft. Pelly, 90 miles north, where he had been. At that place there is a trading post, a Mounted Police station, and some officials concerned with the Indians, besides a few settlers—but strange to say, though this place has no postal service, it has a telegraph office, and all their communication with the outer world is by the latter. I suggested that loving bachelors would be awkwardly placed in such a situation—he, however, said no such class existed there—all were married. Behold how kind Providence is in the disposal of human affairs.

After a three miles walk I got to the Stewart's[6] farm. Both are Perthshire men, where they had been sheep farming. Latterly

5   John Adams, 34-22-28.
6   Walter Stewart, 14-22-28.

Duncan had a business in Southport, England. Here again I was invited to [?] at the dinner table. They are very pleasant people, plenty of money, and the inside of their house literally covered with Graphic pictures.

What induces married men to come to this country? I can't see it is a good country to earn money, but I know where I could get the most enjoyment spending it had I had time.

I purposed going over to Cribbon's place, another independent gentleman, formerly a schoolmaster in Bradford or somewhere thereabout, [has] been at all the interesting spots in the world, a great linguist and the comedian of this settlement. Yet here he is, lord of 320 acres wild land and but a few acres cultivated, just beside himself with anxiety to see someone. I plodded on three miles farther and arrived at Frank Bryant's just in time to see Frank and his wife almost ready for the bachelors' ball. How I did tease them for being singular specimens of married men.

I drove with them two miles farther on to Alf Bryant's, passing Arthur's house on the way, astonishing Arthur and his wife with our levity about Alf Bryant. I was ignominiously expelled from the sleigh for being a money-grubbing, crabby bachelor. I hardly expected to find anyone at home, but my joy was great when my knock was responded to by Mrs. Glover (Miss Bryant formerly) asking me to come in. The mild day had resulted in a stormy-looking cold evening and I was dreadfully cold. After talking a little I was at the door to start out again when Walter Gordon, an Edmonton man, appeared and forbade me going any further, and really the look of things made me favourably disposed to accepting Mrs. Glovers' kind invitation to stay all night. In a short time Mr. Glover arrived from Russell and we four had supper. When so engaged I had reason to be glad I had not started out. The wind rose to a fearful extent so that I could never have found my way over the trackless and snow-covered prairie to our trail, a distance of two miles, so I contentedly remained, and we all played cards till midnight, when Walter Gordon departed for his place a short distance away. Then it was clear beautiful moon-light night.

Next morning was a fearfully cold one—25 below zero and blowing a perfect gale. I bade the Glovers good-bye and started like a deer for Gordon's place. Though it was only a short distance

I thought I would have been frozen. Once inside I was glad to be content till after dinner. Walter Gordon and his brother are bachelors. Walter particularly is the most perfect specimen of a Scotchman I think that I have seen in Manitoba. While at dinner he was remarking that Clara's pancakes the previous evening had been simply splendid, and we concluded that nowhere had any of us been so much reminded of our ante-Canadian days, everything so quietly and neatly done, the dishes particularly. During the whole time I never noticed a dish being washed, although that must have been done in the same apartment. Canadian ladies delight in showing that they can and do work, and washing particularly is so arranged as to attract the public. This may encourage the Misses Pounds.

After dinner Roderick McLellan came in, and glad was I to know that he would accompany me home. He was a Canadian schoolmaster, but now farms and owns a threshing mill—he at this time was collecting threshing [accounts?]. We started out, he on snowshoes walking serenely and placidly on the snow crust, while I laboured in it up over the knees, and he was great on the conversation. I managed to keep it up in a desultory manner, but "a haughty spirit goeth before a fall," and after about one mile had been accomplished his cap described a quarter circle whose tangent was 6 ¼ feet, and the snowshoes and the man were hopelessly mixed up and buried in the snow. I laughed and laughed again, and no effort of his could get them—the snowshoes—fixed on securely, and I inherited them for a time. Now I became talkative, but Rod would answer not a word. I left him at the Pagans' in due course, and about sundown reached home tired and satisfied with my long walk.

Since my last letter the weather has been exceedingly cold—the only exception has been the mild day I started out on my excursion. The frost has been very severe, and every day the wind blows and intensifies the cold. It is almost impossible to do much work outside—the half of our energies are expended on beating the cold out of the hands. I trust it may be a long time before we have again such severe winters. Everybody is grumbling and talking of a removal to the tropics.

We are still hauling logs when we find opportunity. Today we made three trips, the largest number we have yet made, but it was cold, cold. In a week or so the weather will surely get milder, when we can get to the building. Bed-time interrupted me, and now I must be off to my work cutting firewood. Andrew is getting out the horses to start for Russell. This morning is a clear bright one, and we seem to be sure of a fine day. I must compliment you on the last letter we received. We all remarked the pleasant change—scarcity of news prevents me this time following your example. We are all well. Father is a great deal better now and is going out this morning. He brought in a trapped rabbit—these animals are very plentiful, but I don't care much for them. With kind regards to your friends and our love to yourself, I remain

Your affectionate brother
Willie

Woodvale, Shell River, Man.
2 March 1884

My Dear Maggie,

We were disappointed of your mail last week—one of the horses had a cold, and we induced the Pagans to go down for it, but they had to come back empty-handed. The government had suddenly altered the arrival of the mail a day later. After this we propose going down on Mondays instead of Wednesdays. This time I cannot refer to a letter of yours—your letter will not likely be got till Tuesday.

Since last letter very little of importance has occurred. The severe cold gave way at last and instead we have had the opposite extreme. Last Monday we had 60° of heat—the snow looked as if it had a mind to disappear, but it didn't. Since that time daylight has brought a thaw and night frost more or less sharp. For two days back snow has been falling very steadily, whitening all the black patches again. These mild days are very disagreeable, causing feet and trousers bottoms to soak with wet and making bush work unpleasant. Last night the wind rose to a perfect gale, driving and blowing the snow in a way that made the house seem the essence of comfort. Tomorrow will I expect to finish the log cutting. In the meantime, and after we have them all drawn to their destination we shall begin to cut fencing poles.

The animals are all well now and getting fat. Should all go well we will have an increase to our stock this year in the form of two foals, a calf, two litters of pigs, and a great increase to our poultry. By the fall of the year when all are roaming around in the friskiness of youth our farmyard will have a very lively appearance. Andrew is now getting very uppish and speaks of turning his attention from slow going oxen to lively stepping horses.

Friday a week ago I had an excursion to Shellmouth. A number of neighbours were there voting on the advisability of introducing the herd law. The law is to save fencing—it insists on the owners of animals either herding their stock or fencing them into paddocks, thus saving the fencing in of grain fields. We are so situated that either way will suit us. We expressed ourselves indifferent and did not vote. The discussions on the subject among the settlers were very entertaining. The matter was ultimately compromised, and only certain districts placed under the law. The reward we have for our impartiality is that half our farm is under the new law—the other half is not, and this would suit us nicely were it not that our grain fields are already fenced. As our grain is under the herd law and our animals enjoy the old system, the result of this being we could be without fencing at all. Instead of voting I sold some flour to the townspeople.

On Saturday I went up to the Assissippi Mill with some grist, and with the exception of a pleasant drive nothing noteworthy happened. On Wednesday I again went up to Shellmouth to deliver the flour I sold. On the way up and not far from the house I happened to look back and discovered what I thought was one of the pups following, but a closer inspection showed it to be a large mink and a huge one. I never had the fortune to see one alive before, as they are very wary and live near water. Their skins are very valuable and particularly so some years ago when you young ladies considered their fur the correct thing. At that time they would be valued about 25/-, now they fetch something like 3/-. You see how your fashions (winter) affect the Indians. This particular one came along quite confidently and passed the sleigh about ten yards distant. In shape it was like a huge weasel or ferret, and larger than a cat a good deal, with a round bullet head, a capacious mouth and dangerous-looking teeth. Had I known their habits better I would have given chase, but I thought that would only fool me into a wade among deep snow. Now [that] I know they cannot travel very quickly, next winter when we are living in the river valley and not quite so busy I must try my hand at trapping, so keep up your spirits, I may be able to give you a fur set yet.

On Saturday Andrew drove back to Assississippi Mill for the flour. Snow fell all day, but it was mild and agreeable. He met Alf Bryant, who had been there on the same errand. Arthur I hear is coming over to buy wheat from us, but I am afraid he is behind—we disposed of a good deal of that commodity very advantageously, and what we have yet we expect to sell still more so.

I think I mentioned in my last letter about Mr. Gibben—he has at last seen the drawbacks he labours under for farming and has accepted what I hear is a very important scholastic appointment in the States. I don't know whether you met Pantelow [?], who came out here with Miss and Alf Bryant, and is a cousin, I think. He has also succumbed to the force of circumstances and has just gone to Toronto to a situation there. More of the superfluities will I daresay soon follow. Pantelow's father is I think Mayor of Windsor. Farrar is, I learn, on his way back from England, but above all Will Pagan who went to Ontario this winter is not only coming back with stock but with a wife and a brother-in-law. You will remember me writing about a Mr. Hardy, schoolmaster at Shellmouth, who lost his way thither and got to our house late with frozen feet. I afterwards drove him to Moosomin and put him on the cars for Winnipeg. He entered the hospital there. At first he got four toes amputated and got on well, but the remainder had to come off a month ago. The report is he appeared to be doing well afterwards, but next day he died from blood poisoning. I was very much shocked when I heard the news. His wife and family purpose going back to the old country. I have just been reading George Eliot's "Middlemarch." It is truly a perfect production ... I mean now to read up about stock. Have you no interesting magazines, pamphlets, or scraps to send? We are thankful for anything in that way here. I do not like to dictate, but still I think you might get some one of the magazines—you would enjoy the perusal yourself—and then send it on, and I am sure ours would be heartfelt enjoyment. You never let me know further about the books you at one time purposed sending. You may with safety send literature with paper covers, but not on any account hard bound. Excuse my impudence. I must now finish up and leave room for Andrew. With kind regards to your friends and our greatest love to yourself, I am

Your most affectionate brother
Willie

Woodvale, Shell River, Man.
26 March 1884

My Dear Maggie,

Father got your last letter, Andrew got the former one, and we were glad to learn the contents of both. I did not write last week and am very penitent. Will you forgive me? Further on you will understand the cause. I cannot tell you how much I appreciated the two magazines you sent—Chambers Journal and Carlyle's Essays— the opportunity of reading them gave me a new interesting life. The "Scraps" did not turn up. The childrens' party must have been very enjoyable. I noticed a paragraph in an English paper complaining of the unsettling influence such have on very young children— probably you saw it—I think the bad effects are exaggerated— certainly a continual round of dissipation would be injurious. We also saw an article exposing the hardships of Assistants under the London School Board. I really hope this is exaggerated, or at least that your school is one exception—we would certainly be very much grieved did we know you were slaving yourself, no matter what the compensation was, where you might as well be out here enjoying a rural and independent existence.

Since I last wrote we have been very busy cutting wood in the bush and afterwards hauling it to its destination in the river valley. During the last six days we have been even more industrious. The weather has been exceedingly mild, and today will, I fear, be the last of the sleighing unless more snow comes. Everything gives one the impression that this is the breakup and end of winter—should that prove to be the case the change will be a month earlier than usual. Fortunately our bush work is nearly concluded—what little still remains to be done can be managed without the snow, although not quite as expeditiously. I like bush work very much provided I am not hurried, but should I be hurried I get flurried, trip up among the cut branches and dead wood, tear clothes and sweat like a trooper. However when one is their own master they can suit their own convenience.

To give you some idea of the work, we have been cutting the logs 26 to 28 feet long and from ten inches to a foot in diameter. Two of these on the sleigh are a handy load for the teams. Last week Andrew and I pocketed our lunches two days and went over to the Assiniboine to cut fencing poles. The snow was very deep and we had to break a track about a mile wading to the knees. We cut in two days 330 rails with side posts additional, and at night we did not require rocking to send us into slumberland. Had you been with us and no snow but leaves and foliage, our luncheons would have had quite a picnic character—not a being within two miles, not a sound but an occasional rabbit passing about, the sun shining down with dazzling splendour—all these render the consumption of sandwiches, cold tea and tobacco very pleasant—I was going to write Arcadian, but a hard seat on a pile of rails and the prospect of again requiring to handle the axes would hardly harmonize with the idea.

After the cutting we had to set to and haul, then followed more log hauling. We had to get some hay, and last Friday I went up to Shellmouth—I took the oxen, as the snow was too deep to make any speed with the horses. All the journey up and back again I employed myself reading Carlyle's Essays, Browns' [?], and Sir Walter Scott. I did appreciate the other two. I could hardly understand the Essays—it seems to me one must be well acquainted with the subject.

At Shellmouth a large quantity of lumber is accumulating, and the prospects are great for a huge increase to the houses. Denmark, the Russell postmaster and storekeeper, will bring his family there soon and make that his home, and there is likely to be two sawmills going soon, with two stores. Another petition has been sent in for a post office and they have agreed about a postmaster—that want will soon be supplied. Mr. Whaley has been mentioned as postmaster—the young men hereaway appreciate that very much, as he has three daughters who can earn fame as well as distribute mail matter.

We are likely to have a rebellion or a revolution in this Province soon. The Manitobans almost to a man are kicking at the way they are being governed by the Federal authorities at Ottawa. Unions are forming all over the country, and delegates have been sent to Ottawa, but got no satisfaction. They now purpose appealing to the Imperial authorities. The misgovernment has been shameful. Most likely it will result in a new Confederation being formed of the Western Provinces, with outlet on the Pacific, Hudson's Bay, and Lake Superior. Railway monopolies will be ended, and free trade will the principal features of the change. These will bring us into closer sympathy with the Old Country; besides, the Hudson Bay route will place us here within ten days' journey of the Old Country.

The animals are all alive and kicking—horses, cattle, pigs, poultry, dogs and cats all in ecstasies over the fine weather. The younger ones cannot understand the black prairie and the streams of water. Everything is sloppy, dirty and disagreeable, but every day is warmer and pleasanter than the previous one, so that their discomforts will soon vanish. This summer will be a busy one with so much housebuilding besides the other work, but [by] the succeeding one we hope to be so circumstanced that we can receive a visit from that almost mythical figure, our sister Maggie. And once here I think the school board would find it hopeless work to persuade you back to resume the work after the holidays. Now I must stop . . .

Your most affectionate brother
Willie

Woodvale, Shell River, Man.
4 April 1884

My Dear Maggie,

I duly received your last letter yesterday . . . The bank note was very welcome. They are rare things hereaway, but quite current—we are very grateful. You must be careful and keep a reserve against a day of necessity. We all congratulate you on the nice long interesting letters you have sent for some time back—you cannot imagine how we prize them here. I am glad you have not been offended at my grumble—your letters are almost the only tie we have to the old country. . . .

A review of our three years' experience seems like a dream or a romance. Time has passed very quickly, still the three years seem to cover a long period, and it is only now we are beginning to realize that we are fairly settled and making headway. We are the only ones of all our neighbours who have made any money from our farming operations, and notwithstanding the poor season, we have realized as much as will pay a lot of old debts and new ones. In a month or so when other accounts become due (and which I expect to be able to pay) we will be independent and without a single debt in Manitoba and have as much as will tide us over till we can realize of this next harvest. Beside this we have money that has been making on the farm for short and long periods—this summer we hope to have two foals, one calf, two litters of pigs and three broods of chickens (one of the hens is hatching just now)—all these mean money to be realized before very long. Now seeing that last year was a bad year, and that many of our fellow settlers have realized no money at all of their farms, and in many cases will have to spend money for seeds and etc., do you not think we have done well? This year we expect a favourable season, and if prices are good next winter we will most likely lay the foundation for making our fortune.

A great many in the country are becoming disheartened, and rumours that the railway is not coming this year are making them even more despondent. A good harvest will raise all our hopes. This mail I am sending to Toronto for garden seeds, and we are likely to have a singularly nice garden again—among other things cucumbers, tomatoes, melons, besides tree seeds—sugar maple and silver fir.

In my last letter I wrote that it looked as if winter purposed taking its departure early. Since then the weather has kept mild, and the snow is almost gone. Whole tracks of the prairie are bare, and for a week back all the animals have been out grazing, kicking up their heels at the freedom and changed circumstance. Last night a flock of geese passed overhead steering for the great lakes north. They fly in long, long strings abreast and keep a horrible cackling. The change in the weather has kept us from getting on with much real work. The soft bare prairie and occasional snow banks cause it to be neither good for sleighing or wheeling. We have been fanning grain and getting the machinery in working order for the summer. We have had very few visitors, and things have been getting on very quietly. Father is quite well again, although for some time back he had been kept a prisoner in the house because of a cold he was troubled with. We are all well and in good spirits.

Last Wednesday I started out for another business tour on foot. The prairie was very soft and the trails, particularly the ravines, were not good for the horses. I journeyed due east from here. The first house I came to was on the adjoining section belonging to McDougall, a Highland man from Prince Edward Island.[7] He has all winter been sick and unable to do anything at Assissippi. His partner Corlett was inside—he comes from the Isle of Man. From there I crossed over the prairies passing south of Farrar's house and Perrin's house, both of which have been uninhabited all winter. Farrar has been in England—he is expected back next week. Perrin has been keeping store at Denmark and Brown's in Russell. The country up to this point was flat plateau, very much encumbered with sloughs and poplar bluffs. After this it descends into a low-lying swampy valley. At the other side are two houses, but I did not know the occupants so I passed on, and going up an opening with a hill on one side and a tree grove on the other I came to Attwood's[8] house, but I was just in time to see his horses first, then he and the sleigh disappear among trees, evidently in quest of firewood. He comes from Ontario.

From this point the country is very rolling with a great number of waterholes and hay flats. To the right the woods are seen in which Alf Bryant's house nestles, to the left the Thunder Creek bank, and away north the banks of the Shell River. The next house is Sennet's, down in the valley of Thunder Creek. He is in Ontario just now—his father is a Canon of the English Church there. By this time Arthur Bryant's house is seen, and you see east up the valley of Thunder Creek a long distance.

In due time I reached Arthur's house. He was from home, away for hay, but Alf Bryant, the brother you met in England was there with a new arrival from England—Mr. Mess. He and a brother have

---

7   John McDougall, 14-22-29.
8   A.Y. Attwood, 29-22-28, became a prominent figure in Russell.

come out to learn farming. He remains with Alf for a year, the other goes with Glover across the Assiniboine—two more unlikely settlers to teach farming they could not have chosen.

After dinner we went over to Frank's. I waited there for some time and then started south for Russell. After a long, heavy tiresome walk in the snow I got there about sundown, and there I was too tired to think of travelling home, ten miles farther, so I got your letter (but no papers, as the mail day had that week been changed to Saturday) and walked up to Butcher's—the schoolmaster's—house and claimed his hospitality. He comes from Devonshire England. After supper and a night's blowing up of the Government we all adjourned to slumberland.

Next morning I loitered around till ten o'clock and then started home. I met a new Glasgow immigrant—his face was familiar—he had been in an insurance office in Ranfield St. He thought this country a great change from Scotland. Everyone hears that the immigration is going to be as great this year as before despite the dissatisfaction and agitation going on.

The walk home was a pretty tough one, and I had not gone far till an [?] step over a creek sent me through the deep snow up to the pockets, and I felt the water underneath trickle sweetly into my boots. On the way I met a neighbour—one of the Irishmen—Archer, on his way to Russell. He was walking in his shirt, trousers, hat and boots, the weather was so warm. In due time I got home feeling very tired. Next day was rather cloudy, and the succeeding morning was dark and blowing. I got up early to take a grist to the Assissippi Mill. Before I got away the snow began to fall, and in a short time the country had recovered its winter garb and put farmers over early seeding and ploughing ideas.

I came back home by Frank and Arthur Bryants' houses. Since I was there on Wednesday Mrs. Arthur Bryant had had a little girl, and Arthur was very important and proud looking. Now I must stop . . .

Your affectionate brother
Willie

Woodvale, Shell River, Man.
16 April 1884

My Dear Maggie,

I cannot this time refer to your last letter—it will not be due till we are down posting this one. Last Saturday we received the book you promised to send long since—"Old Faiths in New Lights," and the little I have read of it gives me the idea that I will enjoy the reading of it very much. I am just as far as ever from believing in the Orthodox Faith[9] and your book gives my doubts more logical expression. . . . We greatly enjoy the reading, and that is rather a scarce commodity with us. Our books are very threadbare now, and during the long winter nights the newspapers were well digested down to the advertisements. Now that the busy season is on we have something more remunerative to take our attention, therefore do not inundate us with too much reading and tempt us to forget our work.

Spring is now on us, and work is the constant order all day long. Winter is leaving us with a hard struggle. A fortnight ago farmers were gleeful over the prospect of early seeding, but these hopes had a dispersal—a snowstorm came and whitened the prairie again. Fine weather succeeded, and yesterday the snow was only to be seen where it had drifted into deep banks. The ducks and geese are getting plentiful, and last night when Father and I were coming home we could not help remarking the lovely spring appearance of the creek valley—the rich brown colour of the shrubs and willows relieved by the yellow hue of the grass gave the long abruptly steep banks a peculiar beauty the long winter helped us to appreciate to the fullest extent. Every tree and bush held myriads of little birds of every variety and colour who made the air hum with their chirping and whistling. Away down below, Thunder Creek was beginning its long prattle over the stones that gives it its name. Everything made us certain that spring had really appeared in full vigour, but alas, alas—during the night I awoke and heard on the roof a gentle patter of something that was too soft and puffy to be rain. And in looking out, the whole valley was again clothed in a snowy

---

9 Presumably the Church of England.

garment. Towards morning the wind rose, and all day it has been very cold and stormy. The little birds have been around the house in countless numbers, evidently anything but pleased over the mistake their migration had led them into in luring them from their winter quarters. Further south the snow will not likely survive tomorrow. Tonight it is freezing and clearing up. The creek is now in flood—the ice will soon break up in the river now.

During the mild weather we got a little ploughing done and seven acres of wheat sown. Besides these, we have been busy housebuilding on our new site in the river valley, and we have the walls of one house up now. This forenoon we were away cutting roof poles. In a day or two we will have the roof on—this will give the broad valley a less deserted appearance.

The newcomers are beginning to flock in. Farrar got back last week from England, accompanied by two English friends, on farming pursuits intent. I have not yet seen him, but I have heard that one of his friends wears eyeglasses. Two of our Irish neighbours have recently been joined by brothers just out from the old country. One of them was here last Sunday—he seems a pleasant young fellow.

Last Sunday Andrew and I drove down to Russell for the mail in the afternoon. A good many people were there. Arthur Bryant drove out as we went in. Frank was going about town—his wife was with him, but invisible—calling, most likely. Four new houses add very much to the appearance of the town. One or two were horrified at my transferring a piece of meat from the store to the waggon—they evidently thought us too awfully impatient at the Lenten fast. Before coming away Major Boulton and Denmark drove in with a waggon load of strangers. They turned out to be six Englishmen just come to the settlement. That morning they had been up at Denmark's farm, and had been induced to rent it for the summer. I guess Denmark will make more money on the transaction than they will. Their strange habiliments amused the loafers. And certainly kid gloves with fingers and long mud-catching ulsters, to say nothing of their platter-looking felt hats, seemed strange and odd. No doubt but they would have their own opinion of the native garb, but the character of the climate and the country will soon settle that.

I am sorry to say there is a doubt about the railway coming our length this summer, although no definite information can be obtained of the railway company's intention. It is rumoured that the capitalists in your quarter of the globe have not given them the encouragement they anticipated and that, though they will grade the roadbed to Shellmouth, they will not be able to lay the rails any nearer than Dow's ford, forty miles from here. I sincerely hope the report is false, as I am heartily tired of long journeys during the winter. My news box is now empty, so I will resign the paper and desk in Andrew's favour . . .

Your most affectionate brother
Willie

[P.S. from Andrew]
. . . We are now timeless. The other night when Willie was winding up his watch he broke the mainspring. My watch has stopped for two years now, it wants cleaning, and Papa's is the same way. Besides this, we have two clocks wanting the watchmaker badly. There is no watchmaker near us, and to send them to Winnipeg they charge such exorbitant prices, and when you get them back they go for about a month and then stop again. We can't get them sent to the old country either, as the post office won't take jewellery of any description. . .

Woodvale, Shell River, Man
2 May 1884

My Dear Maggie,

We are very busy seeding just now, and I have been forced to let the writing of your letter remain over till the last moment. Saturday a week ago Andrew received your letter, and all the good news it contained was greatly appreciated . . .

Let me tell you that the Bryants are what I consider rather "snobby"—they have a desire to be considered "tony" with neither education or money to back it up. I cannot speak of the Davies. The brothers out here, so long as they kept together, did very well.

Their separate annuities combined helped them to live independent of farming, but since the division, the £60 each has left them pretty hard up. Arthur is the only one who can juggle money, but all of them are now pretty well depending on their farms, and so far that has only been an expense. They have never been good workers, and from all appearance I should not wonder if they have hard times ahead. Were Mrs. Davies a witness of things as they are out here I imagine a great many of her stately notions regarding her connections would receive a bad shock. A small pension and little inclination or ability to work hard are about the greatest obstacles a pioneer could have.

6 May ... The most of our seeding is now over, and for three days back the wheat ground has been daily getting a more grain appearance. For three weeks now the weather has been simply glorious—mild and warm, and not a vestige of a cloud, scarcely. Now we would be pleased to have a shower of rain. The leaves are beginning to show on the trees and the prairie where burnt, is quite green. During April the ducks had a very restless time of it. All around the shooting was going on at a great rate. They are exceptionally plentiful this season, and we had our share of them. The first of May, however, began the closed season, so that we have now to break the law if we would indulge.

I think I mentioned last time that our poultry stock has been increased. We have now seventeen little chickens, and as they are a novelty, and we do not possess anyone with a feminine objection to a mess or a quantity of very unmusical whistling, we allow them to roost in the house at night. It is exceedingly amusing to watch their antics. They are so tame that the wonder is some of them do not get hurt or tramped. The contrast is a little peculiar—that while you were making yourself uncomfortable with a view to greater comfort by indulging in a spring cleaning, we were indulging in an innovation turning our drawing-room into a hen roost. Let us hope the poultry will not learn bad manners.

For some days back Father and I have been stable building over in the river valley. We are making things appear over there now as if we meant business. The house has only to be plastered and the roof covered to make it habitable. Andrew was away a day and a half ploughing for Teulon, and the reckless young man desires me to bring him a pair of boots from the store tomorrow with the proceeds—twenty shillings—that is the way things are done in this country—easy come, easy go.

Saturday a fortnight ago I was down at Russell. When I got back with the mail I found Teulon waiting on. After supper by way of a change we went over to the Pagans. There we found some of the neighbours. We spent a very enjoyable evening. When it got to twelve o'clock we changed from discussing politics to religious subjects. So engrossed were we that the sun rose on our deliberations and startled us rather. We got home just in good time for breakfast. You see how prairie loneliness affects our sociable instincts.

Last Saturday I went up to Shellmouth. The ferry boat is plying now, and the store has been opened. Surveyors will now be engaged surveying the town into lots. Will you kindly excuse my stopping this hurried scrawl—next time I hope to give a more satisfactory account of our doings. Will you kindly remember us to your friends the Misses Pounds, and with our best love I am

Your affectionate brother
Willie

Woodvale, Shell River, Man.
24 May 1884

My Dear Maggie,

We did not go down to Russell last Saturday—we were very busy— the Pagans however went down and brought back our mail, and it included a letter from you. We were pleased to hear all the good news, especially that you were so singularly situated in comparison to the general experience of assistant teachers. I was interested in the account of the earthquake, although it lacked one important item, and that was your experience—and I say, Maggie, it cost us ten cents. The post office seems to think you want too much bulk carried at the low rate of 2 ½ cents. This is the second time we have been so dealt with . . .

I am glad you can get me the violin strings. Any song book with tuneful accompaniments, or music that does not deal too extravagantly in upper ledger lines will also receive a hearty welcome.

Speaking for myself I do not grudge a little of my own time fiddling. Father and Andrew are of course partial to literature. We would like a photo of you very much—in fact if you do not keep us so reminded of you, you will be in danger of becoming a very visionary personage only realizable by a powerful employment of our faith faculties...

We are having delightful spring weather—too much so. I keep a diary of the farm work, and for a long time back the weather entries have been "warm pleasant day" until the pleasing information has become quite too monotonous. We want a change, such as "dark and looming," "raining like fury," "thunder and lighting and a perfect deluge"—and the crops look decidedly as if they desired a change. The wheat and oats are pointing above ground thickly, and hopefully tomorrow will finish up our seeding and planting experience for this season. Earnestly do we hope the results will equal our expectations. Everything is looking gloriously beautiful. And if the grain and plants would only come up spontaneously, and afterwards walk into the granary to be shorn I could be tempted to spend my dignified leisure on artistic pursuits. But alas, we must work and behold, and wonder and work.

The cold leafless winter causes us to think no foliage was ever seen before so green and verdant as the present. The creek valley is just a long line of enclosed splendour, and the deep hum of insect life and the musical whistling and chirping of birds causes one to forget that there are any dark shades in this world, that all is sunshine and glory. The river valley is also grandly beautiful, but on a more extended scale. The yellow grass is charmingly relieved by the brilliant green hues of the poplar groves dotted here and there on the broad plain. The dark banks on the opposite side are entirely clothed over by dark-leaved trees towering their tops over other to the top. The extensive horizon on the opposite prairie, flat and unbroken, extending uninterruptedly for a hundred miles, is bounded closely by heavily-wooded groves. To the south the headlands jutting into the river become less distinctly blue and more hazy as they are distant from the viewpoint.

Williams, who lives with the Pagans and hails from [?] England, is charmed with the scenery hereaway. Our portion he thinks equal and beyond any English gentleman's artificial attempt to make his surroundings beautiful. So there now, are you not tempted to bid the city smoke farewell? On Monday we purpose devoting all our energies to housebuilding, and before the week is over we hope to be in our new quarters.

Last night while fishing, I saw the first beaver I have seen. It came down the river and passed so close to Father that I expected to see him poke it with his rod, and then past me. A slight noise I made caused him to dive, and then it showed its broad tail as it went down headfirst with a splash. Only for a second did it remain under—back it came towards me, anxious evidently to go up Thunder Creek. I was standing on the little neck of land at the mouth. After a little while he came on the bank below us and critically inspected a dry stick, sampling it in a knowing way with his teeth. We then saw his whole body. He looked very much like a small bear in the water when swimming. It gave a peculiar low wailing sound. Their skins are not as valuable now as they at one time were, and after the first of May they, and all the fur animals, lose their winter and most valuable coat.

At Shellmouth a new schoolhouse is at once to be built. The teacher has been changed, and the village is now graced with a lady teacher owning the somewhat [?] name of Miss Ewillues, and reported to be very good and pretty. At present she is dosing the children with knowledge in a large canvas tent. No doubt the young settlers will be more likely to Church Service—now you see what a power you may have, even outside your educational duties, for doing good, provided you are winsome and wise. I have a very small stock of news this time . . .

Your affectionate brother
Willie

Woodvale, Shell River, Man.
6 June 1884

My Dear Maggie,

Last Saturday Andrew got your letter. We were extremely glad to learn from it that the Inspector's report of your work was so exceedingly favourable and creditable. We are sorry to know that

Miss L. Pounds has been so ill—we trust she is quite recovered ere this time. I was quite overjoyed to receive the violin string and the rosin—both helped the fiddling very much. Last night I was giving full vent to my musical feelings when the first string snapped unexpectedly and wounded my sensitive musical inclinations, so that I hung the fiddle up to be repaired, when once I had recovered from the shock.

The tie and the seeds were very welcome. The former had such an effect on Andrew that he is now bent on having a suit of new clothes. The seeds we must reserve till next Spring... Since my last letter we have been working away quietly and steadily. Thursday a week ago we moved over into our new abode in the river valley. After a week's experience and getting settled, we find ourselves very comfortable. The improved pasturage commends itself to the animals we had some good fun removing. The pigs were the most obstreperous, but all are now contented with the idea that this is the new abode. Many, many years will likely pass away before we again change. We consider ourselves settled for good, and are accordingly putting up buildings with an idea of permanency.

Since the removal we have been busy building a stable. The framework is now finished—the roofing, plastering and flooring are next considerations. At present all the animals have their sweet liberty night and day on the prairie. The pigs are in an open pen, the poultry we have roosting in a canvas addition at the end of the house, and the rooster takes full advantage of his proximity to our sleeping quarters to call us early with his chanticleering row. Last Saturday we had a pretty calf added to our stock, a regular beauty. And now we have plenty of milk for household purposes.

The weather continued exceedingly hot and dry till yesterday morning, when we had a decided change—cold, raw, cloudy weather. Today has been pretty much the same, with the welcome addition of some rain. This has been of great benefit to the crops, giving nature a different appearance. I only hope we may have more rain, as we wanted it very much. There is the promise of an exceptional abundance of wild fruit this summer. The blossoms have so far, and will likely now, escape frost.

Andrew and I went down fishing this forenoon, but caught naught. They do not seem easily tempted during wet weather. When we got back we found Father and Henry Pagan keeping each other company, and only a few minutes ago Langford went home, so that we are still well off for company. The Irishmen have been having a great time hunting a big brown bear a mile north of us, but although they wounded it twice, it managed to escape them. About a month ago I saw the same gentlemen galloping around and having a good time near Langford's shanty.

You made a great mistake qualifying yourself for a teacher in Scotland. In Manitoba they get over such trifles easier. The Board of Education has appointed a Professor to travel about the central points in the province, where he holds an educational grinding mill for three weeks, to which all who wish to become teachers are invited. A short time ago, this Professor, Goggen by name, came to Birtle, had a three weeks' Normal course attended by a goodly number of males and females, held an examination at the close, and without more ado granted certificates. All these certificate holders are now in charge of schools (and of the latter number is Miss Ewillues, the Shellmouth teacher) and receiving $35 a month salary. What do you think of that plan compared to your experience?

I was up at Shellmouth on Monday night. I wanted to see Venables, so I crossed the ferry boat, a proceeding the horse objected to very much, rode along what is termed the "dump"—a high embankment like a railway running over the river flats—and from the dump rose up the opposite bank. I was very much struck with the extended and fine view of the river valley north and south, for thirty miles clear and distinct like a birds-eye view. I rode on for about half a mile. The country is excessively flat, but pleasantly relieved with trees and lakes.

Mr. Venables has his house beside a lake, rather a nice site, but oh, what "shacks" to live in. Venables is a former Londoner and has a good deal of the Cockney, wears an eyeglass and looks the gentleman. He was formerly a brewer. His wife and family are with him, and I imagine he has had a [setback?] in business. His partner, Mr. Venning, comes from Ceylon, where he has a coffee plantation. I guess if their friends saw their circumstances now they would faint. During the winter they lived in Shellmouth in a rented house and seemed to have plenty of money, but that commodity seems to be scarce now.

The whole settlement are getting very downhearted over the railway. American railway schemes are in bad favour with capitalists just now, and the company could only get 46 cents to the dollar on their bonds, so the railway will not likely come our way this year. At least a number are getting disgusted, and like fools, instead of waiting, they are leaving. A little patience and all will come right. Prosperity will not be forced. We are well off compared to the majority because we realized some money on our last harvest. Now I must stop and leave space for Andrew. We are well and in good spirits. Kindly remember us all to your good friends the Misses Pounds, and with our very best to you, I am

Your affectionate brother
Willie

Woodvale, Shell River, Man.
20 June 1884

My Dear Maggie,

Father received your last letter. We were glad to know that your examinations are now over, and trust your efforts will be rewarded with success. You seem to have been enjoying a good deal of outings. I envy you your Whitsun[day] holiday. I would think a stay at the coast a great novelty. It is somewhat singular that I, so fond of the sea and shore, should be as far distant from it as I could possibly be anywhere—a good time will doubtless be coming.

I wonder what you would think of our circumstances now. Not so long ago I was writing you of zero cold and zero experiences—now the scene is reversed, and decidedly so. For some days back the thermometer has been almost at 100 degrees in the coolest shade we could place it. Today, in the morning, it began at 77 at five o'clock—in an hour or two it climbed to 80 degrees, and since 9 o'clock it climbed up gradually to 99 degrees. Roasting is about the only term that could be applied to the experience. Last Saturday it was too much for labour of any description, so Andrew and I adjourned to the river, where we emulated the cool habits of the little fishes. The change was simply delicious and held us spell-bound for a long time. Even the simple attire of hot shirt, trousers and boots is a burden in weather like this.

On Saturday evening we had our first thunderstorm, and it was terrific while it lasted. The sky was black with great ugly raging clouds, round which the sheet lightning played incessantly, while the forked lightning would dance and caper all over, devising the most fantastic figures. The thunder rolled, thumped, and cracked continuously, and in a most peculiar manner, throbbing like the beat of a steam hammer, far beyond even human imagination to realize. The beating caused the ground to quiver like an earthquake. The rainfall was not particularly heavy, certainly not so much as we could have wished for. But to the north the rain seemed to be pouring down like water spouts. With this exception the season has been unusually free of thunderstorms.

Since the rain the grain crops have taken a new lease of life. One could almost imagine they saw them growing. Everything betokens a remarkably prolific harvest of hops, strawberries, raspberries, currants, cherries, plums, and cranberries. All we want to make the next winter an enjoyable experience feasting on them is you, accompanied by a huge jelly pan and a lot of sugar.

Since my last letter we have been getting along very quietly. The most of the time Andrew has been ploughing, while Father and I have been well-digging and stable-building. We have not reached water yet, although we are down 35 feet, but the prospects are good. When we got 24 feet we found the track of a deer, distinctly marked, that must have been made in pre-historic times. Just now we are taking out a soft rack that looks exactly like coal, but after it has been exposed, somehow it becomes more like a slate pencil, and is good for marking wood with.

We have been very unfortunate with our young stock. Our disasters did not cease with the young pigs. Today I buried a pretty colt, and for a little it seemed as if the pony would require the same service. Fortunately she is getting all right again. Better luck I hope awaits us next spring. The calf and chickens are getting on splendidly ... Williams, who stays with the Pagans, expects his organ on Friday. After that you may picture to yourself the prairie in a tremble of excitement over the combination of melodious sounds that will after that be wafted over it. The violin string you sent is a perfect treasure . . .

Your most affectionate brother
Willie

Woodvale, Shell River, Man.
3 July 1884

My Dear Maggie,

We duly received last Saturday your long, long, and very interesting letter addressed to me—notwithstanding the great length it underwent a careful perusal, so much so that we almost participated in the enjoyment of the holiday you spent at Folkestone. . . I am under the necessity of writing you on scrap paper—my stock of note paper has run out. You must therefore excuse my patched looking letter. Since my last letter we have been having a big time of it in the way of thunderstorms. The Saturday I posted your letter I walked down to Haworths, and from there got a ride to Russell. Ben Haworth, formerly a chemist in Manchester, and Williams, who lives with the Pagans, composed the company. The forenoon was excessively warm, 103 degrees in the shade, so we were roasted to a turn on the way down.

After we got our business finished among other things—Williams getting his organ was the great event—we started home, and had not gone far till the thunderclaps began to make a noise, and when we had gone about a quarter of the way, a fearful-looking thundercloud scudded up on us with the speed of lightning, and for about half an hour actually poured its water supply on us, the hurricane causing us to dread we would be blown out of the waggon. Oh, but we got drenched! The like I never got before, my good fortune favouring me so far that during such tempests I was under coverage. After the deluge the rain still continued, much to our amazement, till we got about two miles from Pagans', where another thundercloud burst over us and gave us another drowning.

We all stopped at the Pagans' and made an attempt to bring about a sense of comfort. The organ was duly unpacked, inspected and performed upon. I had a try at it, but the harrowing recollection makes me blush. Since that time I have made two or three attempts, and can scramble and read through a piece slowly and surely. Williams is an atrocious player—seems to have had no training, and wades through defiant of anything like an attempt at fingering systematically or playing in time or in tune. It seems to me his $300 organ will be a long time in repaying him by any enjoyment he can get out of it. The organ is very nice, has ten stops, a sugary tone, a magnificent case, two knee swells and etc., but after bowing a fiddle I believe I would prefer a piano. Andrew came over before dark when the rain ceased, and together we wended our way home.

Last week the most of our time was occupied ploughing down on Andrew's claim. On Friday when there we ate lunch beside the ploughs. We did not go home for dinner because of the distance, nearly half a mile. We saw two waggons with oxen and horses on the opposite bank of the Assiniboine, like specks. They seemed to be shouting at us, but though they were opposite, the distance was too far for us to make anything of them, and they drove off. This was the first sign of humanity we have seen on the other side of the river, so we considered they were lost. This I afterward learnt was the case. They had come from a colony out west and were looking for Shellmouth.

We dug the well down forty feet and got no water. As we had to get on with the other work, we gave up for the time being.

Last Tuesday, the 1st of July, was Dominion Day, and Andrew and I as in duty bound had a holiday and prepared to go to Russell and see the sports. When we were about starting with the waggon and horses, along came Teulon and begged me to keep him company. He had his waggon and oxen. I was very loath to do so, but he was so persistent, dreading the loneliness of the journey himself, that I consented. Andrew quickly disappeared, and together we thrashed the oxen to a decent creeping pace, while we discussed music and politics. Both of us had been reading Hawres'[?] "Musical Memoirs." We had not got half way when it commenced to rain, and soon it changed from light rain to heavy, and continued drenching us till we got about half a mile from Russell, when it cleared away.

We got there feeling very cold and miserable. After some dinner we adjourned to the sports ground, and it was not long till Andrew appeared, warm, dry, and affecting to smile at my clammy-looking habilaments.

The sports were a great success, a great deal of horse racing and etc. Mrs. Frank Bryant competed in the married women's race and did not come in a winner. A great crowd of people were there, 300 I daresay. I spoke to Mrs. Glover a little—her sister Mrs. Davies had been writing that you were a great stranger now. I apologised as best I could by telling her of the magnitude of your work and the long distance you were from it. The last she readily understood, as she said she knew the road thoroughly. Mrs. Glover is now wonderfully changed for the better, both in looks and in manner. She and her husband purpose going next day to their homestead. It is a long distance north of this, and in a district very poorly settled. They will have a lonely time of it—probably they expect their own company will be sufficient.

In the evening there was a concert, a very poor affair compared to last year's. A Miss Hogg, daughter of the Presbyterian Minister at Binscarth, played the organ very well. I did not expect there would be a concert, so I had somewhat hurriedly to harass my memory for a recitation. It was very well received. We left Russell about eleven o'clock and had a long cold wet ride home. The latter portion of the journey was got over despite the pitch darkness. We got home at half past one o'clock.

Next morning we went to do our statute labour. The law provides in Canada that each settler occupies a certain number of days working on the roadways or, as with us, making roadways. Seven of us were two days cutting a trail through the bush across Thunder Creek at the north side of our section.

Yesterday Father went down to Russell for the mail, while Andrew and I ploughed. Today, Sunday, Andrew and I were away in the forenoon picking strawberries. Every kind of fruit is unusually plentiful this year. The quantity of strawberries we ate would frighten the digestive organs of any old country person.

On the morning of the 1st of July the grass was delicately whitened with hoarfrost, a spectacle that filled the most of the settlers with feelings of lively anxiety. We escaped remarkably well. The tops of the potato plants just burnt a little on the top, but in a large number of cases the potatoes have been burnt black to the ground, and in consequence the sufferers are very much disheartened—Frank and Arthur Bryant are especially so. For four seasons now their potatoes have been destroyed.

Things are going ahead at Shellmouth. In addition to the store already there, another one, a branch from Moosomin, will be opened, it is expected, the first of August. The prospective proprietor, Mr. Hill, is now resident with his family. And still another is reported, on which concern our neighbour, Perrin,[10] is rumoured to be a partner. A woollen factory and cheese factory is proposed at Assissippi,[11] but still no word of the railway. It is rumoured that no further extension of the line will be made this summer owing to scarcity of funds. This is deplorable, still I suppose we ourselves will not suffer much. Our grain is simply splendid, and promises a good and early yield—in the majority of cases, the opposites are the prospect. So railway or no railway we will in all likelihood get a good market for our grain. The weather just now is very broken, cloudy and wet to an extent unknown to us before. I trust it will clear away and let us have a good hay harvest. Now I must conclude. . .

Your affectionate brother
Willie

Woodvale, Shell River, Man.
25 July 1884

My Dear Maggie,

Andrew received your last letter, and we were glad to learn from it of your welfare. The change to Folkestone must have wrought wonders. . . I have been so long in writing, but really it is almost impossible to accomplish a letter during the busy summer months, from sunrise to sunset always something to take up the attention, and no time for artificial light, which really is the best thing to cause

10   Herbert B. Perrin, 24-22-29.
11   There was a cheese factory there by 1907.

one to forget outside surroundings and endeavour to strengthen the bonds of trans-atlantic friendships.

. . . Since my last letter we have, I might almost say, been making progress backwards. Before that we had been digging a well—we sunk it fifty feet and I am sorry to say got no water. Had we continued working amongst clay we would have persisted, but we struck a thick bed of sand, and the presence of that shifting material would have necessitated our lining the well from top to bottom, a rather expensive item. Even had we got water it would have been rather a long haul, so we decided to give up. We tried another place some distance away, but after getting down about sixteen feet we struck a huge boulder stone that we could not circumvent, so it also had to be filled up.

This completely upsets the programme we had sketched in the spring. All the buildings we have put up are useless till we shift them to a new site where water can be obtained. This next winter we have decided to go back and live in Thunder Creek valley. But to prevent a like conclusion to our work there, we are hunting for water now at the proposed site. We have a hole dug out fourteen feet deep, and our work on it tomorrow will decide likely whether we will get water or not.

In the summer months water is a plentiful commodity. The winter brings the trouble—for six months every pond, stream and river is frozen up. This has been a great want to us. We got water from a spring oozing out at the bottom of the valley, but it was not conveniently situated. This winter we are bound to have a well. We expected no difficulty in finding water in the river valley and put up buildings with every confidence—now we are wiser. Should we get water in the creek valley we will shift our former buildings down there and have a cosy time during winter. The buildings will be in an open glade surrounded by trees and protected all around by the valley banks, 200 feet high.

Fully a week ago we commenced haying, and though we have not been engaged steadily, owing to the showery weather, yet we are getting on well, got nearly the half up. When you receive this letter we will be busy harvesting. The crops are looking splendid—not their equal to be seen within fifty miles. We hope it will escape damage from hail and frost. If you meet any Kilmarnock friends, ask them what they think of a country where wheat can be seeded the 17th April and have the berries perfectly formed and ready for ripening by the 23 July. We feel quite proud of ourselves. Everyone is complaining, and they have late seeding to thank for their poor prospects. Next year we expect to have 65 acres under crop, and if we have another good year, as the present promises to be, we will surely begin and make lots of money.

Our garden is getting on well. We are getting potatoes, peas, radish and lettuce now. The livestock is all well and hearty. We had a brood of twelve little chicks the other day and they are getting on well. Won't we have a superabundance of eggs next summer!

The crop of wild fruits is wonderful this season just now and for some time back. The Saskatoon berries have been hanging in black clusters, bending the branches with their weight. They are peculiar to Manitoba and very sweet and luscious. Today I picked a pitcher full in about an hour. The Indians, before they were acquainted with wheat, made bread from them. The strawberry season is over now, but the raspberries are beginning to ripen and promise abundantly.

The Shellmouth females and children are having great fun berry picking just now. I was up there last night, and things are getting on lively—a lot of new houses going up. Besides two new stores—one a provision, the other a furniture store—the schoolhouse is completed now and is a credit to the place. A nice little belfry adjoins the roof, and a bell will likely soon be sending chimey echoes down the valley. There is a likelihood of the government putting a bridge over the Assiniboine this winter, and that will start a stir there. Major Boulton has gone off to Ottawa regarding it.

I crossed the river and went over the boundary into the Province of Assiniboia. The prospect reminded one of our pioneering days— the land is all taken up but very few houses adorn the prairie. We can see a tent opposite our place across the river—some new settler doubtless beginning prairie life.

One of our neighbours, Farrar, was in England last winter. Since he came back he has been busy housebuilding. This week a load of new furniture arrived for him, and now (the truth will out!) he is going to get married. The Pagans went out to Moosomin to meet their brother last Monday. He has been enjoying himself in Ontario all winter.

I get a tune on the organ once a fortnight or thereabout and really I am making great progress. My violin experience has helped me to keep good time. Probably I may be a church organist yet.[12] If you have an old piano about that you have no use for, you may post it out to me and then I could make progress. Now I must conclude. Andrew will not manage to write this time, as we have changed our programme of work—tomorrow he will start away for Russell early in the morning.

We trust you will all thoroughly enjoy yourselves at Arran. We poor miserable souls are confined and shut up to a prairie life. No coast holidays for us. Is it not strange our health does not suffer? Could you not manage to come and spend your holidays with us? The Atlantic can be crossed in little more than six days, and the journey here by rail would only occupy four days. After a sojourn here companying with prairie boors and bears and berries, you would, I am sure, conclude Arran after all was poor fun in comparison . . .

Do you know that we expect a post office at Shellmouth shortly. Had it not been for a blundering among the settlers we might have had it long ago.[13] Do not make any change in the address yet. . . .

Your most affectionate brother
Willie

Woodvale, Shell River, Man.
29 July 1884

My Dear Maggie,

Father duly received your last letter, and we were all greatly pleased to hear of your continued success at the school work, and the pleasing result of the inspector's report, and above all of your good health. . . . You were quite correct in your estimate of the teacher's salary, but the young lady, I am afraid, will not have a great surplus.

---

12 In later years he was organist for the Presbyterian and the Anglican churches in Shellmouth.
13 There was rivalry over the position of postmaster.

Board and lodgings are very expensive, and extras, I am afraid you would think, were to be had only at an exorbitant rate. . .

Just now we are exceptionally busy taking advantage of the fine weather to put up our winter supply of hay. We have a lot of mouths to feed for seven months, and it takes a large quantity of fodder to satisfy them. At first we had very unsettled, showery weather that delayed us very much. All this week, however, the weather has been simply glorious—nice warm days and not oppressively so, few mosquitoes and cold nights that made the resting of our tired bones a luxury. Tonight we will all feel very tired, so you must not think hardly of me only sending a short letter—besides, my attention is partly diverted firing loaves in the oven.

We have been living quite luxuriously for some time back. The quantity of wild fruit was simply extraordinary, and besides, we have eggs and butter and new potatoes, without mentioning milk and etc. Think of that, you city resident. Do you indulge in porridge yet? Next week the shooting season begins for ducks, chickens and etc.

I think I told you in my last letter that our proposed permanent homestead has turned out a failure—we could not find water. The site chosen in the creek has furnished the necessary at a depth of 18 feet. As soon as the hay is all up we will set to housebuilding again.

Our grain is looking exceedingly well, and promises a bountiful yield. In a fortnight we expect to be harvesting. It had a narrow escape a week ago from damage by hailstones—a fearful heavy whirl-storm crossed the south part of our claims and left hailstones bigger than marbles on the ground.

I was up at Shellmouth on Wednesday night, and really it is getting to be a busy, pretty-looking place—if only the railway would come, what might it not be. The railway company, we heard, is constructing fifty miles westward this summer. And if they do as much next, that will bring it to Shellmouth.

One of our neighbours, Mr. McLennan, is just now building a concrete house, so you can judge how quickly we are advancing. Last week Will Pagan came back from Toronto, and has since been indulging in cigars and limejuice. He brought up two new teams of horses, and the farm, with four teams about it, looks quite a horsey establishment. Now I must stop ... Be wary of the cholera—on the first show of danger take shipping for here, and Jack Frost will intervene and scotch the dread malady. I remain

Your affectionate brother
Willie

Woodvale, Shell River, Man.
22 August 1884

My Dear Maggie,

We are afraid your last letter must have gone astray. It is now two weeks overdue, so if you had anything noteworthy in it you had better repeat. The want of it was a great disappointment. . . . Just now we presume you are luxuriating and enjoying yourself under the patronage of Goat Fell.[14] We do hope you are getting sunny weather and are laying in a gigantic stock of health and fresh air. Certainly you have all that could be desired in the way of society. Strange to say out here we have our holidays yet to look forward to, and the grim visage of Jack Frost, under whose patronage we enjoy them, is looming in the distance, and the prospect is nerving our working capabilities to their utmost. Since the last letter we have removed and rebuilt the stable, and for two days back we have been excavating a cellar. Horrible and to our dismay, instead of digging, we had a good bit of it to quarry. Heaving, rolling and breaking big stones causes one to feel pleased to go to bed early, but it is over now. Yesterday afternoon we began shifting the logs from their old site, and today we rebuilt a good bit of the house.

Tomorrow I am under promise to go up to Teulons to assist at a house raising "bee." "Bee"ing is an American institution, and means the gathering of all the neighbours to assist at some particular work, and if it had no existence, solitaries would have a bad time.

Sunday a week ago Father and I went up to the first Presbyterian service at Shellmouth. That was the first time we had been at church for months and months. The service was held in the new schoolhouse, and really I was surprised at the nice interior of the new building. It

---

14 The highest mountain on the Arran Islands.

is quite a credit to the place. Mr. Jones, the missionary, was late in turning up, and we had somewhat a tedious wait. The congregation numbered 22, not a bad turn-out considering that the Whaley family and we are the only Presbyterians.

The scarcity of support will in the meantime, I am afraid, interfere with the continuance of the service. Mr. Jones last year did not succeed very well at Russell, and the Mission Board cancelled his appointment. Lately, however, he was reappointed to a district farther north, including Shellmouth, but with this proviso—that the Board would not guarantee more than $200. Mr. Jones says he must have $600 to live on. This would imply that he expects $100 from each of the four stations, and he doesn't want any promise—nothing less than a written obligation. I for one object. If he is not willing to wait and exercise patience and a little frugality like the rest till the place grows, then he may go.

The English clergyman has got into a mess. He is a farmer first and a clergyman odd times. The settlers at all his stations passed resolutions that they considered him amply rewarded with the $400 granted by the Missionary Board, and also that it would be advisable to introduce a fresh man. So much for clericalism in the Northwest.

On Monday or Tuesday at the latest we expect to be harvesting. The grain has prospered exceedingly well this year, and we have reason to anticipate overflowing granaries. The only drawback is, today it is blowing just now a regular hurricane, and the ripe oats will be shaking off pretty badly. You must pardon my again sending a short letter. Our time is very limited, and little of interest is occurring—from morning to night it is work, work. We are all well. With our kindest regards to the Misses Pounds, and our united and best love to yourself, I am

Your most affectionate brother
Willie

Woodvale, Shell River, Man.
12 September 1884

My Dear Maggie,

Can you pardon me my long three weeks silence? So busy have we been harvesting that what little opportunities I had for writing I was too tired to take advantage of them, and even now I must ask you to accept a very short hurried epistle . . . Since last letter we have been exceedingly busy, first housebuilding and latterly harvesting. Our binder would not work satisfactory this year. Again it made larger sheaves than it could bind, so we had to engage the Pagans' binder to cut the crop. It is fortunate that we made no settlement for the machine, nor are we likely to till it is made to go satisfactorily.

We have all cut now but eleven acres of oats and barley on this side of the creek, and the binder is over and ready to begin to that. Yesterday we finished stacking the wheat. I wish the oats were all secured too, as the blackbirds are flocking in myriads and harvesting it. Our grain was the first ripe in this settlement, and the blackbirds take this way of rewarding us for our smartness.

Last Sunday morning and again on Thursday morning we had very heavy frosts, forming ice on the water. This has done great damage to late grain. The most of our neighbours have suffered seriously, and we only have escaped. The Pagans have all their oats frozen, and seven horses depending on the crop this winter. Teulon had a splendid crop of wheat ruined, and Haworth will have only chaff to thresh out this time. The Bryants, I hear, may save themselves the trouble of harvesting, and this is the second time they have been so treated. These frosts are to be deplored, and will hurt the credit of the country very much. The settlers themselves are a good deal to blame for not pushing forward their work—both years we have escaped. This year we will have a thousand bushels of grain to sell, and surely we will make some money of that quantity, particularly if the frost has been in any way widespread in its effect.

Shellmouth is booming away. Another house has been erected— the Grand Central Hotel.[15] The railway is coming nearer at the rate of four miles per day, but the frost will stop that soon. Now

---

15 In its early days it charged $1.00 for supper, bed, and breakfast.

this winter a bridge is to be built over the Assiniboine there by the government. This will help the town greatly.

One of the prominent townsmen, Graham Boulton, a nephew of the Major's went off last Sunday to join the Manitoban contingent of warriors to relieve Gordon at Khartoum.[16] Nobody envies him but some of our neighbours, the Irishmen. We have had very unsettled wet weather delaying and adding to the harvest work. Just after we finished the wheat stacking last night it came on very wet, and we were thankful it did not come down earlier. Now you must excuse my concluding this short epistle. After harvest the long nights will give me more opportunity for writing long letters. We are all well, and with our kind regards to the Misses Pounds and kindest love to yourself, I am

Your most affectionate brother
Willie

Woodvale, Shell River, Man.
31 October 1884

My Dear Maggie,

You will be thinking hard thoughts of us here for not keeping you regularly informed of our well-being. We are over head and ears in work and discomfort, and must ask you to deal leniently with us, and if possible pardon our shortcomings. . . . We have this fall been in a perfect hurry-scurry. The disappointment with our house site augmented our work, and a great deal of wet weather during harvest increased and delayed us so that our ploughing is very far back. Only about 25 acres done, and to climax, the whole winter set in stern and fierce about a fortnight earlier than our previous experience led us to expect, and found us quite unprepared.

Had the weather kept open for a week longer we would have been safely ensconced in snug quarters. As it was, last Saturday, and for some days previous, the wind was high and cold, and our summer

---

16 A contingent of Canadians joined the British expedition sent to rescue General Gordon at Khartoum, but saw no action.

quarters a mere apology against it, and the stable even worse. But Sunday morning startled us—the ground was white with snow, and more snow driving down in a keen strong gale. Necessity knows no law, and the animals had to be moved over to their unfinished winter quarters—an improvement so far that they are situated at the bottom of the creek valley, probably 200 feet deep, and consequently out of the wind.

On Monday we also changed our abode. And since then, till now, we have been hard at work plastering up the daylight in the walls and scrambling around as best as we can in the confusion for our bed and board. The snow kept falling, and the wind kept blowing till yesterday, Thursday, when in the afternoon it made a sickly attempt to clear up. During the night it made a bolder effort, and this morning succeeded with a vengeance, clear and bright but with a frost revelling away down somewhere in the zeros. But we are approaching household comfort rapidly, and if we had our winter clothing donned we would be able to smile at even the lowest extreme of temperature.

Tomorrow the team and sleigh go down to Russell, and the dollars will trot likely lively, and the wool will come. Fortunately all our potatoes are secure under our feet, but the turnip and carrot will require to be lifted with a mattock.

So unexpectedly early has the change been that great quantities of grain are still out in the fields. And it does not look like farming under inauspicious skies to see the shocks standing like white stones over the field. Pagan's oats are all out, Haworth the same with barley, and a number more with crops ruined in a like manner. A great number of settlers have to mourn over loss this season in some form or other. Frank and Arthur Bryant, as if frozen grain was not sufficient, have both had hay burnt by a prairie fire—the former pretty nearly losing his house. The fire started east of us on the Shellmouth trail. Who was to blame can't be discovered, but it quickly swept over a large piece of country, burning hay, stacks of grain, and two or three houses. Another fire started on the other side of the river from Shellmouth, careened away out west for a day, then wheeled round and came back opposite our place and raised a terrible smoke. A whole afternoon the sun was like a copper ball, if not obscured, and at night the country was lighted up by the flames.

This fire has done great damage among the new settlements. Venning, at Shellmouth, formerly a planter in Ceylon, is credited with accidentally being the cause, and he will pay smartly for it. The penalty is $200, a pretty expensive outdoor smoke for him. It is getting late now and I must conclude. I cannot think of anything more pleasant to finish up this rather dismal letter than that we are all well and the animals are well. The poultry had a cold time latterly over in the river valley, but now they are strutting around with all freedom. An additional seven pigs help to make things more lively. With our kindest regards to the Misses Pounds and a whole mountain of live and good wishes for even an increase of your happiness during the new natal period you have entered upon—that these periods may be numerous, and each one bring an increase to your peace and property is our earnest hope.

Your most affectionate brother
Willie

P.S. Please be more generous with postage when enclosures are sent. Received Sunday Talk and are grateful.

Woodvale, Shellmouth, Man.
10 November 1884

My Dear Maggie,

We duly received your last letter addressed to Andrew. You appear to have had quite an extravagant experience on your birthday. Your friendships are surely accumulating. You must really let us know something about this Mr. Bond—we are getting quite interested in him.[17] Now if you had only been on this side of the Atlantic, how gladly would we have set about showing you how we could commemorate your birthday.

---

17 Maggie married John Bond in April 1890. They came to Canada in 1904 and settled on the same section as Peter Wallace.

You will note that the address at the top has been altered. The long-anticipated post office has been established at last. Had there not been a rivalry about the postmastership we might have got it two years ago. But that is all over now, and our long eleven mile drive to Russell ceases to be a weekly necessity.

"Misfortunes never come singly" it is said, but in our case it is blessings. About a fortnight ago the railway surveyors passed through the district and definitely located the line to Shellmouth passing our place about a mile to the north. They promise to have a train running over it by next winter. So if you just exercise a little patience you will be rewarded by getting steam conveyances almost to our very door.

My last letter you would think a little doleful, but we were at loggerheads with the weather. Every shabby trick it could manage it played on us till we got our new abode in a habitable state. When that stage was reached it cleared up, and for a week back we have had balmy clear days followed by brilliant moonlight, frosty nights. The snow is almost gone again, and we could almost delude ourselves into the hope that winter is past and spring has been ushered in. But alas, I fear old Jack Frost is only a short distance north, furbishing his weapons for a terrible onslaught. Never mind, we are ready to give him a warm reception and "heap coals of fire on his head."

I wish you could see our new abode. I am sure you would assert all in one breath that it was grandly picturesque and enchantingly cosy all around. Nothing to be seen but wood and heights. A climb must be made to the top to know what kind of weather it is.

During the night however is the time for fun—the cats wailing on the city tiles is quiet music in comparison. The wolves are numerous and blest with good lungs. Judging from the tone you could imagine one old fellow sneaking among the timber and snubbing his snout on a stump, and giving vent to his feelings afterwards by emitting a long powerful groaning howl, audible within a radius of four miles. And scarcely is his tale half over when it is almost drowned by a series of the most unearthly shrieks and yells, caught up and repeated by the innumerable echoes up and down the glen—giving one the idea that the old fellow with the bass voice was being laughed at in his discomfiture by a whole chorus of irreverent treble-voiced grandchildren. This causes Jess, the dog, to get into a perfect frenzy of rage.

To a newcomer I should think it would be a little nerve-shaking, but we do not mind it much. The wolves seem this winter to be more than usually plentiful. One of our neighbours trapped one. He preserved the skin with head attached. It had tusks in it longer than my forefinger. Twice I have had the pleasure of meeting them—they are surely sneaky looking thieves. Fortunately for my peace of mind they did not appear to be hungry.

The prairie wolves are very numerous, and generally become more so for some little time after first settlement, no doubt owing to the richer harvest falling to their share from wounded game and civilized wanderlings, and scraps. They are about the size of a good big dog, slate grey in colour, and have the same ugly mischievous pair of oblique eyes, but are very shy and cowardly. This afternoon one of them set up an unearthly shriek apparently just from the skirts of the wood. I got the gun and with the dog tracked him, but his bashful disposition caused me to come back empty-handed. Captain Langford, when here on a visit, described them as making more noise than the howling jackals in India. In many respects they resemble these Eastern scavengers very much. I think I wrote you of the scare a neighbour and I got from them on Silver Creek. . .

Do not send any more violin music. Now and then I have a good long spin at Williams' American organ. That, and hearing Teulon playing, has given me a disgust at my own fiddling effects. For too long time we were too busily employed outside for me to get time to improve towards excellence, and about a fortnight ago, when I went for the fiddle in despair, the blamed thing collapsed like a pistol shot—and when I recovered after the panic and calmly surveyed the cause and extent of damage, I found the bridge, the soul of the violin as it is termed, lying around the house in separate and detached pieces. This was the climax, and, I judged, a symbol of what my efforts would lead to.

I can play the organ very well now, feel quite at home. As often as I can manage on Sunday afternoons, I go over and the Pagans and company loosen their vocal organs on hymn tunes to my accompaniment. Williams has no notion of playing at all, and as he purposes going to Ontario this winter he wishes to sell the instrument. But alas, my wishes are far ahead of my purse, and even were it otherwise, it would not look well for an ambitious pioneer farmer laying out the price of a cow on a musical instrument. But good times may yet be ahead, so my hope is in the future. How are you situated for an instrument, and is it a good one?

You ask what we do for light. We burn what is commonly termed coal-oil, but really kerosene, in tall crystal lamps, somewhat after the style of the lamps used on a grand occasion in Ayrshire. The light is bright, clear, and steady, no flickering or uncertainty—a grand substitute for gas. The oil is very inflammable and has a horrid smell. Its former quality occasioned numerous accidents throughout America, but its latter feature has been our only trouble so far. We are very neighbourly and obliging, and when at the store a neighbour gets you to give him a lift home, you are apt to feel bad for a week or so when you discover that his innocent-looking coal-oil tin has a leak.

The settlement is making great progress just now. At Russell the new hotel has been opened, and whiskey is no longer either a forbidden or a scarce beverage, and a pretty new schoolhouse has been built. At Assissippi the proprietors of the flour mill have ousted all their stone grinding machinery and are enlarging the premises and fixing in the new patent roller machinery. Last Tuesday Andrew was up there and came home with a double notion of his own and Woodvale's importance. Mr. Gill[18] had been escorting him and explaining the strange things, and telling him that our wheat hadn't its equal in the district, and that we appeared to be most fortunate in every respect—first class oats and etc., and etc. A new livery stable has been put up there.

At Shellmouth the improvements are more marked. The ferry boat is to give place to a new bridge. A fine new livery stable has just been opened, and the same proprietor is laying the foundation for a large new hotel. In addition to this there are now three other accommodation houses. The new store was opened on Monday and a keen competition has now begun, much to the farmers' benefit.

---

18 Henry Gill was a representative of the Shell River Colonization Co. When it dissolved he became first postmaster at Assissippi, and with his two sons and Fred Richardson built a store there.

A sawmill will be in operation next summer. A camp of men are up north in the woods already, cutting logs for it. Last Sunday the Archdeacon from Winnipeg preached the sermon. Now are we not getting on? But these are small doings compared to what will likely be done next summer and when the railway shows up.

We are still busy plastering and fixing up things. In a week or so we expect the threshing mill, when we shall have a better idea of the summer results. Seven little pigs got their freedom yesterday, and now they are squealing around everywhere and getting in everyone's way. In a day or so we intend changing pigs into pork—this will tend to enliven the humdrumness in prairie farming. We are slowly diminishing our large stock of young roosters—these, with the large number of rabbits, prairie chickens and partridges. The prospects of a royal larder are good. Do you not feel tempted to join us?

On Friday I expect to pass another milestone in my life's journey.[19] And wonderful to relate, I am still pretty much as I was when we bade farewell—a little stouter and stronger looking, and a complexion tanned pretty much by the sun, but still I am sure the intervening 3 years has made no change so great but what you would readily recognize me. Now I must stop--I am getting into a sentimental mood . . .

Your affectionate brother,
Willie

Woodvale, Shellmouth, Man.
28 November 1884

My Dear Maggie,

Last mail brought us no letter from you, but instead we received the book you sent, the "American."[20] We thank you very much for sending it, and enjoyed the reading of it. I think the Yankee was rather hardly used and in the end dismissed in rather an unsatisfactory manner. I suppose that is the new style of story writing, but I prefer the old,

---

19 His twenty-sixth birthday.
20 By Henry James, published in 1877.

where the writer causes the hero or heroine to undergo a great deal of bad usage and trials, but in the end rewards the principal with some substantial, if not a wedding. . . .

Since my last letter we have been making great and marked endeavours to get level with our arrears of work. The house is now more comfortable, and things are settling down into some form of order. The stable is also snug and comfortable now, and the animals, though a little crowdy, are cozy and begin to know their winter quarters.

Last Friday and Saturday caused them to do so a little more readily. We had then a pretty sharp frost snap—25 below zero. This is the lowest temperature we have yet seen at this early stage of winter.

Early in the week we smothered our conscientious qualms and became butchers, killing two big pigs. Three minutes sufficed to put them out of pain, and we were very successful at manipulating them afterwards. So now our winter supply of bacon is assured, and that with an overabundance of game, we ought to become corpulent when the work is neither plentiful or pressing.

We are now anxiously awaiting the steam thresher. The one coming here is not working very well, causing delay and uncertainty. Saturday, a week ago, I started out after it on an intelligence hunt. Among other places, I called at Arthur Bryant's—he was from home at Russell, but Mrs. Bryant gave me a very kind reception, insisted on my coming in, and treated me to new cakes and milk, and a eulogy on their little baby girl. But the little customer can't speak, and I do not understand or appreciate youngsters till they can do so. As an offset to this, however, she confided to me the news that another of Arthur's sisters intended coming out next spring. My, didn't I prick up my ears and calculate on possibilities!

On the way back I came by Shellmouth, and after a little delay got the mail. Last Saturday I again set out on a like errand, this time accompanied by Will Pagan. We had to go farther north, and so kindly were we received that we got two dinners and the chance of two suppers, but nature forbade us accepting more than one. It was a treat. The Thresher was at Will Adam's. He comes from Nova Scotia, and his wife recently induced a sister, Miss Sutherland, to join her. Rumour has it that she is open for proposals. Anyhow, she received us very politely and looked awfully pleasant, ladled out jam and sent around the bun slices in a reckless fashion. If instead of being hard-headed, hard-handed pioneering Kanucks we had been schoolboys, the pleasant treatment must have opened our hearts sure. But alas, alas, that sugar supper had such an effect on us that we could not guide the horses home.

After a struggle with darkness we got to Fred Gordon's,[21] a real bachelor establishment, where the best place for anything is where it can be quickest thrown out of the hand at the door. We had to sleep on three layers of bags on the floor using our own rugs for blankets—two blankets and a buffalo robe. After waging war with the numerous cats and dogs who wanted to help to keep us warm, I went to sleep dreaming that I had tried but failed to discover the north pole. It was cold, cold, and no wonder. Next morning we discovered that we had split partnership—Will Pagan had the blankets while I had been trying to raise perspiration under the cold, greasy buffalo skin. [It was a] 25 below zero morning, and we had a sneezer of a drive home facing the wind, both our noses touched a little by the frost.

At home our principal work has been drawing home hay and firewood. The country is all white with snow, and driving is pleasant, sitting on the smooth gliding sleighs behind the horses jingling their bells. It is wonderful how pleased horses are when they first get on the bells. Tomorrow afternoon I go up to Shellmouth to post this. Now I must conclude—it is time we were getting out to finish up the stable duties for the night (8 o'clock). I must leave space for Andrew. We all join in sending you and the circle of friends you are in our kindest love, and I continue

Your most affectionate brother
Willie

P.S. A loud report came from the wilderness that Mrs. Glover (Miss Bryant) has had a baby boy . . .

---

21 He homesteaded on 4-22-28.

[Editors' Note: by this time Andrew and Willie seem to be living in separate houses, because in Andrew's letter of 22 January he speaks of "driving over to Willie's house." The following letter is from Andrew.]

Woodvale, Shell River, Man.

11 December 1884

My Dear Maggie,

You seem to be getting very discontented with your London life, when you are thinking of changing your school and talking about coming out here. We would be very glad if you were with us. It would be so nice if we were together again. We have been greatly disappointed with the thresher. We expected to have had it here about a month ago, but it broke down and has not been working for a time. They had to send for repairs to Winnipeg, which caused the delay.[22] Last week Willie and I drove up to Mr. Lillans[?], the owners of the mill, to see when they would be likely to do our threshing. They promised to come this week, so in a day or two we will be having a lively time of it.

Rod McLennan[23] was married a short time ago, so we were introduced to the first lady who has married a settler in our township. She is very good-looking and quite a credit to the locality. He was a schoolmaster and she was a schoolmistress in Ontario . . .

With kindest love from

Andrew

Woodvale, Shellmouth, Man.

12 December 1884

My Dear Maggie,

My stock of paper has again become exhausted, and I have to make use of some of the scrap paper you sometimes send. We were

---

22 The Wallaces bought their own threshing machine in 1904, the first in their neighbourhood.

23 He was the first teacher at Asessippi school. (Asessippi was the spelling later adopted, though Wallace spells it Assissippi).

pleased to receive your last letter. The long silence made it the more welcome, but we were sorry to know that you had suffered so much from toothache. You may be thankful that you were not suffering the affliction in Manitoba, as here clever dentists and gas are perfect strangers, and the sufferer has only to grin and bear with the best grace possible. We trust you are now free from your misery.

To get a substitute for the violin bridge I had to prey on the old writing desk—you must remember well, but I cannot say that it is a success. It causes a muffled grinding tone, and the first string is quite limp, like thread. And though I have not tuned it up to high pitch, the least creak causes me to wince of a probable whack. Could you send me a new bridge and another first string? I could get them from Winnipeg, but run a great risk of getting rubbishy material.

We have been still enjoying open mild weather. The other night it became murky and dark, and next day we had a steady fall of snow. About sunset it was particularly wild and boisterous looking—ugly indeed. Now the ground is in good order for sleighing. We have been busied principally cutting wood and making other preparations for the steam thresher, but we seem doomed to every disappointment with it. On Wednesday we saw them steaming away at Gordons, five miles away—after that we made sure of them, and yesterday Andrew and I started out for Haworths with the intention of making a beginning on this circuit of threshing. It was so misty we could see no distance till the afternoon, and then we were chagrined to find them still further away at Arthur Bryant's. This year will close that account—we will be no more bothered with them. They will have lively sport threshing out the five acre patches next year to make a fortune. It annoys us very much, the loss of the fine weather.

I can think of very little this time that would interest you. We are all well and the animals are in the best of health, with the exception of one of the cats that foolishly allowed itself to be tempted into a strong steel trap set for wolves. It is now sorrowfully and industriously nursing a smashed limb.

By the bye, regarding the skunk furs—a skunk skin is valued by the Hudson's Bay Co. at 3 [shillings] and three at the most would be all that was required, so somebody must be making money on them. Last summer we killed at least five, but I would not put my fingers on the smelly things for a good deal. The stench is their great protection from other preying animals, and if Miss Tuer would like a sample of it I will gladly send it next summer. The skunks, if they get a chance, are rascals on poultry. Last summer I made a narrow escape from an unpleasant experience. Sometime after dark I was walking home through the creek and saw something black and white gliding down the trail. I thought it was one of the cats. You can imagine my dismay when I stooped down to give it a reassuring pat to find myself face to face with a big skunk. You may guess I backed up considerable. Why the brute did not drench me I cannot understand. I was relieved to see it glide among the bushes. Teulon killed one in the Langfords' abode over a year ago, and you can detect the smell to this day. We wish you all a pleasant Xmas holiday and unite in sending you our kindest love.

Affectionately yours
Willie

1885

Woodvale, Shellmouth, Man.
7 January 1885

My Dear Maggie,

You will by this time have given me up in despair I fear, but uncontrollable circumstances have kept me from writing. Saturday a fortnight ago the steam thresher came to Haworths, and it was hurry, hustle everywhere making preparations. On Monday, Andrew and I started out for the thresher, and it was a "sneezer," 40 degrees below zero, and cold, cold, and remained so all day. And frozen noses, ears and fingers were plentiful. The frost also kept the steamer from working well, causing a great many stoppages, so that keeping up the heat by exercise was impossible. Though we threshed till about 9 o'clock at night, there was not a creditable amount of work done.

Next day the scene of operations was changed to Pagans', and the cold was still as intense, so that the delays and freezings were repeated. Next day we had to go back again. It was a shade warmer, but the steamer would not keep up speed and Xmas brought with it the correction that still another day would be required to finish there. The mill men left [for Christmas] with the promise that they would be back after holidays, a week later. Since then we have all had more or less colds, etc., and I have been sick. Neuralgia and a disorganized liver, so Dr. Haworth says, and I have had a pretty bad time of it— medicating myself in the first instance, and swallowing quantities of horrid stuffs, castor oil, salts, senna, belladonna, and even sulphur, but all to no purpose, and getting little rest day or night. Yesterday I went down to Haworths and got a mixture of rhubarb and goodness knows what else, and this morning I feel greatly better. Can you in the circumstances forgive my long silence? . . .

With regard to the £10 you purpose sending me, we trust you are not doing so rashly. Surely I did not give you the impression that I wished the organ. I will not deny the fact that I would like to get it, and meant sometime to get one, but at present it does look like a judicious investment. I will let the matter hang for a month. The selling price of the instrument is £30. As an agent, Williams bought it in Ontario for £16, but the freight is something considerable, probably £6 or £7 additional. It is a splendid toned instrument, ten stops and two knee swells. If prospects are good I will offer him £15. If he doesn't bargain at that he "kin just kape it." He offered me it as low as £18. I will let you know further, meantime I cannot express, but I think you will appreciate, my gratitude. Do you remember the Saturday afternoon hunt we had after a harmonium in Glasgow?

On Xmas night we ate our plum pudding at the Pagans'. Face ache prevented me enjoying myself to the full, but all enjoyed themselves till daylight next morning with music, cards, etc. etc. New Year's day we spent very quietly at home. For about three weeks we had a spell of very, very cold weather—the longest and coldest snap that has been here for a number of years. Since Saturday morning the weather has taken an agreeable turn, mild and pleasant. The pity is we are not threshing. We hope to be doing so at Pagans' tomorrow and on Thursday at our own place, and we hope our big expenditure will be realized. Today is voting day at Shellmouth, and we must be getting our dinner and starting out . . .

Your most affectionate brother
Willie

Woodvale, Shellmouth, Man.
22 January 1885

My Dear Maggie,

We were glad to receive your letter . . . [it] came to us when we were busily occupied threshing. While the thresher was here I was cook, and you can imagine the busy time I had. The scarcity of water for the engine delayed operations somewhat. To get anything like a quantity Andrew had to bring it from a lake 2 miles distant. The creek valley prevented us taking advantage of the river.

The millmen came here Wednesday night a week ago, and took Thursday, Friday and Saturday to finish what grain we had on the other side of the creek. On Monday they set about bringing the engine and machine through the gully. The engine had not proceeded far when it slipped and toppled over the bank, the smokestack buried into the snow. All the neighbours had to be collected, and on the afternoon, after a great deal of halooing and manoeuvering, it was put up in its natural position again. But some breakages had to be put right by a blacksmith, and it was not till Thursday again that work was resumed, and that day finished up our stacks.

We did not realize the grain, but still we have cause for gratitude for what we did get. We got 438 bushels of wheat, 245 of oats, 108 of barley—after all is cleared up, fully 800 bushels of grain, all of first-rate quality and good for the highest price. A bushel of wheat yields over 40 pounds of flour with bran and meddleys additional, so you can in a manner realize that we can satisfy the appetites of a good many. I had fifteen mouths to make dinner and supper for, and three threshers at every meal, so you can guess I had some lively work cooking.

On Friday morning Andrew and I with the greatest good will put the two teams onto the engine and dragged it up to Teulon's. For three days he had the benefit of their company, but there it was pretty much a threshing of grainless straw. From sixteen acres he only got 136 bushels, grain of a very inferior quality—just chicken feed. The last afternoon was almost wholly taken up with a stack of wheat that only yielded five bushels. In fact, the farming operations of all our neighbours will yield no income. So do you not think us fortunate and deserving of credit?

Throughout the threshing the weather was intensely cold, down to 40 degrees below zero and seldom above 20 degrees below, and the effect has been in my case, an intensely severe attack of neuralgia. Today I am greatly better and more like myself again. I seem to be blessed with a weak stomach and bad teeth. Never mind, when I make my fortune I will have sweet revenge on the latter.

At Shellmouth they are preparing for a grand demonstration in February. And do you know, I have received a flattering invitation from Arthur Frank Venables, late of London, now Chairman of the Literary Society, and the possessor and wearer of an eyeglass, to join a party of the upper select who are getting up a theatrical performance. They have costumes all completed, I understand. Will you not come and see me dancing on the stage with a ringletted wig, surmounted by a feather, a sword and tight breeches. I rather think I will steer clear of the business. As it is I'm not a member of the society and have no intention of becoming one. I have been elected onto the committee to get up the performance, so you see my elocutionary efforts have not been judged amiss.

Last night I was down at the Pagans', and I hardly know whether to blame myself or congratulate myself, but I bought the organ for £16. It is a dirt cheap bargain, and I will have plenty of opportunity to part with it at an enhanced price. What I dislike most is the putting money away just now in an unnecessary thing . . . but surely the problem of life is not so hard that it precludes one indulging in recreation to a certain extent. In any case, the deed is done, and our home will once more occasionally—and particularly in the long winter nights—be filled with volumes of musical sounds . . . I do sincerely trust you are not scrimping yourself sending the money you speak of. If you send any music, please see that you do not overdo it. Send it secular, catchingly and popular. I have lots of sacred music. Of course, something particularly good will be welcome, but I wish to impress you with the fact that you are not in any way to bankrupt your pocket money. The less music, the better practiced, and maybe I will yet be organist at Shellmouth. I will get the instrument home soon on Saturday, and next letter I will give you a full description. I must stop and leave Andrew space. We are all well and in great spirits. To your homefriends we send kindest regards and our kindest love to yourself.

Your most affectionate brother
Willie

Woodvale, Shellmouth, Man.
11 February 1885

My Dear Maggie,

We duly received last Saturday your registered letter with enclosed note for the latter. I am especially grateful to you. I fear you will be taking exception to the want of regularity in sending your letters, but the fact is I have been very much bothered body and mind for some time back. My old friend neuralgia keeps me close company. The cold, windy weather aggravates it very much, and causes me to be rather glum and dispirited, and takes the rosey hue from existence. Up till a month ago we had great hopes of being at last able to make some money, but these must now be delayed over now. The grist mill in our district was recently entirely remodeled and new patent roller machinery put in. When all was ready to begin the immense business they purposed doing, it was discovered that the water power was not sufficient to make the wheels go round, and the whole affair has been shut down till next summer. So here we are with plenty of grain but no market, and for a month or two I will have a nice time staving off money claimants. This bothers us very much. As soon as spring comes we will be all right. . . . A large portion of the wheat we will make into flour and sell that as opportunity offers during the summer, but you can understand the difference between doing that and taking the wheat to the mill and bringing back money.

Last week I was from home four days. I was at the Birtle Creek, 45 miles distant, with a load of wheat, and I brought it back in flour. I had a very tough journey—the days were stormy and made the trails very heavy with snow. I got very nice flour.

I really wish the railway would come along so that we could get a cash market at Shellmouth for grain, and put an end to these long journeys and this pioneer life. After all, the railway will come no nearer than forty miles this summer. The company have great difficulty getting money for their enterprise. We have the sure hope however that it will be our length the following year. A large sawmill is to be put up at Shellmouth in the spring that with the [?] building may mend matters somewhat. Beside this, we hear that a large number of old country people are coming to settle on the other side of the river under the auspices of the Church of England Colonization Society, so that probably better times will be in store in the near future than we anticipate.

I have got the organ home now, and we have great concerts. The fiddle bridge and strings came all right, and Andrew is now producing music, weird and unearthly no doubt, but still progressing. The organ does splendidly in our house. It has a far better tone than before, probably owing to the upstairs floor. It stands six feet high, has five octaves, any amount of artistic cabinet work, and a solid rosewood case. The ten stops are Dulciana, Diapason Viola, Bass Coupler, Forte, Divideo, Swell, Treble Coupler, Flute, Melodia, and Echo. It has also two knee swells. All this with a stylish cloth-covered music stool, sets off the house immensely. How does it compare with Uncle Hugh's? I bought it very cheap. Williams, its former owner, takes his departure for Ontario next Thursday and the eldest Haworth goes with him. But he is bound for England, thoroughly disgusted with Manitoba. I will see him before he leaves, and if he expects to be in London I will try and persuade him to call on you. I think you would enjoy a talk with him.

Friday week there is to be a grand demonstration at Shellmouth. I send you a programme. You see I backed out from the farcical affair. . .

With the exception of my old [neur]algia we are all well. The stock are doing well with the exception of the pigs, and they are all going wrong with cold. We have lost two, and three are just now under medical treatment. I hope they will get better. I must now stop. I purpose going down to Russell, and starting early in the morning, and it is now bed time. . . .

Your most affectionate brother
Willie

Woodvale, Shellmouth, Man.
1 March 1885

My Dear Maggie,

Many many thanks for the registered letter addressed to Andrew. The enclosure was all right . . . Since my last letter we have been enjoying the luxury of a mild spell of weather. For some days back, and especially today, the contrast to what it was ten days ago is startling. Then we exposed as little of our skin as we could possibly avoid—now only the decent notions consequent to civilized habits tempts us to wear clothing at all. All the animals are lounging around luxuriating in the heat. The working ones will, I expect, be bracing themselves up for spring work. But the first swallow does not always prove the arrival of summer, and Jack Frost is only a little way in bringing a vengeance dose for us yet.

But the days are now nice and long, and the sun is gaining power. We are able to put some work through our hands now. At present we are busily employed cutting and hauling logs for our new homestead. In a fortnight or so we expect to be building. Before the year is out we expect to have a double house, two stables, pig house, and hen house added to our number of buildings. After that we will set about getting the other buildings, i.e. granary, two houses and stable moved to the new site. The other granary will follow after, and if eight buildings do not make a display of prosperity, then the country has no display.

My only grumble this time is the loss of pigs. Out of seven bought last year we will only have two. The investment has been a black loss—they got infected by some catarrhal disease. Next investment will be more fortunate, I hope.

Did you get the programme for the concert at Shellmouth Friday a week ago? It was a grand success and a notable event in the short history of this town. I had to help with the preparations, and started on foot immediately after dinner. When I neared Teulon's house I heard him at his violin, scraping away as if for dear life, and aiming to perfection. On entering, I beheld him arrayed in his best, shaven and clean, and after the fiddle was boxed, in his right mind. Together we continued the journey, and quickly we got to the scene. A few of the leading ones soon gathered, and after the schoolchildren were off, the work began.

First the piano had to be got up, then all the chairs and lamps within a decent radius collected. And with sweeping out, fixing up stage and curtain, etc., we had good fun. Everything was complete—drop curtain, footlights (candles), dressing rooms, reserved seats in front for those of aristocratic notions and a reckless regard for their half-dollars. After the fitting up came the rehearsal, and for two or three hours the piano, violins, and vocal organs made a great din. Just before dark the sleighs and cutters began to arrive and discharge their occupants, and after supper the hall began to fill up till it was completely blocked.

A party of Englishmen came here a year ago and now are settled across the river from here under [the name of] the Wolverine Mixed Farming Co.[1] Their leading man is a Mr. Goldsmid, who was for a long time on the English stage. At the concert he gave a descriptive sketch of an amateur theatrical performance in London, and it certainly was the best and most enjoyed item in the concert programme. He acted as stage manager at the burlesque afterwards.

It would only waste paper to attempt to describe the whole performance. The dressers were well got up. Mr. Venables' acting was certainly the best, and the curtain dropped in a highly artistic manner. I enclose a copy of the chorus that was afterwards sung, composed by one of the actors, Mr. Price. The concert was certainly the greatest success that has been here yet.

After all was over, the hall had again to be cleared and swept for the dancers. After supper in the hotel, the ball began, and with the number of piano operators present, a specially engaged violinist and a flutist, the dancers had rare times till daylight. Andrew and I did not start home till then, but enjoyed ourselves very well one way and another in the ballroom, hotel, or store. The settlers are just now greatly excited over the herd law, or whether it is better to make the law insist upon the cattle or the farm being fenced. So that though we were not dancing, we had our attention employed. Alf Bryant was present with a hired team and a lot of news. Wallace,

---

1 The Wolverine Settlement was founded in 1884 by P.W. Goldsmid and Herbert Vyvyan.

the H.B.Co. officer at Russell, is a good piano player—he was an organist in England.

I am sure there must have been about 200 people attracted. On Saturday you may be sure little work was done. I understand the Literary Society cleared £7. This was remarkably good, and enabled them to lay in a stock of books. Very generously they presented the Sunday School, recently started, £1 to help its funds.

I am enjoying the organ greatly and rapidly improving. I can read much very much more quickly than I could in the old country. At present I am murdering the marvelous work, "Caliph of Bagdad," (your old favourite), "Tancrede," and "Somnambula." The three latter I got from Teulon—I expect him down this week with the violin parts. They are however just a little too far advanced for me ... The music I think must have charmed the neuralgia away. I am all right now. It is as you suggest—my teeth are bad, and swell sometimes so that I can hardly eat anything hard. You must excuse my now concluding ...

Your most affectionate brother
Willie

Woodvale, Shellmouth, Man.
18 March 1885

My Dear Maggie,

Last mail brought us no letter from you, so I must start right away with Manitoba. Since my last letter the weather has kept mild pretty much, and now that the days are a reasonable length we get a good day's work done. Our work has been cutting and hauling logs for building purposes. Another three days will, I expect, find them all over at the building site.

Saturday a week ago I went to Shellmouth, and among other things paid a visit to the new store. Teulon was with me, and we both got treated [to] cigars. Before I started home I arranged with Mr. Whaley,² who is one of the Councillors, to go down to Birtle

---

2   The postmaster.

fifty miles distant, to get a load of planks for the new ferry boat. There is not much prospect of the bridge being built till next winter. I started on the journey on Tuesday morning before sunrise.

It was very, very cold, a high wind blowing. Whaley drove into Russell just behind me, and so cold was he that he had to stop up for dinner. He has been over twelve years in the country, so you can guess it was pretty cold. We started again just after noon, and jogged on till we came to Binscarth, the central point of the Scotch colony. Splendid buildings, church, store, smithy, hotel with a great many stables for their immense stock. After a warmup we went on and got to the Halfway House, our first resting point, about sundown. Next morning off again and travelled the twelve miles to Birtle before nine o'clock.

This place gained its prominence from being on the main trail to all points west before the railway came. It is prettily situated at the side of the Birdtail Creek, and surrounded by steep high banks. The whole town was excited over a lawsuit, and as no business could be done, we with the rest of the town attended court. Some of the wild boys had been rambling about after nightfall, and seeing some clothing hanging outside a negligent storekeeper's premises, thought to have some fun, and quickly the clothes were transferred to the office of the lawyer. So far the joke was good, but when the clothes were sent back, the dealer insisted on an apology. This was not forthcoming, and during this difficulty, the clothes went amissing—were stolen in real earnest. The storekeeper took out a warrant against the lawyer for stealing his clothes, and this was the case before the court. It was a perfect burlesque. Nearly everyone in town knew the guilty jokers except the storekeeper, and do all he could, he failed to make a case or find out the real perpetrators. The magistrates were in [on] the fun too, and what with speechifying and laughing it was dinnertime before the case was dismissed.

To soothe us somewhat for the delay, the wood merchant treated us to dinner. He lives in a fine house on the heights above the town. We were shown into a nice furnished room. It did bring back old country feelings to see carpets, piano and small ornamental fixings. At dinner we had no wines. We had at least napkins and the presence of his smiling daughter, just home from an eastern boarding school.

In the afternoon we got loaded, but too late to start, so we went to a lecture on astronomy by the Doctor, and before going to bed we had quite a lot of music—violin and piano. Next evening found us back at the Scotch colony, and the succeeding one at Shellmouth, tired and glad to be home. I got £3 for the journey, but rather than go freighting again I think I would suck nutriment from my thumb.

My stock of news is somewhat limited this time, and I hardly know how to fill up the paper. The cabinet organ comes in for a fair share of my attention. I enjoy it very much, and flatter myself that I am making great progress. The hymn music is just a little tiresome now. I fully intended picking up something, if I could, at Birtle, but time would not permit.

The hotelkeeper [at Birtle] told us a good story of the way musical instrument [agents] do business in this country. A year ago he bought an organ and put it in his sitting room. Of course everyone began studying elementary music, till the instrument became a nuisance rather than a pleasure. The hotelkeeper happened to be in Brandon, and meeting an agent, he, more in joke than anything else, said he wished he would take the organ away and put a piano in its place. What was his surprise on getting home to find a splendid piano occupying the place of the organ, and an account valuing it at $550. That was rather a smart way of doing business. Considering that it had come 90 miles by railway and 40 by road, it was really a fine piano. When do you mean to come out and try the organ?

You will remember Shaw, who came out from Glasgow with us. A Glasgow lassie came all the way to Winnipeg, where they got married. She brought a piano out with her. Last winter she had three friends died, and she went back all alone to Glasgow. I expect she was tempted by legacies. She returned last spring. Again about the middle of this winter, a sister's illness tempted her back again to Glasgow, where she is now. Do you not admire her contempt for distance on land and sea? I met Shaw a fortnight ago, and he was vowing this was the last old country trip his wife would take for a long time.

His partner Walker heired a handsome legacy some time ago—he is now independent. Since ever he came here he has only blackguarded the country. He went back to England last fall, and I thought we would see no more of him here, but he is writing back now that he is completely disgusted with the old country and wishes himself back at Shell River. He means to come back with Mrs. Shaw in April.

Poor Ben Haworth will be back again in his Drug Store [in] Manchester, sadder and wiser. The man to whom he sold his business has become blind, and Haworth left here with the intention of becoming his manager. This country fairly cleaned him out. He had to take steerage passage, and until he got to New York he meant to keep his Manitoban attire—cap, overalls, and a huge pair of homemade rawhide moccasins. My, but he would make the down-Easters gape! I wonder if he regrets leaving Manitoba.

I think I would get crazed were I to awake in Glasgow and find out that my Manitoban life had been all a dream. I could not live in the city smoke again. Even American towns I am glad to get out of them. In the old country you cannot possibly realize the charms of a country life. I must now stop . . .

Your most affectionate brother
Willie

Woodvale, Shellmouth, Man.
2 April 1885

My Dear Maggie,

I have mislaid your last letter to Father, so I must trust to memory regarding the questioning portion . . .

The days are gradually stretching out—daylight till seven o'clock now. This makes a wonderful difference in the work, although it is hard to break off winter habits till the snow goes, and that event is not coming to pass quite as early as we anticipated. For a week back the weather has not been agreeable, dark and cloudy and sometimes very stormy. A good deal of snow has fallen, but the thaw continues, and the depth is not increased. Last Monday we had a regular old country snowfall—damp, clinging stuff that fastened onto everything. The trees and shrubs are loaded, and it made snowballs. Generally the snow is so dry that one might as well have a pelting battle with chaff.

Our work has principally been farming and hauling away grain and drawing fencing rails. Grain is selling very slowly and prices are low—we are looking forward to business getting brisker. We are all well and in good spirits.

I daresay old country habitants will be exercising their minds over rebellion reports from Manitoba. These are only too true. But as the scene of the trouble is 400 miles Northwest from us, it does not and will not affect us much. It is rumoured that they have taken possession of Prince Albert town, and put a regiment of Mounted Police to flight, killing six. But as the telegraph wires have been cut, reports are not very reliable.

Perhaps you will remember some of our Manitoban prospective plans before we left the old country. One of them was that we would settle at the forks of the Saskatchewan River. That is the district where the rebellion is, and that is the objective point of the railway that passes through our district. You need not be the least bit alarmed regarding our safety. Hereaway the Indians and Half-breeds are not numerous, and are contented, and should the field of operations be extended, Shell River is out of the course and has no attraction for a disturbance. . . .

On Saturday I went down to Russell with a load of wheat. The sun reflected from the snow was very dazzling and trying to the eyes. When I got to Russell I was surprised to find crowds of people, and was more than astonished to learn that the cause of this was the rebellion out west, which has extended to alarming proportions. And fears were entertained of a general rising among the Indians.

Major Boulton was that day enlisting volunteers and buying horses for cavalry and transport purposes. He succeeded in getting a corps of sixty men, two of them neighbours—Langford and Thomson—and as many horses, beside buying and engaging a number of teams for transport purposes.[3] Really there was a lively and exciting bustle. The men and horses were to leave next morning for Moosomin station on the C.P.R., from there by the cars west to

3   Boulton's Scouts were made up of two volunteer companies of mounted infantry, 66 in Russell troop and 57 in the Birtle troop. They saw action at Risk Creek, Duck Lake and Batoche. Three men were wounded and one, D'Arcy Baker, was killed. A monument was erected in their honour at Russell.

Regina where they will be drilled for a fortnight and then for the seat of war. They did not persuade me to enlist or sell my team.

It was reported that the Mounted Police had been worsted in a fight and had to retire, leaving Prince Albert in the hands of the insurgents, and that a number of lives had been lost. Troops are on the way up from the East, so it is likely the rebels will soon get the quietus, but in the meantime the disturbance will have a deplorable effect on the immigration prospects of the country—although I believe ultimately good will come out of the evil insofar that the government will be under the necessity of introducing new attractions to the country such as the Hudson's Bay Railway and an extensive system of branch lines. Had we free trade additional I could see a near prospect of making a fortune, so we live in hope.

Do not be alarmed for our safety. We are at present too isolated, away from central points, and it is to these the Indians will devote their attention. Plunder and whiskey are the only things that can have caused them to join issue with the rebels. We seldom see Indians here—a hunting party once a year probably, and in the neighbouring villages so far there have been no Indian roustabouts. There is a reserve at Fort Pelly, eighty miles from here, and should they take to the warpath they would come down the trail to Fort Ellice, and that passes east of us a good many miles. So do not be in the least alarmed even if matters do get worse, and that is hardly likely. In Manitoba the Indians are more contented and civilized than in the Territories farther west.

It was very late before I got home that night. I had to wait a considerable time on my grist, and the sun had made sad havoc with the snow trails—some places a foot of slush, other places quite bare. The one was bad footing for the horses, the other hard drawing for the sleigh. We have now 2000 lbs. of flour on hand, so you may be sure that so long as that is to the fore we will not starve.

On Sunday the thaw continued, and yesterday the creek came down in full flood. Our house is now built at the side of it, and we were pleased to hear its familiar roar again. Ducks and geese have again put in an appearance, and a number of other little birds have looked up their old haunts and are again making the woodlands echo with their songs. Now is the only time that their plumage can be seen to advantage, as the trees are bare of their thick foliage. This last winter seems to have come and gone exceptionally fast, doubtless owing to the fact that we always had some work on hand. Yesterday Andrew and I were cleaning out seed wheat and preparing fence posts. For some months now the work will be very pressing, and we will have little spare time.

Owing to our housebuilding disappointment the ploughing is very far back. Everybody is however pretty much in the same fix. We mean now to go more in for stock—this will divide the work more equally over the year, more work in winter and less hurry rush in summer, and those so engaged claim it to be more lucrative. Certainly, in the event of disappointment, the eggs are not all in one basket. Wouldn't you think it nicer to be making butter and feeding pigs—such affectionate animals—[than] pounding knowledge into juveniles?

Last night the cattle gave us the slip and got away on a stroll. I hunted them unsuccessfully for some time till a threatening sky warned me to get home, and I got there just in time. A furious hurricane set in, the worst one we have had since coming here. It made the trees crack and howl dreadfully. The cattle would have a cold campout. Andrew is on his way back with the wanderers now. Today the wind is very high and intensely cold, so I fear we will not get seeding as we purposed.

Andrew has told you, I see, the prospective feminine additions to our neighbourhood. It is hoped the rebellion will not scare them from coming. A settler, Lochead, two miles east of us, has recently come back accompanied by his infant children. So we are getting our locality more civilized looking. Space will not permit my continuing further...

Your most affectionate brother
Willie

[P.S. from Andrew]

... Last Saturday I went to a house-raising bee at Lee's. He did not get his house up—there was such an excitement over the war news and the contingent of volunteers leaving Shellmouth and Russell that none of the other hands turned up. He expects his sister will leave Dublin in a month to join him here. He is rather put about, as it will give him pretty hard work to get the house ready for her reception and get his crop in. . . we will soon have plenty of ladies in our township . . .

[from Andrew] Woodvale, Shellmouth, Man.

10 April 1885

My Dear Maggie

. . . The rebellion out west is getting rather a hot affair. A week ago there was a battle fought—of the troops, twelve were killed and forty-seven wounded.[4] Of the contingent that left Russell and Shellmouth, one was killed and seven wounded—it is not known how many Indians and half-breeds were killed. You need not be the least alarmed for our safety, as the fighting is three hundred miles west of us. . .

With kindest love from

Andrew

P.S. Kindly excuse me this time, awfully busy . . . Will write next mail,

Willie

Woodvale, Shellmouth, Man.

24 April 1885

My Dear Maggie,

We duly received last Saturday your letter of 18 March. . . . You really must excuse my remissions replying to your questions. It is very hard for us, working about all day outside, to keep things as orderly inside as they might be. In fact, sometimes it is more like a scramble around trying to do everything. Your letters come, are read and appreciated, and put away, sometimes in the desk, sometimes on the shelf, and when replying, time is often so much taken up that

---

4   The battle of Duck Lake.

to limit [?] for the last letter would have serious effect on the length and value of the epistle on hand. In time I hope to remedy this—meantime pray be charitable.

Now we are again heels and head over in work. This year it promises to be of a more diversified nature. We have just bought two cows, both milking, and this is seeding time, and neither of them will brook delay. And in the midst of this we have business in connection with last year's grain. The cows are remarkably quiet good milkers. This morning I had my first churning of butter (7 lbs.). When the other cow is milking, three weeks hence, it will be a case of churning three times a week.

The seeding has been very much delayed by wind, snow and rain. The ground is very wet and not in good order. Still, we hope to have a good harvest and certainly we have the prospects of better prices for grain. Andrew will tell you of the four broods of little chickens and the pretty, frisky little calves. We are now getting into stock, and we may reasonably hope that now we are laying the foundation of the fortune in store for us. I have not much news this time.

Our military contingent are now, we hear, at the seat of war, and a decisive battle with the rebels is, we understand, about to take place. This we hope will put an end to the rebellion. In Manitoba all is peace and quietness. Hereaway the departure of the warriors brought some money into circulation. The outfit of the sixty men and horses cost the government $20,000. War is rather an expensive game.

The ferry boat is again running at Shellmouth, and we hear nothing more of the bridge. The Railway Co. are, we hear, preparing to come at least sixty miles nearer us. The millwrights are busy preparing to put up the new sawmill, so that on the whole, things are looking up.

Saturday, a week ago, I was with others helping Lee to put up his house against his sister's early arrival. The Peytons will shortly, I expect, be asking a like assistance in view of Mrs. and Miss Peyton's arrival, and we hope shortly to be in the same situation in view of your early appearance.

We were glad to learn definitely your mind in the matter in your last letter. So far as we can judge, you do not seem to be very contented or well at your present work. . . . What with cattle, pigs, poultry and 65 acres of crop, we want a housekeeper very much now. And as you say in your letter, that whenever we want you and whenever you could be any help to us, you will, on us letting you know, come out at once—well, we want you badly and you can be exceeding great help to us. But independent of all these considerations we long very much, all of us, to see you again and to be together. But before discussing the matter of coming fully, I may as well admit to you that we could only with the greatest difficulty send you money to aid you on your journey. Since we have come here we have had a pretty tough experience of scarcity of money—in the first place, because we commenced with too little capital, and disappointed calculations did not mend matters. For some time now, a year probably, we have been pretty comfortable insofar that we had produce to dispose of. Now we are, beyond all doubt, assured of everything we can desire in the way of provisions and clothing. But any little cash we can get hold of, in spite of this bartering and tricking, finds a channel in the shape of taxes, etc., and other items that insist upon a hard cash settlement. I think you will appreciate the position. We are prospering though we may not be coining money. We have comforted ourselves with the idea that at least you had money for all your wants, and we can understand how you could be unwittingly led into expenditure that though you would rather have dispensed, yet your position was such that it could not be avoided. I only hope for all our sakes that you have sufficient money to bring you this length, and I would infer from your last letter that you had.

So far as outfit is concerned ... that need not cost very much, I take the liberty of thinking. In the way of dress I presume you have a good stock. Good wool is the hardest thing to get in this country—a small parcel of that would be of great service, and you would find the advantage both on the journey and here of having a good heavy tweed ulster.[5] There is no necessity to buy any furs— we have plenty of raw material for the catching about. We would, if you come, require to extend our household equipment. It would be a great saving if you could bring a full stonewear dinner set for a dozen, with forks and knives and spoons, and also the china tea set you already possess. Stonewear and cutlery are excessively high here.

---

5   A long, loose, heavy overcoat, usually belted, originally made in Ulster of frieze or other heavy fabric.

A supply of linen thread would also be an advantage. All this will not cost an extra amount of money.

The passage money is, I think, not more than £25, and you would be none the worse for having at most £3 or £5 for incidental expenses when railroading in America. On the steamship you are boarded and have little or no expenses. On the cars you will buy your meals en route. The trip will last about four days, and the meals cost from 2p to 3p each. With Allan line you can book direct through from Liverpool, England to Moosomin station, C.P. Railway, our rail point. This will enable you to figure out and see if you have money sufficient. If so, Henry with his other kindnesses will learn for you the exact passage money, and if you have not sufficient we must keep our counsel and devise ways and means later. You might write and ask the Steamboat Co. yourself what the fare by the all-rail route in American would be. Bear in mind that the cabin rates vary, and do so from the position of the berths. The cabin passengers all share alike at the table. £40, I should imagine, will be ample to meet the whole expense. Of course, once you are at Moosomin station, we will take care of you, rich or poor. I will be minute in succeeding letters.

Meantime, so as to enable us to make preparations and give us a zest for doing so, reply at once and let us know how you receive the proposal. Whether you unhesitatingly decided against, or are uncertain, or would like time to think it over, or mean to come, do not trouble yourself about scruples on our account—they have no value.

The work we want you for is to cook our meals, keep the house and dairy clean, and stitch our garments. The hardest feature of it will be an occasional floor scrubbing, and I'll bet a good deal you are not two months before you are so strong and eager that you will be cultivating a flower garden. Andrew and I will see that the cows are milked, that you have plenty of firewood and water, and I'll take care of the churning . . . We would like you to start out the first week in July and get here about the beginning of August. And if you let us know soon that you decide upon coming we will be as gay as larks. I would earnestly advise you to come and give the country a trial for a year. If you do not like it, or cannot stand it, I'll guarantee that no obstacle will prevent me arranging so that you can get back to the old country. In my succeeding letters I will presume that you can and will come. . . .

Your most affectionate brother
Willie

Woodvale, Shellmouth, Man.
21 May 1885

My Dear Maggie,

I was exceedingly sorry that time would not permit me to write you last mail. I had about a fourth of a letter written and was busy getting on with it when Peyton, a neighbour, came in and distracted my attention, and as there was a likelihood of my missing the mail altogether I had to bundle up and make for Shellmouth in his company. Father duly received your letter and we were glad to learn all the news it contained.

. . . We were glad that Miss Bryant afforded you an opportunity to meet her before she started for here—the socks will be a real blessing. Is she not alarmed over the rebellion? We are not in the least affected by it, although a foolish report got somehow into the papers that this district had been plundered and pillaged, and caused a good deal of excitement amongst Major Boulton's scouts out west, who all come from this district. There is not the least likelihood of such a thing happening.

I wish you could see our home now. Nature is making rapid strides. The leaves are out on the trees and the prairie is getting green again. We had a delightful spring shower yesterday and another this morning, and everything is growing just like mushrooms. The grain is getting every chance this year, and everything bodes a splendid harvest. Prices are also likely to improve very much, and we gleefully anticipate making a lot of money this year. With the two extra cows we can greatly economize our housekeeping bills, but they leave one very little leisure time, constantly at work.

Between times I have managed to finish a letter for Uncle David. I am dreadfully behind with my correspondence. I wish you were with us—I would quietly shoulder a lot of it over on you. How would you like that? We trust you have a letter on the way letting us know your mind on coming out. The possibility seems too good to be true. It would make a wonderful difference to us here. I think you need not fear the change so far as health is concerned—what with the bracing dry climate, pure air and exercise, you will grow fat and strong.

We have not made much progress with the house building yet, but in a week or so we purpose getting right at the work, and very shortly we hope to move over to the site, and this will enable us to make more speed with the work. I am going down to Russell today to see about house-fixings, and should I not get satisfaction, the likelihood is I will start for Birtle at the beginning of the week. With the other work we are getting along well. With the exception of barley, all our seeding is done.

The next item on our farm programme is fencing, then a little draining and after that reclaiming new land. The cows continue to do exceedingly well. I have already sold a [?] of butter. We expect the other cow will be milking in a day or two. We are also increasing our number of poultry very much—the last brood of chickens are exceptionally good and pretty. There is a possibility we may get the railway thirty miles of us. If you come out however, you will require to come by the C.P.R. to Moosomin Station, seventy miles distant. It is also reported that the bridge across the Assiniboine at Shellmouth will be commenced in a short time. This will be a great boon to the town in many ways.

I think I told you that we had a resident Presbyterian preacher at Shellmouth now, but he has such an extensive district to overtake that he holds service there only once a fortnight. Father and Andrew were at service last time and were greatly pleased with him. I have very little time to play the organ now, but many of the pieces in the last book you sent I like very much. . . . Andrew has a letter scrolled but he will not be enabled to write this time, I fear, as the rain induces me to start for Russell a day earlier than was intended. The sun is now shining brightly, so I will have a pleasant journey . . .

Your most affectionate brother
Willie

Woodvale, Shellmouth, Man.
9 June 1885

My Dear Maggie,

Pardon my not writing last mail. I had been from home all week, and on Friday night I felt so tired and loath to bother that I determined to again trespass on your good nature. Your last letter duly reached here. We were pleased to learn all it contained. Your next one will, we hope, give us tidings of whether you mean to join us, and we anticipate it very much. Andrew received the atlas and it is, though somewhat ancient, a welcome addition to our library.

We have been busily employed seeding, housebuilding and fencing. The seeding is now over, and we have a promise of a fair crop—the only drawback is weeds. Some of the land we will rest next year and summer fallow—this will remedy the nuisance. We purpose having the most of the fencing done this week. After that housebuilding will occupy the whole of our attention.

During my absence the old cow presented us with a nice, strong heifer calf, and now we are getting gallons of milk, about sixty quarts per day. What do you think of that? The mosquitoes are now quite plentiful and help to keep us lively.

I am glad to say that we now see the end of the rebellion. Affairs looked pretty ugly sometime, and had the government troops suffered a reverse I fear all of us would have had to clear out for awhile. The government sent up rifles and ammunition, evidently they had a fear of the result. The Indians are very quiet and humble now that Riel has been made prisoner, and their last state is worse than their first. As no gunpowder is allowed to be sold to them, some of them must have recourse to the habits of their fathers and use the bow and arrows. A band of them passed the house today and were so civil they even called their dogs beneath their carts lest their fangs should taste some of our chickens.

At the last battle[6] another of our neighbours was killed—Ted Brown, through sheer reckless exposure of his person. He was well liked. Since he left here he had been advanced to Captain in Gardner's place. The latter is now home in a pitiful state, quite

---

6   Batoche.

helpless. Perrin is coming to pay a short visit, after that he leaves for home. He will feel the loss of the arm very much. Langford is back with the troops, although the bullet has not yet been extracted from the wound. The boys are all very glad the fighting is over. Some of them will likely remain out west all summer. The settlers in and around the seat of war are in a deplorable state—no provisions and no prospects of a harvest this year.

The latest idea here is finding gold. Some old Californian has turned the heads of the Shellmouth people, and some of them are industriously washing out little specks that glitter. I think we will still continue farming.

Last Sunday Haworth and I (by the bye his brother has settled into a situation on the Isle of Man) went over to Arthur Bryant's, and I met Miss Bryant. Mrs. Glover and her little boy were also there. The latter I could understand and converse with, the former I couldn't. I did all I could to gain information from her about you, but to my questions she invariably said "Wha..?" and silence seemed to be golden with her. So I came away about as wise as ever. One thing I could learn was that you were not at all well, and as Mrs. Glover says that the Balham air has a relaxing effect, our advice to you is clear out and come to our bracing atmosphere—the Davis', she says, are removing for this very reason.

We did not get your parcels, as Miss Bryant still awaits the stage driver's convenience at the Railway depot. Next mail I may have some word for you of them. The socks especially will be a blessing. The pair I at present wear are devoid alike of cloth at toes and heels.

I had to go to Birtle last week about my land. I wrote the Government agent some time ago, but he wishes an interview, and I had to waste five days for ten minutes' conversation with him. The trouble with my claim was that I have not resided upon it as required by law, but I will get my title now by ploughing twenty acres additional. When I get my patent I mean to take up another homestead, and this will give us 1120 acres of land. After that I think we may be satisfied. The lot I purpose taking up joins Andrew's, and is alongside the river. We had a high old time travelling to and from Birtle with Teulon and Butcher, both of whom were down getting their deeds. I left on Sunday night, and we all three slept at Haworth's so as to make an early start on Monday morning—this, according to my companions, was seven o'clock. At an ox pace, and slowly, we wound our way to Russell. Before getting there it came on rain, and continued doing so till we got five miles beyond, where we camped for dinner. When we were so engaged it faired up. Just before starting the mailman came along in distress and wanting help. One of his horses had kicked itself clear of the harness all over the prairie. I went back to the scene, half a mile distant, and gave him a hand, and we had a lively time. The horse had one of its forefeet tied up, but despite that it kicked up behind fully six feet. After a deal of trouble we got the brute hitched and he, with much charity, drove it fully a mile on three legs.

We got to Silver Creek about sundown and there we pitched our tent. After supper another party arrived—Price, the Shellmouth comedian, and two new arrivals from England, all bound to take up homesteads. Still later, another three Shell River settlers came, and together we basked before the campfire till late, late, telling stories—Price particularly entertaining us with stories of the rebellion. He had been at the front as a newspaper correspondent, and was just back. We slept the sleep of the just, and next morning awoke to find the valley densely enveloped in mist. By the time we were ready to start (and this was not hastened by the Englishman's cooking of delicacies, etc.,) the sun had dispelled the fog. We had great fun down the trail. Speed was no object, and a good time the great thing. We got into Birtle at four o'clock, but I must resume our Birtle doings next letter. I had intended getting some time today to finish this letter, as I was baking and churning, but my time was fully occupied, and now I am under necessity of immediately starting out to catch the mail.

We sincerely hope you keep strong and well now—these examinations have, I fear, an adverse influence. We are all well and in good spirits. Kindly remember us to your lady friends, particularly the one for whom I am to hunt the bear this winter. We all send you our kindest love, and I remain

Your affectionate brother
Willie

Woodvale, Shellmouth, Man.
25 June 1885

My Dear Maggie,

We got your eagerly anticipated letter last mail, and we all studied and discussed it fully. At first we were extremely disappointed, but after a little when our minds grasped the full certainty that we would not meet this summer, we realized the wisdom of your choice. I confess that I had qualms over the possibility of your being reconciled to the change, things are so different here from the old country. But I thought the pleasure of being all together again would atone for a great many drawbacks. Now, however, speaking for myself, I see the great folly of your giving up a comfortable certainty for a doubtful uncertainty, and here I may remark that we are all extremely pleased to learn in unmistakable terms that you are so pleasantly circumstanced and your prospects are so good. Father would have desired exceedingly to have had you with him, but now we all accept the fact that your sphere is not in Manitoba. Probably in the near future the possibility of a visit our way may open out.

I trust you will appreciate the impossibility of us having the slightest knowledge how you stood financially. It certainly comforts us to know that you have enough and to spare. We earnestly hope that this may continue to be your experience. I regret to think that my organ idea may have somewhat scrimped you—by all means spare yourself no expense, certainly none on our account.

I am happy to say that we are now in the paths of prosperity and soon I hope to be able to say that you can depend on us in case of mishap. The lack of money has caused us in the past some pretty tough fights—now affairs are so that we will easily make income and expense tally, with ordinary luck, and every season now will do so more amply. It would certainly comfort us very much if you kept us better informed on your money matters. Say we each turn a new leaf in this respect.

It is very fortunate that you can now take a pleasure in your work. When that is the case life has a charm about it. I am very unfortunate in my choice of a time to write you. Somehow I am induced to delay till a more fortunate period, and that generally resolves itself into the last moment. This time I have been so busy that I put the letter off till today, when I expect to be churning and baking, and between times I thought to find an opportunity—but alas, Bob Haworth dropped in on us last night, and his presence induced us to stop up till late, and we failed to get up as early as we ought to this morning. The work got behind, and to cap the whole, the cattle gave me trouble, and here I am scrubbing as if my life depended on it. The possibility of your coming made me a little careless with the letter, but now the new prospect will aid me to turn a new leaf. . . .

The Rebellion is now happily at an end, and the boys with Major Boulton are expected back next week. A great demonstration is spoken of.

The Pagan boys got a big surprise last Sunday morning when their father walked in upon them unexpectedly about nine o'clock and caught them dishabille. Since then they have been holidaying and having a good time. He leaves again next Tuesday. The Peyton's friends are now here—a mother, sister and brother and a whole pile of stuff, American organ included, and things look prosperous there now. The ladies declare the journey from the railway would deter them from going back to the old country if nothing else did. The young lady was a church organist. Their experience was pretty rough. The boys had only oxen, and the loads were so high that the ladies could not be prevailed upon to mount, and they walked all the way. Lee's friends are coming out next month. We are busy housebuilding yet, and will be so for some little time. A few welcome showers have improved the harvest prospects very much.

I must now draw this shabby letter to a close . . . Remember us to your friends, especially the ones who help to knit the luxurious socks we are now appreciating . . .

Your most affectionate brother
Willie

Woodvale, Shellmouth, Man.
10 July 1885

My Dear Maggie,

. . . You cannot imagine how much work we have done and have yet before us. This summer, to begin with, we have forty acres to plough, then 65 to seed down and that not under the most favourable circumstances. After that, a lot of fencing, followed by house-building. We put up two buildings for stables—one of them we are living in now—a mile distant from our former habitation, and that distance nearer our work.

Just now we are breaking up a twenty acre patch of new land. This will secure me my right to my land title. Presently we shall be haying, and between times we must put up a dwelling house, sink a well and generally fix up our new homestead. Then follows the harvesting and building a granary and fall plowing. With all these before us I trust you will in charity forgive any remissness in my correspondence. Probably we are attempting too much. But really, our past efforts have had so little success financially that we are induced, notwithstanding our change of abode, to increase our area of cultivation. . . .

The clergyman you speak of assuredly deserves respect. His English clerical brother here is just the other extreme, careless and callous, although a very pleasant man to converse with, but not to deal with. He runs a farm short funded. Last year his parishioners refused to augment his grant from the Mission Board one cent.

Our Presbyterian missionary is a very young man who has neither education or eloquence, but he is sincere, earnest and eager. His district is very extensive—he has four preaching stations each distant from the other about twelve miles, yet he has a Sunday School, Bible class, and singing class at Shellmouth.

Our work is progressing favourably, and the crops have taken a new lease of vigour since the damp showery weather we are now experiencing set in. A sharp frost damaged vegetables greatly two weeks ago, but these too are now pushing forward. We are again in the van so far as early headed grain is concerned. Mr. Whaley was here on Monday, and last week he had been forty miles east at Rossburn and saw no crops so far forward as ours. Previous to ten days ago the weather was oppressively hot and fatiguing—it did damage to our grain in the granary. The better part of seventy bushels of wheat heated and will not now be available for flouring purposes.

I wish the country would enter on a prosperous career again and enable us to roof and floor our buildings properly—defective accommodations means waste. The government have committees—another huge blunder that will I fear delay the day of prosperity. However, we may not complain—numbers around us are feeling the pinch very badly. Just fancy, some of them have £5 to pay for taxes, the greater part for school purposes. Those who can't pay are now to be forced to by the threatened sale of their lands. I sympathize with them so much that I would like to see a rebellion on our own account, although we have our taxes paid. Fortunately we are just a mile outside the school district—all the same our taxes total five guineas,[7] but I must quit grumbling.

I daresay you already know that our western rebellion is finis. Colonel Boulton is expected home daily with his men, and we will have a full feast of war anecdotes and experiences. The gallants in and around Shellmouth are just now having a great time escorting the ladies over the country and being picknicked in return. Miss Peyton, north of us, is with the others, having a good time. Don't you envy her flirting about with Canadian farmers? I don't think the boys are progressing as well with the ploughing as they might—society is turning their heads. They seem to be very pleasant people anxious to be friendly. Father and Andrew called in on the way home from church last Sunday, and Andrew was made extremely happy with an unlimited invitation to go up in the evenings and play lawn tennis. I rather guess the stock give us another kind of amusement.

The gold fever at Shellmouth is not so active just now from the want of quicksilver. The process is very interesting—the shining metal is formed in small specks among the gravel and sand beds about the river. An expert can tell a likely place by the colour of the deposit. To separate the gold, a tripod is set up and inside, a box with handles is swung like a barrow with no wheel, and styled a cradle. This is filled with the sand, and by adding water and shaking to and

---

7   Five guineas equalled £5/5, or $26.

fro and tipping, the dirt is got rid of and the bottom is covered with little gold specks. Quicksilver is run over these, and the chemical absorbs them up and disgorges them when distilled. The cradle should properly be made of copper. It is claimed that an ounce can be so obtained in a day easily, and an eastern jeweller, who came specifically up, declared the prospects good and bought some gold. So far, however, we have not been tempted, and do not feel the want of the quicksilver. And now it is after bed time, and I must say good night. I trust to still further supplement this letter tomorrow night.

We are as usual working away, seeing and hearing little of the outside world. Seldom but on Saturdays when we go for the mail do we see anyone. Last Sunday was, however, an exception. Father and Andrew brought down with them Mr. Butcher, the schoolmaster at Russell (formerly Plympton, Devonshire) and Jackson, hotelkeeper at Shellmouth. Mr. Butcher was greatly impressed with our scenery and position, and seemed very anxious to know of any vacant land, but too late. Harry Pagan was also over for his mail. His father went back last week after a ten-day stay—most of the time he spent at fishing, the boys ably assisting him.

On Monday we had two visitors—McLellan and afterwards Whaley. The day was damp and showery and we did not do much work. In the afternoon I started off for a walk to Haworth's and Lochead's. The former has now got his land title, and as his farming operations have been mostly expenditure, he has like his brother departed for the east. I bade him goodbye with regret.

Will Pagan accompanied me to Lochead's, and when we were about a mile from the house a drenching rain set in, and we got there soaked and had to make ourselves comfortable for the night, as the wind and rain continued with exceptional fury. Next morning I got home. Since that time we have been earnest in the ploughing. Tomorrow I am going to Assissippi Mill with grain, and there I hope to post this letter. I will come back by Shellmouth and get the mail. The animals all take kindly to their new quarters.

We are living on Andrew's claim now and propose to settle permanently. It is the most convenient for all things except wood, and for a time we will have sufficient, and we have the command of abundance more. Within the mile we have unlimited pasturing, haying, watering, fishing and hunting facilities, all great blessings.

We are particularly well provided with the houses being put up inside the belt of timber that stretches midway between the river and the valley banks. Towards the river and to the west are the hay marshes, and beyond are the timber-clothed banks on the other side. In front are the bluffs and groves of our own side, north and south is our cultivated land. The view from the upland prairie is magnificent. I forgot to mention the large lake northeast a half mile, where we will have splendid opportunity for skating, if we have time.

We are still uncertain about the railway—want of money is retarding work. But we can at least expect it within forty miles of us, if no further. Then we have a lot of cold drives this winter with grain, but even at that we will be grateful. The scarcity of money is a great drawback—our last year's harvest will not pay expenses. We have great hopes of the cows and stock doing better for us. I am getting on well with the butter-making, and so apparently is everybody. The price is now 6 cents per pound, and only barter at that, but in a little more than a year we will earn from the young stock. We are in good spirits, all in good health and living on hopes of the good times coming.

The sawmill at Shellmouth has had a serious check. The proprietor, after expending a fortune, has acknowledged himself unable to bring the logs down that were cut last winter. The low water has been the drawback. He now proposes to buy logs all the same. The machinery is being rapidly put in.

I am sorry that the change of abode has interfered with my organ playing. I could not think of risking it in our temporary abode. The want will help to spur me on to help get the house up. Mr. Pagan was profoundly disgusted at my lack of Scotch music. He promised to send me a collection, but out of sight, out of mind, I hear.

Now I must conclude with that you continue getting on happily. Remember us very kindly to your lady companion, particularly the stocking-weaver. How deliciously comfortable my toes feel! I expect you will gladly accept the substitute for Andrew's supplement—the mosquitoes are luxuriating all over—enclosed find a few as a present, the brutes. Take great care of yourself, and accept our great love,

Your most affectionate brother
Willie

Woodvale, Shellmouth, Man.
15 July 1885

My Dear Maggie,

I am afraid you will think me very careless and unreliable. I fully purposed writing last week, but what with cheese-making, butter-making, etc. etc., the work gets behind outside, and I get bothered and feel in a mess. Then the heat has been something awful. Since the first of July the sky has been cloudless, and the sun has been holding furious [?] away between 90 and 100 degrees. One day it was at 106 degrees in the shade. All this has had a deterring and depressing effect, and particularly so when it is blighting the grain growth we are so dependent upon. Old timers are again to the front, dismaying all with the time-worn expression that such had never been known before. . . .

I fear we must give up the raising of grain for market purposes and get into stock as quickly as decency will permit. Those who did so at first are comfortable now. Had we known to do so first, we would now have been similarly situated, but it was all, I have no doubt, for the best. We have experience now we had not then, and probably we gained that in the cheapest possible way. All around are now of the same opinion.

As it is we are again comparatively better off with our grain than the most. We will again have a harvest—if not remarkable for quantity, it will be so for quality. Had we the experience of the most, we would have been penniless and somewhere else. Providence seems to delight in giving us enough and no more, and you can imagine how the straitened policy gives us anxious thoughts. This year I thought we would come out well ahead, but is just going to be the usual thing—a tight fit.

Now please do not imagine from this that we are hardly placed—quite the contrary. [We have] abundance to eat and that of a quality that would make city people stare. Our produce can only be disposed of by barter. My complaint is we can't make [money?], hard cash cannot be got, and the anxiety arises because it is required sometimes. It is a blessing I did not manage to charm you here last year, as I could not have provided you with the many conveniences I had in view—such as a nice house, well-furnished, pony, etc. So you may rest content with the idea that what might not be, could not be, and in this way Providence verifies the course you have chosen. May this idea give you contentment to find your mission in your present sphere.

With regard to your contemplated engagement ... you must consider me deeply interested, and a sympathizing onlooker. As such I might say that you might, from a worldly point of view, hesitate and do better, but really, bread and butter and entertainment is infinitely superior to diamonds and heart disappointment. And these days it seems to me the talented are not so well rewarded as the persevering, and especially those who realize and plot after a particular thing. Do not have anything to do with Mr. Bond if he thinks that he is less likely to be successful at school teaching than he would have been at, well, for instance—fiddling.

I am a powerful adviser just now in this respect, as I last winter and this spring felt the dilly-dallying effect of thinking of another course from my present, and I blame the neuralgia for it. The aching, day after day and for weeks, caused doleful thoughts and foolish reminiscences, and I thought I had walked contrary to my ordered pathway—that I must speedily provide for a return. . . . don black clothing and be a clergyman or a lawyer. Well, I have overcome these fancies, and though I want [encouragement?] till I get from beneath the shade, yet I think the neuralgia has taken its last parting kick at me—and a powerful heavy one it was too, as evidenced by my swollen chops and weak digestive organs. And to resume my story, I can only repeat what my last letter contained and wish you Godspeed in your journey through life . . .

We now have a young man in training for farming. He comes from London, was a trained electrical engineer, and talks of investing capital in stock farming. He stands 6½ feet, somewhat of an exquisite in his manner, but willing and handy, and his name is Dove. "Gentle Dove" he has been christened by the boys at Shellmouth. He is a very great assistance to us. The little extra time his presence spares, gives us time to clean and wash up and live like Christians. He was for some time with Teulon, but he got disgusted with his trifling attempts at farming. The likelihood is he will remain nine months with us. We could do with one such every year, and if you meet any anxious inquirer, mesmerize him and send him out.

I glanced over Dove's stock of enticing pamphlets that had fired his imagination in the old country, but having so much experience of the dross probably takes the glitter of the gilt away. If only one could subsist for shooting and fishing and riding around, this would be an exceedingly enjoyable country. Just fancy, since this time last year I do not suppose we have had 48 hours rain.

Our present missionary is from Glasgow, and he declares that he never dreamt that he would ever see as much sunshine in such a short time. He is a very pleasant, talkative gentleman. How his talk reminds me of Glasgow. But he has no influence, and as a preacher he is the worst failure I ever heard of. His addresses are the weakest nonsense possible and brimful of the most absurd statements. I am so sorry, as people if they [?] are intelligent. No Brete Harte character here, and such a display brings the whole cause into disrepute. I hope when he goes back in the autumn that he will become an insurance agent.

The railway is pushing ahead lively. The cars are now coming into Birtle, and they have the roadbed graded twenty miles beyond the Assiniboine Crossing. Shellmouth is quickly removing to a so far unnamed city south of us. The sawmill is now there. For two weeks back surveyors have been staking a branch railway through by the Bryants and away north, but nobody, even those interested, believe it will be built. They are simply endeavouring to deceive the public till elections are over.

We are now busy haymaking, and hard work it is—the hardest and hottest in the year's routine. We have given up hoping for rain, as it would do the wheat no good now, as it is changing colour and will be ready for reaping in little more than a week. And we will, for the first time in our experience, harvest hay and grain at the same time.

Many of our neighbours are almost eaten up by little burrowing animals—they call them prairie dogs, but I think they are better named ground squirrels. They seem to be the climax to further grain growing hopes. We are fortunate in being so far free from pests. Our inaccessibility and isolation doubtless favour us. The drought has dried up all the springs and ponds, and the grass is like tinder, and all complain of poor pasture. Today we had to drive our cattle down amongst the mosquitoes and the long succulent grass in the marshes. So again we have reason to rejoice a little in a Pharisaical mood....

Your most affectionate brother
Willie

Woodvale, Shellmouth, Man.
24 July 1885

My Dear Maggie,

I duly received your letter last Saturday, and we were pleased to know of your welfare. The change into the new school will doubtless be a great event. It is fortunate you got the weakheaded old lady removed with so little disaster. The farm work out here is progressing very well, and each day we are adding to the convenience and improving our new abode. The crops are coming along fairly well, but compared to previous years they are going to be poor, very thin and choked with weeds. This is a complaint more or less all over. I suppose we must thankfully take things as they come.

For two weeks back we have had a good many thundershowers, and these are not in our favour just now. Our roof is not very tight. They are checking the maturing of grain and keeping us from haymaking. I miss the organ very much. I could not think of risking it in our temporary abode—this may account for any grumbly mood. In about a month I hope to have it over.

Friday, a week ago, I was at the gristmill in Assissippi. On the way back I met Arthur Bryant thither bound. On Saturday afternoon I went to Shellmouth, and on the way back I stopped up at the Peytons, had tea, then a game of lawn tennis. But either I am a duffer or it is a difficult game, and when Teulon, Pagan and Thomson put in an appearance, I decided to become a spectator. After sunset we had music, and that I could appreciate and enjoy. Miss Peyton is really a good player and can handle the organ well. I think I told you she was an organist in the old country. How she will suit this country is a problem—she seems to interest herself in little else.

On Sunday Father and I went up to church. When we got back, Will Pagan was keeping Andrew company. Will Pagan, Charley Peyton and I had arranged to go down to Birtle next day, and as Peyton was very bad with toothache, we deemed it prudent to go up in the evening and see how he was feeling regarding the journey. Again we had music and hymn singing, and I got home about 11 o'clock. Next morning we were up at 4 o'clock and away at 5:30, the toothache man and all. That night we camped within seven miles of Birtle, and next morning got there.

Our first business was with the government land agent. He and I had a big talk and a near approach to a row. Before giving me my title he wished me to sleep three months on my homestead. I would not have minded so much had it not been my second journey— before, he said nothing about the requirement. In the end my cheek, as the other boys expressed it, induced him to accept my application. It has yet to be approved by the Chief Commissioner. Generally he does so—I hope he will not make mine an exception. But for a fortnight I will not know. Peyton got his put through, but Will Pagan was sent to put in his three months' sleep. The folly of the land laws would make one weep.

The land business occupied a lot of time, and after it we, with other citizens, gathered to welcome the arrival, from the rebellious country, of Major Boulton and his Scouts. They numbered fully a hundred, and all our old friends looked pretty rough and sunburnt. They had ridden straight through, all the way from beyond Battleford, camping out all the time. They rode in two and two, Major Boulton at the head, and the cheering, bell-ringing, whistle-blowing, and gun firing was great. After a great deal of handshaking, etc., they rode back over the river and camped, and afterwards came back to partake of a huge dinner provided by the Birtle people. And poor fellows, they need and enjoyed it, as they had partaken of nothing since morning and then only some tea biscuits and unseasoned tea. Langford was the most changed, very thin looking. He got a bullet in his collarbone, and there it still remains.

Towards evening Will Pagan and I started homewards, Charley Peyton having been induced to wait and come up next morning with the troopers. We had a wet drive, but got a comfortable camping ground, and notwithstanding many drawbacks, slept the sleep of the just. Next day was dry and pleasant, and we had a nice drive home, and I got here about nine o'clock. The troopers are all home now, and the atmosphere is heavy with tales of the battlefield and etc. etc. Now I must stop this letter. Somehow I am not in a writing mood tonight, and I have the returns to make up for the Government crop report. Next letter I will have the great reception to the Scouts to tell you of. It comes off next Thursday—sports, etc. I daresay fully $500 has been collected for prizes ...

Your most affectionate brother
Willie

Woodvale, Shellmouth, Man.
5 August 1885

My Dear Maggie,

... Since my last letter work has been progressing under our hands surely if a little slowly. There has been two breaks—the first the Volunteer reception at Russell, and today heavy rain showers. Monday, a week ago, we commenced haymaking, and good weather favoured us all the time till today.

I was very loath on Thursday to go pleasure seeking to Russell, and if the settlers had not turned out so well I would have felt somewhat ashamed. As soon as the cows were milked and the other necessary work done, Andrew and I started out with the horses for the scene of festivities. We enjoyed a pleasant drive, and found the quietude of Russell transformed into joyous activity, all the flags in the place fluttering in the breeze. The H.B. Co. post being first in the place, the buildings erected afterwards followed its lead in having flag poles erected. This helps the town to make a good display.

It was the largest crowd I have yet seen at the place. A goodly proportion of ladies were congregated, and interspersed among them were men driving rigs, on the move and motionless, and a goodly number of equestrians, military and civilian. Altogether the place had a gay aspect and caused my regrets about haymaking to vanish.

When we arrived, the shooting competition had begun, troopers against the stay-at-homes. And the troopers, after the expenditure of a great amount of powder and balls, came off victors. After this followed the excitement incident to horse races. A detailed description of these would have no interest for you. One item in the programme caused some stir—one of our Shellmouth boys who had been out at the front was riding past us as quickly as his horse would allow him, when Denmark's dog, no doubt recognizing an old friend, ran onto the course and got mixed among the horse's front feet, and rider and steed came to grief. The latter turned a complete somersault, but fortunately not on top of the rider, who got up protesting he was all right, hoped the dog was killed, mounted, and continued his mad career. The dog did likewise, but in another direction.

I presume after this the troopers were treated to dinner by the Committee—there followed a long speech by Colonel Boulton. This concluded our interest in the programme, as we very shortly afterwards started for home. The weather was everything that could be desired. The intense heat of the preceding few days had given way to cloudy sky and a cool atmosphere.

With this exception, affairs here continue in their usual humdrum way. Everybody pleads guilty to poverty, boasts of his crops, and wonders where a market will be found. The railway is, we hear, making rapid progress toward us, and will undoubtedly be within forty miles of our place before winter. Now that Major Boulton is back, the prospects of a bridge across the Assiniboine at Shellmouth are better. I sincerely hope the works will go ahead at once and give us a market for our flour and butter.

The large saw mill there will presently be making a noise. The proprietor has had a pretty bad time. Last summer he constructed dams and widened the river at considerable expense where he cut the logs last winter. Alas, the dry spring caused an insufficiency of water to float the logs down. Nothing daunted, he employed about seventy men, went up and set to work to drain a large lake into the stream—this also proved ineffectual. Completely disgusted, he brought the men back, and they were not long dispersed when the rains came on and flooded the creek. But before he could gather his men again, the water had ebbed again, and now he proposes to cut logs bought from another company. I have little more to say. We are all well and prospering as well as circumstances will permit. The knowing ones in high places prophesy a return of prosperity very shortly. I hope they will be correct . . .

Your most affectionate brother
Willie

Woodvale, Shellmouth, Man.
29 August 1885

My Dear Maggie,

I am very sorry indeed that I could not write you last mail. We were so anxiously moving out of the stable and fixing up our new abode, and matters are not one whit better this time, as we are busy at the wheat harvest. I expected to get a little time last night, but it was 8:30 before I got seated, and I felt so tired that I gladly clambered out of view into the land of nod. We received no letter last mail from you—we trust you are well.

At the beginning of this week this neighbourhood got a bad smirching with frost that damaged to such an extent, that this year a great quantity of grain will not be cut, and the sufferers are for giving up in despair. The outlook for many is black indeed. Fortunately our grain is only slightly damaged. Had we had time to finish our ploughing last fall, we would again have escaped. As it is, we are very fortunate. I do not know yet whether the frost has been general over the province, but I imagine it has. The general verdict is that this district must go altogether for stock raising. It pleases us very much that we are doing a little that way. But I must hasten, as Andrew is rampaging around to get away to Shellmouth . . .

Your most affectionate brother
Willie

Woodvale, Shellmouth, Man.
8 September 1885

My Dear Maggie,

... We are getting on very well with the work. Another good day and we will have the wheat all stacked and secure—five long, high stacks. The barley is all cut and awaits the stacking process. Five acres of oats and five of wheat we will not harvest, they are so poor. Weeds have been unusually prevalent this year and caused very light crops, but the great trouble was the frost on the 13th of August. It has done dreadful damage. Thanks to our housebuilding last autumn that caused so much ploughing to be done this spring we did not escape scatheless, as we were fortunately able to do previously. But we have little cause to complain.

With the exception of some showers yesterday and the day before, the weather has been very favourable. It has cleared up again, and I hope we may have steady settled weather for ten days or so and let us get over harvesting. We must do our best to get the ploughing all done this fall. Next winter we will have a lot more bush work, as the cattle have lately annoyed us a good deal, and we must provide a pasture field for them. The wolves have also been making havoc among the poultry—eight or nine have disappeared. This also we must provide against next summer.

Did I write you that the Government have ordered me to sleep three months more on my land before they will grant me my title? Pleasant prospect! Must get the rascals turned out!

Things are very dull here—with the exception of the sawmill, nothing doing. I have 100 pounds of butter I can't possibly sell, and before that I was disposing of it at 6 cents per pound—a good price for housekeepers but a bad one for the makers. What we will do with the grain this year is a problem. The last harvest barely cleared expenses, and this promises to be worse. No money here and no railway outlet—the railway seems as far in the future as ever. They will, I understand, come this season to Birtle Creek—after that I do not suppose they know themselves what will be done.

The frost has been a bad job. Next summer I expect we must, to make a living, turn our attention to cheesemaking and beef and bacon raising. These commodities we can keep some time and transport easily a distance if need be. So we have not yet lost faith in our prospects for our future. Now that we are firmly settled in one spot, we can make permanent arrangements and not have to be bothering and scrambling among the difficulties of apologies for buildings.

It is getting very quickly early dark now, and the cows milk-up and evening feed-up are now dreads of darkness. The arrival of winter and the consequent leisure for deliberation and meditation will be welcome relief. And afterwards, I hope that our summer work will not be on such an extensive scale and so hurried. At odd times we are putting up the fourth building. This summer, another, the fifth, is yet to finish off, and we have still the sixth to begin from the foundation—two houses, that is, a kitchen attachment and house, three stables and a granary. Beside this we have winter pens and perches to erect for the pigs and poultry yet. So for some little time you must pardon the style of my letters.

Alf Bryant got married last Monday to a Miss Simpson—her brothers farm about sixty miles from here. Her father was a vicar in England and a sister is married to the Birtle clergyman. I imagine she will bring him some money . . .

Your most affectionate brother
Willie

Woodvale, Shellmouth, Man.
3 October 1885

My Dear Maggie,

. . . I trust my former letter will have induced you to view my silence with complacence. We were so busy stacking the last of our harvest last Saturday, and we grudged very much to delay it, so we did not go up to Shellmouth. Though we have still a great amount of work before us yet, but we have the satisfaction of knowing that we keep well forward, and in a fortnight's time we hope to be quite prepared to welcome Jack Frost with a smile.

For the last three weeks we have been favoured with splendid weather. A good soaking shower would not go amiss. Now the leaves are nearly all gone from the trees, and just previous to their disappearance they showed a gloriously variegated appearance. It seems strange now to be able to see right into the heart of the woodlands.

For some time back the prairie fires have been very numerous, and the smoke gave everything a dull, coppery appearance. Down in the States the fires did a great deal of damage, and I fear the other side of the river will have the same story to tell. The fire swept down opposite us this afternoon, and for a time things looked so that you had a faint notion of what the end of the world will be. Fortunately our side is well intersected with water and watercourses, and we escape remarkably.

The other night the moon was eclipsed during the night. I got up and gazed at the phenomenon. My ideas were so hazy and sleep-bound that I daresay the astronomical world would hesitate to interview me.

The harvest, I am thankful to say, is over now, and stacks all fixed up. The next excitement therewith will be the threshing and then follows the great trouble—the disposal of the grain. How I wish we had more stock and did not need to sell a bushel of grain. There seems to be little chance of making grain-farming pay. In the meantime I am thankful we have had the three cows this season. They saved us quite a lot of money. In fact, we had not the money to spend. Without the butter, I do not know we could have got our store good. Next summer I mean to try cheese-making—anything to make a living.

Sometimes I envy salary holders, but I suppose we must accept the fact that no matter how situated, existence has uncertainty about it. And we have pleasing hope that in a few years at the outside, affairs with us (if they progress as they promise) at the lowest calculation will bring us assured prosperity—even if it is not in the modern form of a huge bank account but in the patriarchal form of a large stock yard—a wealth of animal life.

There is not much of interest going on hereaway just now. Next Friday the annual Cattle Show will take place at Russell, and that generally draws out a crowd. Everything is prepared to commence the building of the bridge over the river at Shellmouth. About $3000 is set aside by Government for that purpose, and will be expended this winter. This will cause some stir and circulate some money. Now you must pardon my bringing this letter to an abrupt close . . .

Your most affectionate brother
Willie

[P.S. from Andrew]

. . . Last Sunday I went up to service. It turned out to be the last service we will have this year. Our preacher seemed to feel very bad about it, so much so that he got to weeping. He gave us all manner of good advice, and set down awful badly on dancing and novel reading. It seems that there had been a dancing party held lately, and most unfortunately, on prayer-meeting night. No one attended the prayer-meeting, therefore the row he gave the dancers . . .

Woodvale, Shellmouth, Man.
29 October 1885

My Dear Maggie,

Again I am remiss in my correspondence, and you will again exercise your charitable nature—later you will learn the cause of the delay . . . Father and I went down to the Russell Show. The day was cool and pleasant, and there was an immense turnout of settlers and stock. It is astonishing how each year these gatherings increase in numbers. I interested myself looking around and meeting lots of old friends. The Bryants were there in full force—Mr. Glover and Miss Bryant, Alf and his bride.

In the afternoon we made our way home greatly perplexed with our prospects, as Lochead wanted to thresh our grain in a week, and if not then he could not say within three weeks when. So we had our choice. And as we were far from ready, the problem was whether we could push and get ready or wait till the weather got colder. We decided to do the first, and this explains my long silence. We had to work like niggers, early and late. And in return for neighbours' assistance we had to be up very early so as to have the pressing work done at home, the horses ready, and two or three miles traversed before 7 o'clock.

Last week we had our first day's threshing on the other side of the creek and as a consequence, we had to re-inhabit our former abode, so that the [ravenous?] might have their food conveniently. Tuesday of this week finished us up here at home, and that evening we were heartily glad to bid the threshers goodbye. The mill worked splendidly, quite a contrast to our former experiences. The yield was in one sense disappointing, in another a surprise. We got about 800 bushels of grain, just the same as last year, although we had then only forty acres cultivated. This year we had sixty-three and consequently, in the spring we hoped for a much larger yield. . . . I do not purpose disposing of a great quantity, just as much as will tide us over, as we mean to keep a great many more pigs next summer.

On Wednesday the first fair was held at Shellmouth. The intention is to hold these twice each year. It was a bitter cold, snowing and blowing. There was a large turnout, people and stock, and everything betokened the undertaking a success. Our wheat carried the first prize, and had we threshed it would have done so at Russell.

Business is booming at Shellmouth. Work has commenced on the bridge across the river, and they are busy making the coffer dam. Two new stores have been opened, one by Goldsmid, the actor I think I wrote you of, the other by an Icelander who for cash sells things at greatly reduced prices. He is the forerunner of an Icelandic colony to be settled across the river.[8] Besides him, we have now a blacksmith and shoemaker, both Icelanders.

I don't remember if I told you we had a doctor now, a Dr. Caesar from Hampshire, England. Mrs. Goldsmid joined her husband a fortnight ago, accompanied by a Mrs. Flynn. And as they and the members of the Wolverine Farming Co. have all been connected with the theatrical profession, the announcement that they mean to give theatrical performances during the winter is no vain tale. The sawmill is close and the men are all up in the woods getting things ready for another winter's wood chopping. Next spring will see the mill started with new energy. I must now stop . . .

Your most affectionate brother
Willie

---

8   There was an Icelandic colony in the area by 1886.

Woodvale, Shellmouth, Man.
13 November 1885

My Dear Maggie,

... We are just beginning to fall into our winter routine, and the change from hurry-scurry to a leisurely, satisfactory way of doing things is pleasant indeed. Tonight I feel as if I did not deserve your forgiveness. Till today our hands have been filled to overflowing with work. This morning we awakened to the fact that we had the prospect of accomplishing the necessary work easily—ourselves comfortably domiciled, cattle stabled, poultry secured, everything pretty well shaped for winter. So we laid out the day's proceedings— fetch home a load of hay forenoon, load of firewood afternoon, and after that Andrew and, I with wonderful audacity, decided to go skating. So when the firewood got here I disloaded and cut the required quantity of fuel, while Andrew fixed the stable and tied the animals. This done, we were quickly and deeply engaged fixing up the old skates and fitting them on a duplicate pair of boots.

After supper we started down past the stables on iron, and after a rough and ready scramble through the willows, the lake spread out before us. Loch Birnie, our old mutual haunt, is a fish pond in comparison. Like winking we changed our boots and declared ourselves ready. Together we skated all over the lovely lake by moonlight, explored all its lagoons and bays, and nothing but a couple of owls said us nay, and they hooted at us in a manner that would have done credit to a defrauded skating-pond owner. We went round the lake, over it, and found all kinds of ice—some places so rough that we would gladly have passed quickly and conclusively over it, and strange to say though so minded, we yet in some instances were compelled to give it the rough kindly kiss of affection—other places so smooth and blue and treacherous-looking that we gave them the kiss of suspicion. When tired of rambling, we retired to a bay coated with black-blue ice, and without a ripple, and there we disported ourselves till tired. Then we started homewards, greatly to the dog's delight, who had been strangely moved at our expeditious way of travelling, and who made strange movements to keep up with us, till he got disgusted and retired to watch us and listen to the howling, prowling wolves.

On the way home I suddenly remembered that it was Friday night and I must write your letter. After dish-washing and cow-milking I am at the desk making up for my forgetfulness. The bundle of magazines came all right last mail, and they were a real luxury like their predecessors.

I have been three journeys up to Assissippi Mill with wheat, for which I received the questionably magnificent sum of $13. This will pay our harvesting and threshing accounts and allow us to hold the rest of the grain for the high prices that every authority prophesies we will yet get.

The weather has been simply lovely. All through, the fall has been an exceptionally splendid one, not a drop of rain for months, and the country still free from its snowy months—bright, clear sunshine everyday, and cool, bracing atmosphere. Too cold, alas, to permit of ploughing in the morning when the hoarfrost clings to the grass, trees and shrubs in big heavy flakey crystals. The sunshine bathes everything in glory, and rainbow tints dazzle the eye at every point, and you crush beauty of colour and form at every step.

Our home comforts this fall are quite a change from those of last fall. Our hurried removal in the snowstorm to the unplastered house makes me shiver. These experiences now in all reasonable prospect are over now, and to all human appearances we are now fixed and firmly established.

The cows still milk well—I have made 400 pounds of butter this season. The market has been low, more so than ever before, 6 ¼ [cents] per pound. And yet, had we consumed none but sold it all, sufficient would have been realized to have paid the price of one of the cows. And that without taking into account the calves and what they will yet realize, or the pigs that have been raised on the milk. So can you wonder at my eagerness to go in for stock? And to the end we are sailing surely and satisfactorily. If the grain realizes anyway well I mean to try and get another cow next summer. Now I must stop . . .

Your most affectionate brother
Willie

Woodvale, Shellmouth, Man.
3 December 1885

My Dear Maggie,

Thanks for the birthday wishes you conveyed in your last letter to Andrew . . . This afternoon our long continued spell of fine weather came to an abrupt end. The day opened dark, with a blustering wind. When Andrew and I were over at our other granary the snow began to fall and the wind to rise, and we had just got back and ensconced inside when it came on a perfect blizzard—blowing and snowing furiously. It is now calmed down, but all around the snow is whirled into fantastic wreaths, and winter now reigns supreme.

I posted your last letter on the concert night, a pretty clear moonlight night. All three of us drove up, and during our absence the dog cared for the farm. Some commissions caused us to be somewhat early up. In passing I glanced into the hall, and it had a magnificent appearance—the broad stage elegantly fitted up, two side wings gave the necessary privacy. The back part had a door and a small recess that served the purpose of a bedroom. One side wing had a door, the other a window. Two life-size sketches at either side helped appearance very much—altogether the effect was quite theatrical.

About seven o'clock the audience commenced to besiege the door and caused a good squeeze. When it was opened, the hall was quickly filled and a great many were unable to fit in. I scrambled up into the temporary gallery, not by any means a safe-looking erection. The attention of the underneath was considerably diverted, viewing a conjuring. I will not tax your letter with a description of the plays. The first was "Turn Him Out," a very weak commedietta and the parts represented in somewhat exaggerated form. The next was "Box & Cox," and it proved a success, notably the landlady, Mrs. [?], acted by Fillzer. The local hits introduced were very amusing. During the plays, Denmark's anciently created piano, the fearful and wonderful tone producer, was elevated on the stage and delighted the audience and amateur musicians. . . . We did not wait out the dance. I understand it was no great success—the most of the dancers had been skating all day and felt too tired.

While we were hitching up, Frank Bryant asked us over to a party they purposed having the week following. The gathering did honour to two events, Frank's entrance into his new house, and Alf's wedding. Andrew and I went over, and the long night was spent very enjoyably. A great number were there—probably a hundred. We started for home after four o'clock and enjoyed the long walk very much, and arrived about seven o'clock, awakening Father and Teulon in time for breakfast. The latter intended going over with us, but came about an hour too late.

During the fortnight our work has been pretty much jobbing around, always employed at something. The mild weather continuing so late is quite a singular and pleasant experience. Tonight even the temperature is high. I am glad the snow has come—the waggoning was very unpleasant on the hard ground and not to be compared to the gliding sleighs. Tomorrow I am going to the mill at Assissippi, and I hope to enjoy my first long sleigh ride this winter.

The town people in Russell and Shellmouth are greatly agitated over the railway—they would not grant a bonus[9] and the company have surveyed a line eight miles south of us over the valley instead of at Shellmouth, five miles north. Should the railway go there the difference to us will not be great, but Russell and Shellmouth will be dealt a death blow. I favour no bonus. We are taxed seriously enough already, and what is more grievous to bear is that 75 per cent fully of the taxes is squandered on salaries and official expenses.

4th Dec.—I was up at Assissippi today, starting in the morning before sunrise, and it was a cold, cold rise. The wind was high and the frost was keen, and fingers, ears, and nose would not keep warm— struggling with cold in true arctic style. The wind is the disagreeable thing. It searches through everything. The sleighing on many parts of the trail was also very rough and hummocky, and will be so till the traffic levels it, and hardens the snow. But sleighing is far ahead of waggoning in speed and comfort. I was home two hours earlier than if I had been wheeling. Now want of newsy material causes me to bring this letter to a close . . .

Your most affectionate brother
Willie

---

9   Railways sometimes blackmailed towns in this way—if towns would not pay, the tracks passed them by.

Woodvale, Shellmouth, Man.
19 December 1885

My Dear Maggie,

I was at Shellmouth last Saturday and received your letter addressed to father. I felt a bone in it, and curiosity becomes so wonderfully developed in this country that I immediately set to and picked it, and to say that I was pleased, proud, and felt myself quite a popular individual is a [?] way of putting it, when I gazed upon your well-remembered features and knew I had such a smart-looking and very pretty sister.

. . . Everybody is in ecstasies over the exceptional season—even the poor disappointed farmers are all ensnared by it to wait and try their fortune again. So you may be sure the change is no disguised blessing. Mrs. Peyton can hardly find words to express her admiration of our clear, pure, shining atmosphere. The deep blue starry firmament is her special joy. At the present time the moonlight is good, and really a walk abroad under such circumstances gives one the feeling that life under different circumstances is a joyless blessing. A very bright star in the west is at present exercising our astronomical idea, and for brilliancy I have not seen its equal, not even Jupiter, when he was [?] some years ago. But outside of this exceptional winter, our varied climate has to the farmer great advantages. The severe frost checks, if it does not kill out, disease. Certainly it prevents the vermin so destructive to civilized ways. No rats, potato bugs, weevil or any other pests. Then again, the frost disintegrates the soil, and though farming proper is an unknown pursuit for six months in the year, yet during that time, the climate does for the earth what the farmers in other countries only strive to do.

The more I experience it, so much the more certain am I that this country has a prosperous future before it, from an agricultural and stock raising point of view. . . .

It startles one to think that a week hence is Xmas day—and ne'er a frozen nose. A happier era has apparently dawned upon us. Our united kind regards to all the friends and our great love to yourself.

Your most affectionate brother
Willie

Woodvale, Shellmouth, Man.
15 January 1886

My Dear Maggie,

... Shellmouth people are in a great panic just now about the railway. The matter is to be definitely decided in six weeks, and there is every likelihood it will go twelve miles south of us. The Allan interest in the company is large and they exercise a powerful influence with Government in the charting power. The object in having the railway go south is to improve a large tract of land owned by the Allans there. The matter does not affect us to any great extent. Even at the point we are within reasonable distance, and undoubtedly Shellmouth will not long be forsaken of railway men. Already a company are petitioning for a charter to run a railway there. Of course while there is doubt there is hope.

A deputation is likely to go to Winnipeg and threaten the Government with a withdrawal of support if they do not coerce the Co. to abide by their original agreement. One great cause of despondence is the absence at Ottawa of Col. Boulton. I am induced to think he has gone over to the enemy and the powers that be will help his interest in another way. So corrupt are the ways of Government here. No old country resident can appreciate the almost Turkish policy that prevails.

I see the Premier, Sir John A. Macdonald, was in London tickling the palates of the Tories. Pity they could not keep him. It is currently reported he fled to escape the dust made by the French Canadians over the hanging of Riel. He has held power for a long time now by courting and bribing their support, but feeling ran so high over the punishing of Riel that he had simply to choose between French and English. He dallied and temporized so long over the verdict that he ultimately brought down on his head the wrath of the one and the disgust of the other section.

I think in a couple of years at the outside this country will be its old prosperous self. Outside of the fact that we are likely to have change of Government and the probable abatement or withdrawal of protective duties, the United States are proposing great improvements of the Red River to the boundary, which if carried out will make a great water highway for the Northwest States. A glance at the map will enlighten you as to the ultimate result of this. Manitoba will be spurred on to greater improvements, and consequently the outlet by Hudson Bay will be established. At present all the influence on the St. Lawrence is thwarting the scheme in real old 18th century principles. When the Hudson Bay route is opened up farmers will owing to the difference in freight rates get marginal prices. Just now produce is of little value—wheat we are asked to sell at a price that will not cover expenses, and the millers here are getting the advantages of the farmers ... but now I must close before I get angry at the course affairs are taking. We are all in good spirits. Next week I hope to be in the bush, getting prepared for what another year's growth will do for us. With united and kindest regards ... and great love to yourself, I am

Your most affectionate brother
Willie

EPILOGUE

L ife for the Wallaces in the decades after 1885 saw a process of small changes rather than one of dramatic incidents. Though Willie farmed for twenty-five years after the period covered by these letters, and Andrew for thirty-five, they never won the riches that Willie had at times dreamed of. On the other hand, they survived periods of drought and other troubles, and most years saw an increase in their grain production and a slowly growing prosperity.

Some of the things Willie wished for took years to occur—the railway, for instance did not come to Shellmouth until 1909, more than a quarter century after their arrival there, though it reached Birtle in 1886, and Willie went there specifically to take a ride on it.[1] In the same year he became organist, choir director and music teacher in the Presbyterian church in Shellmouth, and continued in the job when a new church was built in 1905. He held the position for 44 years, until 1930.

In 1887 Willie finally achieved a steady source of cash income when he was appointed Secretary-Treasurer of Shellmouth Municipality, a position he still held in 1904. His annual salary of $160, rising over the years to $360, provided much-needed cash. The only unpleasant part of the job lay in the necessity of collecting taxes from his neighbours, which kept him from his farming work. He maintained an office in Shellmouth, working on Saturdays and staying in town overnight to attend church service the next day.

---

1   The closest station on the railway to the Wallace farm was at Endcliffe, two miles to the east. The line was abandoned in the late 1970s and the tracks torn up in early 1979.

Willie also continued to try innovative ways of improving his financial prospects. In 1888 he bought a new churn for butter-making, and with the Shellmouth storekeeper tried to promote a plan for a co-operative cheese factory. But though his neighbours recognized the potential of the scheme, they could not agree on its details, and the plan fell through. Butter continued to be in surplus locally—as late as 1891 it was still bringing only four to five cents a pound, and Willie was despondent about its future as a source of income.

As the Shellmouth district grew and matured, William Wallace recorded its growth. During good times he was optimistic—"Canada is the greatest country under the sun" he wrote in 1888. At other times he was depressed, dreaming of "getting away to a more lively district," "turning Indian" and striking out west to the wilderness. His letters to Maggie continued to reflect many of the beliefs held by his neighbours—in 1887, writing about the Barnardo home in the neighbourhood, he said that the residents of the district were perturbed over the prospective arrival of "a lot of little paupers." In 1893 he called them "useless and disagreeable." Yet in 1897 he hired a "home boy" and found him satisfactory. He continued to be critical of the Macdonald administration until the death in 1891 of the "Old Chieftain." He was particularly bitter about the Canadian Pacific Railway Company's monopoly of railway traffic in the west—it and the equally evil protective tariff affected him and his neighbours "to the extent of many hundreds of dollars in the year," he wrote in 1887.

From time to time Willie became involved in the kind of squabble that often occurs in small communities. In 1889 he had a sharp quarrel with the Presbyterian Church ladies who flatly turned down his scheme to raise money to clear the debt of the schoolhouse where services were held by running socials—they thought the scheme unseemly. They also rebuked him for singing in the Anglican church choir, for Willie loved music so much that one choir was not enough for him. He wrote Maggie that the Presbyterians in Shellmouth were half a century behind those in Scotland, and ignored their objections, travelling around the country to collect funds for the church. In 1899 he bought a second-hand camera, and was launched into a new hobby which he eventually used as a means of fund-raising for the church, giving illustrated slide lectures around the district.

In April 1890 Maggie married her fiancé, John Bond, another schoolteacher and a keen amateur photographer. The event depressed Willie, since he could not afford to go to Britain for the ceremony. It had not been a good season—wheat was sixty cents for a bushel of number 1 hard wheat, and they had harvested only 640 bushels the previous winter. He contented himself with writing the couple in the self-consciously humorous style he had always fallen into when writing about love and marriage—he told John that it would be a change for Maggie to be under authority, and hoped that she would be "very obedient." He also suggested that the couple migrate to Canada, and proposed that they settle on the Wallace homestead.

In 1894 the Wallaces built a substantial two-storey, four bedroom home, and continued to make additions to the outbuildings. In 1899 they laid the foundation of a new barn which was expected to cost £175. They were still short of cash, however, and Willie had to appeal to Maggie to donate £5 for furniture for Father's room. It was a bad year for agriculture—there was a general economic depression, and wheat was only forty cents a bushel, and oats twenty-five cents. That year they harvested 660 bushels of oats and 390 of wheat. Willie consoled himself that things were even worse in the cities.

Willie continued his interest in public affairs. In 1895 he told Maggie about the Manitoba Schools Question, an issue which he thought was overblown; the important questions, he thought, were free trade and the possibility of a railway to Hudson Bay. He was on friendly enough terms with Major Boulton, the most prominent though not the wealthiest man in the district, and by this time a Senator, to arrange to have him visit Maggie and John Bond while he was in England as an official representative to Queen Victoria's Diamond Jubilee of 1897. Of Boulton he remarked in 1890 that "his military prowess and public-spiritedness are acknowledged all over Canada but his financial credit is below zero." In 1897 he noted that "Galicians" were beginning to settle in the district—the "men in sheep-skin coats" so famous in the Canadian history books had arrived in Shellmouth. Though Willie was not as racist as some of his neighbours, he did think that Scots made the best pioneers—"it is no small honour to be a Scotty" he wrote in 1886, explaining to Maggie that Scots were well adapted to Canadian life.

In the winter of 1900–1901 Willie managed to afford a trip back to the old country—local gossip had it that he was returning for a wife. Father wanted to go, but he turned eighty that year, and his health was not good enough. In 1902 it was Andrew's turn to return to Scotland. The same year Maggie and John visited Canada, and Father went to Winnipeg to meet them. The gossip about marriage was ill-founded—neither Willie nor Andrew ever married, and since Maggie and John Bond were childless, the Wallaces left no descendants.

In 1903 Maggie and John announced their intention to move to Canada. Willie took out a homestead for the Bonds, and in the last letter in the collection, dated 4 January 1904, he assured his sister that the homestead was protected until May 1st, and closed with this blessing: "we shall all be thinking of you and John. Keep up your courage. May the winds blow soft for you both, and with united love, I am your affectionate brother, Willie."

With the arrival of Maggie and her husband the correspondence ceased, though fortunately she brought the entire collection of letters with her to Canada.[2] The Wallaces continued to prosper, and Willie in particular continued the varied activities that caused him, near the end of his life, to be called "one of our most respected citizens" by students writing a history of Shellmouth as a class project in 1942. On their arrival, Maggie and John Bond moved into the Wallace house, which Willie and Andrew enlarged for them. Later they built a house of their own on the adjoining section. John Bond, who had no experience of farming, looked after the garden and the poultry, while Maggie cared for her invalid father until he died in 1906 at the age of 85.

The great change in Willie's life came in 1909, when he was injured in a railway accident, gave up farming, and moved to Shellmouth, where he became postmaster, a position he held for 27 years. Andrew continued to work the farm with hired help until 1919, when the land was sold, and Andrew moved to town to live with his brother. The two brothers lived in a four-room house which served as a dwelling and a post-office—two rooms for business, a bedroom and a living

---

2   The Brandon University Archives has a synopsis of the entire collection that contains a short description of the contents of each letter.

room. After selling the land, the two brothers went on a world tour, as Willie later wrote "to satisfy our wanderlust in Britain, Europe and the two Americas."

The reputation of the Wallace family in the community was later described by Mrs. Sarah Wileman, who as a young girl had lived on the Wallace farm with her father, who worked for the family:

> The Wallaces were a typical Scottish family who lived Godfearing lives. All members were active in community affairs ... Mr. [Peter] Wallace was president of the Russell Agricultural Society from 1884 until a few years before his death in 1906. At the conclusion of this time in office, he was presented with a Morris chair. Willie Wallace always took a keen interest in all community affairs. He was organist and choirmaster of both the Presbyterian and Anglican churches for many years, and gave his service freely for all the village entertainment. Mr. Andrew was also an active participant in these affairs. He was also a director of the Russell Agricultural Society while he was on the farm, and was a staunch member of the Masonic Lodge—first in Russell, then in Shellmouth. Mrs. Bond also gave freely of her time and talents to the Presbyterian Church, and was president of the Ladies' Aid for many years.[3]

The Bonds lived on their farm until 1923, when they built a house in Shellmouth. John Bond died in 1933, and when Andrew Wallace died three years later, Maggie moved in with her surviving brother in the post office building. She was the last of the family to die, in 1948.

Two years before his death in 1943, in his eighty-fifth year, William Wallace offered his letters to Professor E. J. Westcott of Brandon College (now Brandon University), describing them as a "unique collection" which he was glad to have "in sanctuary care and complete." Reading them over he was inclined to regret some of his earlier judgements—"my [1881] remarks about the Elton neighbours were quite uncalled for," he wrote Prof. Westcott, "later in 1884 we returned, and their kindness and hospitality was overwhelming."

---

3   Shellmouth Historical Club, *Shellmouth, Our Century* (n.p.: 1982–83).

Nonetheless he deleted nothing, perhaps knowing that his letters constituted a priceless record of pioneering in Manitoba. No doubt he would have been delighted to see them in print as a witness to present and future generations of a way of life now gone.

After William Wallace's death, Shellmouth began slowly to decline in population, as did many Manitoba towns of its size. Its population, 98 in 1941, peaked in 1951 at 107.[4] As farms grew larger and families smaller, and young people went elsewhere for jobs, fewer people came every Sunday to the Presbyterian church—since 1925 the United church—where William Wallace had for so long been organist and choirmaster. Eventually the church was closed, except for an annual service and the occasional wedding or funeral. In 1998, a group of descendants of original pioneers bought and began restoring it.[5] The Anglican church was abandoned and eventually demolished. The school also closed, as did the post office, and the children were taken by bus to schools in Inglis and Russell. One by one, as their owners retired, the small businesses ceased operation. Finally the railway, for which the Wallaces had waited so long, was abandoned, and the tracks torn up.

But Shellmouth is still a proud community, though now a tiny one, with fewer than ten permanent residents. The United church still has an annual service. The organ that Willie played is still in good working order. In the year of the community's centennial a handsome volume of commemorative history was produced by a civic committee. Though by 1990 nothing remained of "Woodvale" except an altered version of the barn built in 1899, the land has not changed. In the spring the hills flanking the Assiniboine turn bright green and Thunder Creek roars to meet it, as it did in the spring of 1882 when the Wallaces first saw it. There are still deer in the neighbourhood and even the occasional bear. A huge dam built several miles upstream to create a lake and a provincial park has eliminated spring floods, but these innovations cannot be seen from the old farm. Looking west from the farm across the Assiniboine valley to the opposite crest, as the Wallaces did every day, there is nothing to be seen which would have looked out of place in 1882.

---

4   Information provided by Monica Ball, Manitoba Legislative Library.

5   http://www.inglismanitoba.com/church.html#shellmouth.

And in the small, well-kept cemetery back in town, just east of the old church, lie, side by side, Peter and Andrew and William Wallace, and Maggie and John Bond, once separated for twenty-five years, but now joined as a family forever.

INDEX

A

Agricultural Correspondent
  Willie's appointment as, 173
Agricultural Show, 55, 179
Allan (rail) line, 265, 295
  See also Hudson's Bay Railway;
    railway
animal encounters
  badgers, 42
  bears, 36, 114, 166, 220; as ferocious,
    103, 114, 120; hunting for, 75,
    111–12, 220, 270; as prowling,
    31, 33, 36–37; sightings of, 31,
    33, 37, 102–3, 148, 166
  beaver sighting, 218
  birds, 23, 159; as plentiful, 15,
    212–13, 217, 260
  blackbirds, 42, 59, 233
  fireflies, 28, 169
  foxes, 57
  grey owls, 153
  hawks, 153
  mink, 204
  muskrat, use of fur, 42, 126
  partridges, 88, 127
  prairie chickens, 19, 125, 149, 215;
    as plentiful, 77, 93, 182, 186;
    shooting of, 48, 59, 79, 127, 176
  prairie dogs (ground squirrels),
    279
  sandhill cranes (wild turkeys), 84,
    103, 117, 121, 159

skunks, 42; furs from, 244; as
  poultry predators, 245
wolves, 13, 45, 58, 145, 173, 285;
  howling of, 101, 120, 133, 177,
  183, 237, 291; as numerous,
  186, 237–38
Assiniboine River, 83, 97
  bridge over, 52, 100, 113, 174, 228,
    234, 267, 283
Assissippi Mill, 186, 204–5, 211, 239, 275,
  280, 291, 293

B

Boulton, Graham, 234
Boulton, Major D'Arcy, 112, 114, 213,
  295
  as leading man in Russell, 94, 113,
    140, 148, 155, 168
  as residing in Shellmouth, 158,
    228, 283
  scouts of, 259, 266, 272, 274, 281–82
Bowles' stopping house, 141
Brandon City, 28, 47, 51–53, 56, 69, 165
Bryce's Stopping Place, 12

C

Canadian Pacific Railway, 66, 112, 122,
  128, 174, 189
  Moosomin station of, 259, 265, 267

Charters station house, 43
clothing
 buffalo robes, 145, 242
 moccasins, 47, 138, 198, 258
 snowshoes, 149, 153, 202
 socks, 197–98, 266, 269, 272
 winter clothing, 47, 50–51, 54, 127
Confederation
 of western provinces, 208
Cook's Stopping Place, 12
crops, 210, 259
 barley: harvesting of, 23, 31–32,
 174, 233
 corn, 14, 33, 163, 171; harvesting of,
 37, 178
 granaries, 177, 181, 185–86, 217, 232,
 253, 273, 292
 grist mills, 35, 107, 113, 148, 183, 239,
 251
 harvesting of, 31, 37, 118, 177, 222,
 232–33, 249, 273, 277, 279, 285,
 287; as providing money, 221,
 228
 hay, 37, 116, 230; cutting of, 31–32,
 114, 172–73, 226–27, 279–80,
 282
 oats, 23, 49, 165, 217; harvesting of,
 32, 233
 seeding of fields, 163, 214, 263, 268
 wheat, 35, 160, 192, 213, 217;
 harvesting of, 284, 291; price
 for, 190, 296
 See also threshing
Crown Timber Agent, 64
culture and entertainment
 American organ (harmonium,
 pump organ), 146–47, 164, 238,
 248, 257, 272
 Ball festivities, 154–55
 card playing, 57
 Carlyle's Essays, 206–7
 Chambers Journal, 206
 Christmas time, 56, 60; festivities
 of, 136, 248
 competitive shooting, 230, 282
 concert: programme of, 189;
 recitation during, 158–59
 Dominion Day: festivities of, 103,
 106–7, 167, 169–70, 224–25
 fiddle: bow for, 111; bridge for, 244,
 252; playing of, 30, 41, 44–45,
 47, 57, 61, 65, 91, 116, 159, 170,
 178, 197, 217, 219, 229, 238;
 strings for, 216, 219, 223, 244
 fife playing, 47
 flute playing, 21, 44, 47, 57, 61, 80,
 170
 Gilbert & Sullivan: Patience, 29,
 147; Pirates of Penzance, 29
 Graphic illustrated paper, 41, 61,
 63, 193
 ice skating, 43, 54, 56, 60, 276, 290,
 292
 Iolanthe opera, 162
 "Middlemarch," 205
 music books, 153, 197
 "Musical Memoirs," 224
 organ, 223, 225, 248, 255, 271, 280;
 music for, 250; playing of,
 229, 238, 276
 pianos, 60, 116, 224, 229; tuning
 of, 68
 theatrical performances, 250, 254,
 289

D

debts. See finances
domestic livestock, 9–10, 17, 44–45, 120,
 171, 208, 284
 calves, 48, 64, 84, 158, 173, 196, 204,
 209, 219, 222, 268
 cattle, 7, 22, 33, 78, 80, 86; raising
 of, 64, 89; as wintered in the
 stable, 44, 61, 68
 cows, 115, 178, 184, 196; milking of,
 44, 60, 65, 75, 158, 200, 219,
 263, 265, 291
 ducks: as plentiful, 84, 93, 159, 180,
 212, 260; shooting of, 42;

wild, 29, 35
geese, 84, 159, 177, 183, 209, 212, 260
herding or fencing of, 204; herd
  law, 204, 254
oxen, 7, 10, 24, 89, 95, 131–32; as
  finding their way home,
  143–44; as hauling in winter,
  13–14, 22–23, 25, 53–54, 137, 142;
  as tiresome work, 83, 88, 204;
  as working in heat, 19, 28, 69
pigs, 158, 182, 196, 219, 252–53;
  slaughtering of, 240–41
poultry stock, 174, 219; as thriving,
  215, 236, 267
rabbits, 127, 186, 203
raising of, as more profitable, 89,
  278, 285
sheep, raising of, 89
See also farm animals; fencing
Dykes, A.B., 41

E

Eliot, George, 205

F

farm animals
  dogs, on homestead, 9, 18–19, 25,
    36, 45, 58, 60, 158; demand
    for, 126
  horses, 89, 139, 174, 178, 182, 204; as
    aiding travel, 16, 189; racing
    of, 225, 283
  ponies, 99–100, 127, 151, 158, 166,
    172, 182, 196
  See also domestic livestock
farm houses. See homesteads; house-
    building
farming
  equipment for, 10; grain binder,
    174–76; mower, 32, 43, 47,
    114–15, 172
  as pleasant employment, 39, 209,
    269

fencing, 59, 163, 165–66
  building of, 88, 167–68, 191, 267–68,
    273
  poles for, 144, 155, 203, 207, 259
  See also herd law; homesteads
finances
  cost of living, 100
  gold fever: at Shellmouth, 269,
    274–75
  market for flour and butter, 283
  money: as invested in prairie
    lands, 24; scarcity of, 27, 54,
    105, 164, 251, 264, 271, 276–77,
    285; as sent from Maggie, 114,
    122, 165, 208
  passage money, 104, 265
  real estate: as booming, 76;
    fortunes from handling, 66,
    75
  situation of Wallaces, 178, 185, 209
  taxes, 264, 274, 293, 297
firewood, 32, 43, 53, 203, 265, 290
Fletcher's stopping house, 95, 129, 133,
  140, 143
Flewelling's Stopping Place, 13
food production
  beef from Ontario, 56, 70
  bread baking, 42, 101, 104, 111–12,
    166–67, 169, 186, 194, 199, 230,
    270, 272
  butter churning, 100, 104, 112, 169,
    199, 261, 263, 265, 270, 272,
    276–77, 287, 298
  cheese-making, 277, 285, 287
  fishing, 97, 166, 168, 180, 218–19,
    279
  shooting of birds and game, 29, 42,
    59, 215, 279
fruit
  in abundance, 219, 230
  apples, Canadian, 166, 200
  gooseberries, wild, 92, 102
  raspberries, wild, 92
  strawberries, 15, 23, 92, 100, 102,
    106, 225, 228

furs
    curing and dressing of, 92, 244

G

gardens, vegetable, 40, 102, 106, 122,
    163, 171–72, 189, 209
    in drought, 99
    as harvested and ploughed, 32,
      105, 179
    potatoes in, 14, 92, 97, 102, 122, 169,
      171, 173, 226
    seeding of, 23, 90, 209
Garfield assassination, 34
general elections, 103, 117, 168, 192

H

half-breeds, 17, 28, 71, 107, 170, 259
    as killed during rebellion, 262
    as spouses of settlers, 94, 162, 177
    See also Indians
Hamilton's house, 132–33, 140, 142
health and illness
    cholera, 230
    frostbite: of faces, 15, 54, 138–39,
      144, 193, 247; of hands and
      fingers, 15, 68, 70, 139, 144,
      247; of legs and feet, 8, 50, 98,
      144, 160, 188, 205
    knife wound in Willie's knee, 79
    neuralgia (Willie's), 185, 247, 249,
      251–52, 255, 278
    toothaches and dental care, 168,
      185, 190, 244
herd law, 204, 254
homesteads, 164, 219, 237, 253, 273
    lack of water at, 230
    land title for, 269, 281
    layout of, 10, 123–24
    and pre-emption rights, 9
    as requiring a house, 89
    squatting on, 66, 71, 76
    statute labour as requirement, 225
    and stock raising, 171

    as taken by immigrants, 270
    as yielding little money, 157
    See also fencing; house-building;
      prairie lands
house-building, 22, 110, 114–15, 208, 213,
    218, 230, 233, 272–73
    delay in, 267–68
    finishing of, 117, 119
    house-raising bee, 231, 261
    with logs, 26, 90, 99, 104, 121, 124
    See also homesteads
Hudson's Bay Company store, 94, 122,
    126, 138–39, 144–45, 244, 282
    as cashing bank drafts, 105
    obtaining provisions from, 129
    selling furs to, 92
Hudson's Bay Railway, 260
    route for, 208, 296, 299

I

immigration, 79, 82, 100, 211
    as affected by rebellion, 260
Indians, 12, 200, 204, 259–60
    burial grounds of, 130
    holiday attire of, 130
    in hunting style, 16
    as marriage partners, 162
    and rebellion, 262, 268
    as trappers, 149
    See also half-breeds

J

journal style of writing, 162–63, 165

L

logs
    cutting of, 203, 207, 253, 255
    hauling of, 195, 198, 202, 207, 253,
      255
    for house-building, 27, 90, 99
    See also house-building

M

Macdonald, Sir John A., 295
Manitoba
  climate as favourable to farming,
    24, 49, 294
  crop report of, 282
  dissatisfaction and agitation in,
    208, 211
  in fall colours, 121–23, 181
  grants for land purchase, 35
  grants from to start school, 48
  Legislative Assembly in
    Winnipeg, 45
Moosomin
  as nearest railway station, 122, 126,
    128, 135, 189
Mounted Police, 84, 96, 123
  as fighting rebellion, 259–60

N

neighbours, 31–33, 49, 57, 76, 101, 103,
    109, 112, 160, 164, 174, 187, 191
  characteristics of, 26–27, 85
  as settling at Shell River, 92
  as wanting to build a school, 48
Nicol's Stopping Place, 14, 30
Northern Pacific railway, 35

O

Ottawa, tensions with, 208

P

pests
  flying ants: bites of, 36
  house flies, as plentiful, 37
  mosquitoes, 10, 24, 35, 37, 118, 153;
    bites of, 36; as plentiful,
    21, 108, 268, 276, 280; as
    troublesome, 15, 28, 30, 98,
    100, 172
  sandfleas: as troublesome, 100

ploughing, 18, 46, 101–2, 105, 117, 273,
    275, 284, 291
  in fall, 43, 47, 122
  in the heat, 34
  of homestead land, 9, 14, 23, 40,
    90, 93, 99, 108
  with oxen team, 28
post office, 47–48, 51, 53, 55, 69, 89, 93,
    101, 146, 154, 207
  as coming to Woodvale, 148
  in Grand Valley, 9, 11, 21
  officials of, 21, 34, 40
  in Qu'Appelle, NWT, 71, 75
  at Shell River, 85
  at Shellmouth, 229, 237
prairie fires, 32, 46, 160, 186, 287
  as damaging settlements, 236
  as destroying crops, 167, 235
  as set to aid ploughing, 18
  as started by smoking, 90–91
prairie groping
  (walking in the dark), 107
prairie lands, 28, 35
  claims on, 172, 267, 269, 281
  creeks in, 8, 10, 14, 16, 19, 21, 24–25,
    31, 34, 54, 57, 86, 95
  as good investment, 24–26
  hunting for, 38, 44, 85–86, 95, 103,
    122
  isolation of, 14, 102, 130, 216, 279
  losing your reckoning on, 73, 132
  Northern lights over, 72, 134
  office for, 85–86
  scenery of, 100, 151, 181, 217
  sky as star-studded, 28
  as splendid for farming, 26
  titles for, 273, 275, 281, 285
  See also homesteads
prairie loneliness. See prairie lands
Prince of Wales coat of arms, 23
provisions, 78, 90, 104, 118, 122

Q

Qu'Appelle district
homesteading potential of, 108
squatting at, 66, 71
stock raising at, 48

R

railway, 76, 92, 237
as coming nearer to Wallaces, 176,
180, 183, 233, 240, 251, 279, 283,
293, 295
as crossing Assiniboine, 100, 113
as monopolies, 208
as not coming in 1884, 209, 214,
221, 226, 230
snow blockade on, 61, 74, 81, 146
strike of, 192
syndicate for, 35, 52
uncertainty about, 276, 285
Railway Land Section 19, 6
reckoning, loss of
in snowstorm, 73, 132
Red River Rebellion, 113, 208, 259, 263,
266, 268, 270, 272, 274
casualties of, 262
effect on immigration, 260–61
religion
Bibles, scarcity of, 30
Church of England, 210, 252; as
predominant religion, 161
church services, 9, 97, 120, 147, 166,
218
Methodist church, 42, 192
missionaries, 30–31, 41
"Old Faiths in New Lights," 212
Orthodox Faith (Church of
England), 212
Presbyterians, 160–61, 231–32, 267,
273
Roman Catholics, 109, 120, 128, 148
Sunday: as day of rest, 13, 33
Sunday Talk, 236
Riel, Louis, 268, 295
Russell Agricultural Society, 115

S

sawmills, 22, 117, 119, 186, 207, 240, 251,
263, 276, 279, 285
schoolhouse
certificate for teaching, 27, 48, 150,
162, 220
as completed, 228
rights to obtain, 48
at Russell, 239
at Shellmouth, 218, 231
teaching as occupation, 48, 63
Scotch Colonization Company, 160
Scott, Sir Walter, 207
Shellmouth, 239, 253, 287, 289
sawmill at, 240, 251, 263, 276, 279
snow crystals
designs of, 63–64, 75
See also weather, snow
snow wreaths, 56, 74, 77
squatting. See homesteads
S.S. Prussia[n], 1, 106, 110
S.S. Waldensian, 3
stables, 60–61, 253
building of, 117, 215, 219, 222, 231,
241

T

threshing, 185, 187–88, 243, 245, 247–48,
287, 289, 291
bushels obtained, 249
during harvest, 40
mills for, 202, 240
See also crops
trade
bartering, 199, 264, 277
free trade, 260
freight rates, 296
protective tariff: as raising price of
goods, 69
transportation
buggy: with hay rake wheels, 99
canoe: as homebuilt, 86
ferry boats, 52, 216, 239, 263
sleighs, 79; as pulled by oxen, 13,

75; with tents on them, 83;
as winter travel, 12, 14, 55–56,
134, 137, 242, 293

steamboat company, 32, 43, 82, 265

steamboats, 28, 52, 85, 89, 96,
163–64, 180; as bringing
provisions, 11, 161; as coming
in future, 151, 158

trapping, 205

trees
felling of, 92, 152, 195
few of on prairie, 26
See also firewood; logs

U

unions, of farmers, 208

V

Venables, Arthur Frank, 250

W

Wallace, Andrew
homestead for, 178, 185
as kicked by ox, 106
land claim of, 224, 275

Wallace, Maggie, 75
as assisting Wallaces with money,
150, 171, 178, 248
as living in London, 58, 162
money matters of, 104, 118, 271
music examination of, 45, 55, 57
as not coming to prairie, 161
as possibly coming to the prairie,
135, 148–50, 152, 271

Wallace, Willie
appointment as Agricultural
Correspondent, 173
injured foot of, 145, 152, 160, 164
as short of money, 150, 164, 171,
178, 248

water, drinking, 31, 74, 77, 227

See also well-digging

weapons
breech loader: for shooting game,
79
revolver, six chamber, 111; and
wolves, 133
rifle, 111; for shooting game, 79
Winchester repeating rifle, 75

weather
drought, 99, 279
frost, 12–13, 22, 32, 40, 42–43; as
damaging crops, 60, 284–85
hailstones, as large as marbles, 28,
230
heat, difficulty working in, 28, 37,
277
Indian summer, 49–50, 122, 125
lightning, 23–24, 30–31, 114, 118
rainy season, 21–23
snow, 258; as deep, 7–8, 13–14;
as drifting, 51, 58–59, 73; as
falling at end of December,
49; quality of, 56; as storms,
64, 73, 291; travelling in by
sleigh, 12
squaw winter, 49, 122, 125
thunderstorms, 23–24, 28, 40, 99,
113, 118, 166, 168, 222–23, 280;
as terrific, 161, 163
tornadoes, 31, 40, 49
winter as severe, 26, 49, 53, 63,
74, 145, 159, 193, 202, 247;
blizzards during, 22, 67, 198,
292; effects of on harvest, 235

Weekly Citizen, 34

Weekly Herald, 34, 39–41, 53, 58, 63,
67, 72
sent from Scotland, 30

well-digging, 32, 222, 224, 227

Wolverine Mixed Farming Co., 254,
289

women
as pioneers, 184
shortage of on prairie, 150, 157, 192,
261–62